The Dead Sea Scrolls

The
Dead Sea
Scrolls

A selection of original manuscripts
translated and edited by
GEZA VERMES

LONDON
The Folio Society
2000

Map drawn by Reginald Piggott.

Typeset at The Folio Society in Miller with Ondine Display.
Printed on Grosvenor Book Wove by Butler & Tanner, Frome,
and bound by them in printed and blocked Art Vellum.

Binding illustration: fragment of the Psalms Scroll, from Cave 11,
Qumran, 30–50 CE. (*Israel Antiquities Authority, Jerusalem*)

Frontispiece: Fragment (with leather fastener)
of the Prayer for 'King' Jonathan, from Cave 4,
Qumran, *c.* 2nd century BCE. 'King' Jonathan is probably
Jonathan Maccabaeus, the liberator of Judea and the
man reviled as the 'Wicked Priest' by the Teacher of
Righteousness (see pages 53–4, 60–1)

Contents

Map   11

Preface   15

A Note on this Translation and Selection   16

Introduction   17

1   Dead Sea Scrolls Research from 1947 to the Present Day   17

2   The Essenes and the Qumran Community   29

3   The Wider World: The Essenes in Jewish History,
    200 BCE–70 CE   51

Chronology   67

The Dead Sea Scrolls

THE RULES

The Community Rule   71

Community Rule Manuscripts from Cave 4   92

The Damascus Document   97

The Messianic Rule   117

The War Scroll   120

The Temple Scroll   143

Miqsat Ma'ase Ha-Torah   173

Purities   177

HYMNS AND POEMS

The Thanksgiving Hymns   178

Apocryphal Psalms   229

Lamentations   236

Songs for the Holocaust of the Sabbath   237

HOROSCOPES, LITURGIES, BLESSINGS AND CURSES

'Horoscopes' or Astrological Physiognomies   241

The Words of the Heavenly Lights   243

Blessings and Curses   246

APOCALYPTIC WORKS

The Triumph of Righteousness or Mysteries   251

A Messianic Apocalypse   253

WISDOM LITERATURE

The Seductress   254

Exhortation to Seek Wisdom   256

On Living a Modest Life   257

Bless, My Soul   259

Songs of the Sage   261

Beatitudes   263

BIBLE INTERPRETATION

Introductory Note   264

The Targum of Job   265

A Paraphrase of Exodus   271

The Genesis Apocryphon   272

A Genesis Commentary   282

Commentaries on Isaiah   284

Commentary on Hosea   286

Commentary on Nahum   287

Commentary on Habakkuk   290

Commentary on Psalms   298

Florilegium or Midrash on the Last Days   301

The Heavenly Prince Melchizedek   303

BIBLICALLY BASED APOCRYPHAL WORKS

Jubilees   305

The Book of Enoch and the Book of Giants   307

An Admonition Associated with the Flood   311

The Testament of Qahat   312

The Words of Moses   313

Pseudo-Moses   315

Tobit   317

THE COPPER SCROLL

The Copper Scroll: Buried Treasure   321

The Sources   327

Major Editions of Qumran Manuscripts   329

General Bibliography   333

Illustrations

COLOUR ILLUSTRATIONS

Fragment of the Prayer for 'King' Jonathan, from Cave 4,
Qumran, *c*. 2nd century BCE. (*Israel Antiquities Authority,
Jerusalem*)   *frontis*

Large limestone goblet, from Qumran, 1st century CE.
(*Israel Antiquities Authority, Jerusalem*)   *f. p.* 192

Sandal, from Qumran, 1st century BCE–1st century CE.
(*Israel Antiquities Authority, Jerusalem*)   193

Herodian pottery lamp with palm-fibre wick, from Qumran,
1st century BCE–1st century CE. (*Israel Antiquities
Authority, Jerusalem*)   208

Pottery inkwell, from Qumran, late 1st century BCE–early
1st century CE. (*Israel Antiquities Authority, Jerusalem*)   209

Fragment of the Songs for the Holocaust of the Sabbath,
from Cave 4, Qumran, mid-1st century BCE. (*Israel
Antiquities Authority, Jerusalem*)   272

Boxwood combs, from Qumran, 1st century BCE–1st century
CE. (*Israel Antiquities Authority, Jerusalem*)   273

Leather phylactery cases, from Qumran, 1st century BCE–1st
century CE. (*Israel Antiquities Authority, Jerusalem*)   288

Twenty-four silver *shekalim* and half-*shekalim*, minted
at Tyre, from a hoard found at Qumran, 103/2–10/9 BCE.
(*Israel Antiquities Authority, Jerusalem*)   289

BLACK AND WHITE ILLUSTRATIONS
Between pages 48 and 49

1a View of the caves at Qumran. (*SCALA*)

1b Interior of Cave 4 at Qumran. Photograph by John Allegro.
(*Estate of John M. Allegro, University of Manchester Museum*)

2a Muhammad edh-Dhib. Photograph by William Reed. (© *William Reed*)

2b Khalil Iskandar Sahin (Kando) in Jerusalem. Photograph by John Allegro. (*Estate of John M. Allegro, University of Manchester Museum*)

3a Professor E. L. Sukenik at work on scroll fragments. Photograph by Yigael Yadin. (© *Yigael Yadin, Jerusalem*)

3b The Thanksgiving Hymns Scroll, from Cave 1, Qumran, early 1st century CE. (*Hulton Getty Collection*)

3c Cylindrical pottery scroll jars with lids, from Cave 1, Qumran, 1st century BCE–1st century CE. (*Hulton Getty Collection*)

4 The 'Scrollery' at the Rockefeller Museum, Jerusalem. Photograph by John Allegro. (*Estate of John M. Allegro, University of Manchester Museum*)

5a Excavation of the settlement of Khirbet Qumran. (*Israel Antiquities Authority, Jerusalem*)

5b Father Roland de Vaux, J. T. Milik and G. Lankester Harding at Khirbet Qumran. Photograph by John Allegro. (*Estate of John M. Allegro, University of Manchester Museum*)

6a The Copper Scroll, from Cave 3, Qumran, 2nd century CE. Photograph by John Allegro. (*Estate of John M. Allegro, University of Manchester Museum*)

6b Professor H. Wright Baker cutting the Copper Scroll into sections. Photograph by John Allegro. (*Estate of John M. Allegro, University of Manchester Museum*)

7 Ruins of the fortified tower at Khirbet Qumran. Photograph by John Allegro. (*Estate of John M. Allegro, University of Manchester Museum*)

8 Graveyard to the east of Khirbet Qumran. Photograph by John Allegro. (*Estate of John M. Allegro, University of Manchester Museum*)

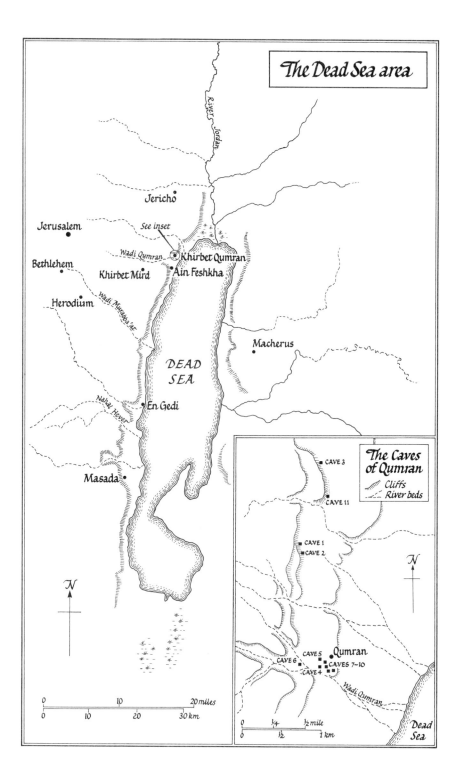

The Dead Sea area

River Jordan

Jericho

Jerusalem

See inset

Bethlehem

Wadi Qumran

Khirbet Qumran

Khirbet Mird

Ain Feshkha

Herodium

Wadi Murabba'at

Macherus

DEAD
SEA

Nahal Hever

En Gedi

Masada

N

0   10   20 miles
0   10   20   30 km

The Caves
of Qumran

CAVE 3

Cliffs
River beds

CAVE 11

CAVE 1
CAVE 2

N

CAVE 5
CAVE 6   Qumran
CAVES 7–10
CAVE 4

Wadi Qumran

0   ¼   ½ mile
0   ½   1 km

Dead
Sea

For M and I with love
and in loving memory of P

Preface

In 1947 a young Arab shepherd climbed into a cave in the Judaean desert and stumbled on the first Dead Sea Scrolls. For those of us who lived through the Qumran story from the beginning, the realisation that all this happened over half a century ago brings with it a melancholy feeling. The Scrolls are no longer a *recent* discovery as we used to refer to them, but over the years they have grown in significance and in 1997 called for particular joy and celebration. Following the 'revolution' which 'liberated' all the manuscripts in 1991 – until that moment a large portion of them was kept away from the public gaze – every interested person gained free access to the entire Qumran library. I eagerly seized the chance and set out to explore the whole collection.

Has the greatly increased source material substantially altered our perception of the writings found at Qumran? I do not think so. Nuances and emphases have changed, but additional information has mainly helped to fill in gaps and clarify obscurities; it has not undermined our earlier conceptions regarding the Community and its ideas. We had the exceptionally good fortune that all but one of the major non-biblical Scrolls were published at the start, between 1950 and 1956: the Habakkuk Commentary (1950), the Community Rule (1951), the War Scroll and the Thanksgiving Hymns (1954/5) and the best-preserved columns of the Genesis Apocryphon (1956). Even the Temple Scroll, which had remained concealed until 1967 in a Bata shoebox by an antique dealer, was edited ten years later. The large Scrolls have served as foundation and pillars, and the thousands of fragments as building stones, with which the unique shrine of Jewish religion and culture that is Qumran is progressively restored to its ancient splendour.

G.V.

A Note on this Translation and Selection

The purpose of this translation is to enable the general reader to come into direct contact with the literary works found at Qumran. The text has been selected from Geza Vermes' acclaimed book, *The Complete Dead Sea Scrolls in English*, and the aim has been to include all the more complete scrolls, especially those which describe the community that created them and throw light on its customs and beliefs. They include community rules and laws in peace and war, hymns, songs and psalms, and a number of fascinating biblical texts and commentaries.

In the interests of readability, the scholarly apparatus and textual references have been kept to a minimum. The scroll translations are in roman type and any hypothetical but likely reconstructions are in sloped roman face to distinguish them from the body of the text. Biblical quotations are in italic. In the more substantial sections, the columns into which each scroll is divided are marked by bold roman numerals (**I, II, III**, etc.). Readers will notice that the text is often more damaged and fragmentary at the beginning and end of each scroll.

For those interested in learning more, the inventory numbers of the scrolls, indicating the caves in which they were found and their place in the archaeological history of the discovery, are listed at the back of the book. There is also a list of the Qumran Manuscript editions relating to this selection, together with a general Bibliography.

Introduction

On the western shore of the Dead Sea, about eight miles south of Jericho, lies a complex of ruins known as Khirbet Qumran. It occupies one of the lowest parts of the earth, on the fringe of the hot and arid wastes of the Wilderness of Judaea, and is today, apart from occasional invasions by coachloads of tourists, lifeless, silent and empty. But from that place, members of an ancient Jewish religious community, whose centre it was, hurried out one day and in secrecy climbed the nearby cliffs in order to hide away in eleven caves their precious scrolls. No one came back to retrieve them, and there they remained undisturbed for almost 2,000 years.

The account of the discovery of the Dead Sea Scrolls, as the manuscripts are inaccurately designated, and of the half a century of intense research that followed, is in itself a fascinating as well as an exasperating story. It has been told many a time, but excuses, and even demands, yet another rehearsal for readers of the twenty-first century.

1 Dead Sea Scrolls Research from 1947 to the Present Day

News of an extraordinary discovery of seven ancient Hebrew and Aramaic manuscripts began to spread in 1948 from Israeli and American sources. The original chance find by a young Bedouin shepherd, Muhammad edh-Dhib, occurred during the last months of the British mandate in Palestine in the spring or summer of 1947, unless it was slightly earlier, in the winter of 1946.* In 1949, the cave where the scrolls lay hidden was identified, thanks to the efforts of a bored Belgian army officer of the United Nations Armistice Observer Corps, Captain Philippe Lippens, assisted by a unit of Jordan's Arab Legion, commanded by Major-General Lash. It was investigated by G. Lankester Harding, the English Director of the Department of Antiquities of Jordan, and

* Cf. the interview with the discoverer reported by John C. Trever, *The Dead Sea Scrolls: A Personal Account*, Grand Rapids, 1979, 191–4.

the French Dominican archaeologist and biblical scholar, Father Roland de Vaux. They retrieved hundreds of leather fragments, some large but most of them minute, in addition to the seven scrolls found in the same cave.

Between 1951 and 1956, ten further caves were discovered, most of them by Bedouin in the first instance. Two yielded substantial quantities of material. Thousands and thousands of fragments were found in Cave 4 and several scrolls, including the longest, the Temple Scroll, were retrieved from Cave 11. The previously neglected ruins of a settlement in the proximity of the caves were also excavated by Harding and de Vaux, and the view soon prevailed that the texts, the caves and the Qumran site were interconnected, and that consequently the study of the script and contents of the manuscripts should be accompanied by archaeological research.

Progress was surprisingly quick despite the fact that in those halcyon days, apart from the small Nash papyrus, containing the Ten Commandments, found in Egypt and now in the Cambridge University Library, no Hebrew documents dating to Late Antiquity were extant to provide terms of comparison. In 1948 and 1949, E. L. Sukenik, Hebrew University Professor of Jewish Archaeology, published in Hebrew two preliminary surveys entitled *Hidden Scrolls from the Judaean Desert* (1948, 1949), and concluded that the religious community involved was the ascetic sect of the Essenes, well known from the first-century CE (AD) writings of Philo, Josephus and Pliny the Elder, a thesis worked out in great detail from 1951 onwards by André Dupont-Sommer in Paris.* The first Qumran scrolls to reach the public, and the archaeological setting in which they were discovered, echoed three striking Essene characteristics. The Community Rule, a basic code of sectarian existence, reflects Essene common ownership and celibate life, while the geographical location of Qumran tallies with Pliny's Essene settlement on the north-western shore of the Dead Sea, south of Jericho. The principal novelty provided by the manuscripts consists of cryptic allusions to the historical

---

* Cf. *Observations sur le Manuel de discipline découvert près de la Mer Morte*, Paris, 1951. His major synthesis in English is *The Essene Writings from Qumran*, Oxford, 1961. For a recent survey, see G. Vermes and Martin Goodman, *The Essenes According to the Classical Sources*, Sheffield, 1989.

origins of the Community, launched by a priest called the Teacher of Righteousness, who was persecuted by a Jewish ruler, designated as the Wicked Priest. The Teacher and his followers were compelled to withdraw into the desert, where they awaited the impending manifestation of God's triumph over evil and darkness in the end of days, which had already begun.

An almost unanimous agreement soon emerged, dating the discovery, on the basis of palaeography and archaeology, to the last centuries of the Second Temple, i.e. second century BCE (BC) to first century CE. For a short while there was controversy between de Vaux, who decreed that the pottery and all the finds belonged to the Hellenistic era (i.e. pre-63 BCE), and Dupont-Sommer, who argued for an early Roman (post-63) date. But the finding of further caves and the excavation of the ruins of Qumran brought about, on 4 April 1952, de Vaux's dramatic retraction before the French Académie des Inscriptions et Belles-Lettres. His revised archaeological synthesis, presented in the 1959 Schweich Lectures of the British Academy, while admittedly incomplete, is still the best comprehensive statement available today.*

A third point of early consensus concerns the chronology of the events alluded to in the Qumran writings, especially the biblical commentaries published in the 1950s and the Damascus Document. The so-called Maccabaean theory, placing the conflict between the Teacher of Righteousness and the politico-religious Jewish leadership of the day, in the time of the Maccabaean high priest or high priests, Jonathan and/or Simon, was first formulated in my 1952 doctoral dissertation, published in 1953,† and was soon to be adopted with variations in detail by such leading specialists as J. T. Milik, F. M. Cross and R. de Vaux.

As long as the editorial task consisted only of publishing the seven scrolls from Cave 1, work was advancing remarkably fast. Millar Burrows and his colleagues from the American School of Oriental Research published their three manuscripts in 1950 and 1951. Sukenik's three texts appeared in a posthumous volume in 1954–5. In the interest of speed, these editors generously abstained from translating and interpreting the texts, and were

* *Archaeology and the Dead Sea Scrolls*, Oxford, 1973.
† *Les Manuscrits du désert de Juda*, Tournai and Paris, 1953; *Discovery in the Judean Desert*, New York, 1956.

content with releasing the photographs and their transcription.

The secrecy rule of later years, restricting access to unpublished texts to a small team of editors appointed by de Vaux, had not yet been applied. The scroll fragments, partly found by the archaeologists, but mostly purchased from the Arabs, who nine times out of ten outwitted their professional rivals, were cleaned, sorted out and displayed in the so-called Scrollery in the Rockefeller Museum, later renamed the Palestine Archaeological Museum, to become after 1967 once more the Rockefeller Museum. If the mass of material disgorged by Cave 4 had not upset the original arrangements, the scandalous delays in publishing in later years need never have happened.

To deal with Cave 4, Father de Vaux improvised, in 1953 and 1954, a team of seven on the whole young and untried scholars. Dominique Barthélemy, who had shared the editing of the fragments collected in Cave 1, opted out, and his brilliant but unpredictable colleague, Abbé J. T. Milik, who later left the Roman Catholic priesthood, became the pillar of the new group. He was joined by the French Abbé Jean Starcky, and two Americans, Monsignor Patrick Skehan and Frank Moore Cross. John Marco Allegro and John Strugnell were recruited from Britain, and from Germany, Claus-Hunno Hunzinger, who soon resigned and was replaced later by the French Abbé Maurice Baillet.

It should have been evident to anyone with a modicum of good sense that a group of seven editors, of whom only two, Starcky and Skehan, had already established a scholarly reputation, was insufficient to perform such an enormous task on any level, let alone to produce the kind of 'last word' edition de Vaux appears to have contemplated.

Yet before depicting the chaos characterising the publishing process in the 1970s and 1980s, in fairness it should be stressed that, during the first decade or so, the industry of the group could not seriously be faulted. Judging from the completion around 1960 of a primitive Concordance, recorded on handwritten index cards, of all the words appearing in the fragments found in Caves 2 to 10, it is clear that at an early date most of the texts had been identified and deciphered. The many criticisms advanced in subsequent years, focusing on these scholars' refusal to put their valuable findings into the public domain, should not prevent one from acknowledging that this original achievement, in which J. T. Milik had the lion's share, deserves unrestricted admiration.

After the publication of the Cave 1 fragments in 1955, the contents of the eight minor caves (2–3, 5–10) were released in a single volume in 1963. In 1965, J. A. Sanders, an American scholar who was not part of the original team, edited the Psalms Scroll, found in Cave 11 in 1956. Finally, with its typescript completed and despatched to the printers a year before the fatal date of 1967, the first poorly edited volume of Cave 4 fragments saw the light of day in 1968.

With the occupation of East Jerusalem in the Six Day War, all the scroll fragments housed in the Palestine Archaeological Museum came under the control of the Israel Department of Antiquities. Only the Copper Scroll and a few other fragments exhibited in Amman remained in Jordanian hands. The Temple Scroll, which until then had been held by a dealer in Bethlehem,* was quickly retrieved with the help of army intelligence and acquired by the State of Israel. Yigael Yadin, deputy prime minister of Israel in the 1970s, mixing politics with scholarship, managed to complete a magisterial three-volume publication by 1977. A gentlemanly gesture on the part of the Israelis, who decided not to interfere with de Vaux, left him and his scattered troop in charge of the Cave 4 texts. As for the unpublished manuscripts from Cave 11, they were handled by Dutch and American academics.

Father de Vaux, whose anti-Israeli sentiments were no secret, quietly withdrew to his tent and remained inactive until his death in 1971. Another French Dominican, Pierre Benoit, succeeded him, but his ineffectual rallying call either elicited no response from his men, or produced promises which were never honoured. In a lecture delivered in 1977, I coined the phrase which was thereafter often repeated that the greatest Hebrew manuscript discovery was fast becoming 'the academic scandal *par excellence* of the twentieth century'.

One may ask how and why, after such an apparently propitious beginning, a group of scholars, most of whom were gifted, had

* Khalil Iskandar Sahin, familiarly known as Kando, a cobbler cum antique dealer, had been the principal middle man between the Bedouin discoverers of thousands of fragments and Roland de Vaux in the 1950s.

turned the editorial work on the Scrolls into such a lamentable story? In my opinion, the 'academic scandal of the century' resulted from a concatenation of causes. Lack of organisation and unfortunate choice of collaborators can be blamed on de Vaux. For the majority of the team members who had other jobs to cope with, the overlong part-time effort caused their original enthusiasm to fade and vanish. J. T. Milik, the most productive of them until the mid-seventies, appears to have been disenchanted by the cool reception of his highly speculative thesis contained in his edition of *The Books of Enoch: Aramaic Fragments of Qumran Cave 4* (1976). 'Academic imperialism' was also a factor. It was easier to hold that 'These texts belong to us, not to you!' than to admit that the procrastinating editors had undertaken more than they could deliver.

In 1986, a year before his death, Pierre Benoit resigned as editor-in-chief and the depleted international team elected as his successor the talented but tardy John Strugnell, who in thirty-three years failed to produce a single volume of text. In 1987, at a public session of a Scrolls Symposium held in London, I urged him to publish at once the photographic plates, while he and his acolytes carried on with their work at their customary snail pace. This request was met with a one-syllable negative answer. To the surprise of many, the Israel Antiquities Authority (or IAA) acquiesced in Strugnell's appointment. His grandiose schemes never bore fruit. In 1990, after a compromising interview given by him to an Israeli newspaper, in which he was reported as having made disparaging remarks not only about Israelis, but also about the Jewish religion – he called it horrible – his fellow editors persuaded him to tender his resignation. It was accepted by the IAA on health grounds. Belatedly even the Israelis saw the light, and *de facto* terminated the thirty-seven-year-old and ultimately disastrous reign of the international team.

After John Strugnell's withdrawal, the very capable Emanuel Tov, Professor of Biblical Studies at the Hebrew University, was appointed chief editor, the first Jew and the first Israeli to head the Qumran publication project. He began his activities auspiciously by redistributing the unpublished texts among freshly recruited collaborators. The new editorial team, of which I became a member in 1991, consists of some sixty scholars compared to the original seven! Unfortunately, Tov did not feel free to cancel the 'secrecy rule', introduced and strictly enforced by de Vaux and his successors, prohibiting access to unpublished texts to all but a few chosen editors.

The protective dam erected around the fragments by the international team collapsed in the autumn of 1991, however, under the growing pressure of public opinion. Almost at once, the Scroll photograph archives at the Oxford Centre for Postgraduate Hebrew Studies and at the Ancient Biblical Manuscript Center at Claremont, previously legally compelled to restrict access only to persons approved by Jerusalem, were also thrown open to all competent research scholars. Moreover, in November 1991 the Biblical Archaeology Society published a two-volume photographic edition of the bulk of the Qumran fragments compiled by Robert Eisenman and James Robinson. How the two Californian professors obtained the material remains unclear, but since vested interests are no longer protected, the rate of publication has noticeably accelerated and from 1992 learned periodicals have been flooded with short or not so short papers by scholars claiming fresh insights. Thanks to the highly efficient stewardship of the editor-in-chief, Emanuel Tov, some thirty out of the planned thirty-eight volumes of the series, *Discoveries in the Judaean Desert*, will be published by the close of the twentieth century, and the whole project is expected to be completed in the opening years of the new Millennium.

Between 1947 and 1956, the eleven Qumran caves yielded a dozen scrolls written on leather and one embossed on copper. To these we have to add fragments on papyrus or leather, the precise number of which is unknown but probably in the order of six figures. Most scrolls are written in Hebrew, a smaller portion in Aramaic and only a few attest the ancient Greek or Septuagint version of the Bible.*

Among the texts previously known, all the books of the Hebrew Scriptures are extant at least in fragments save Esther, the

---

* The claim that several minute Greek scraps from Cave 7 represent the New Testament is unsubstantiated. Most of the fragments are likely to represent the Greek version of the Book of Enoch.

absence of which may be purely accidental. Even Daniel, the most recent work to enter the Palestinian canon in the mid-second century BCE, is attested to by eight manuscripts. There are also remains of Aramaic and Greek scriptural translations.

Furthermore, the caves have yielded some of the Apocrypha, i.e. religious works missing from the Hebrew Scriptures but included in the Septuagint, the Bible of Greek-speaking Jews. Caves 4 and 11 revealed the Book of Tobit in Aramaic and in Hebrew, Psalm cli, described in the Greek version as a 'supernumerary' psalm, and the Wisdom of Jesus ben Sira or Ecclesiasticus in Hebrew. Part of the latter, chapters xxxix–xliv, has also survived at Masada, and hence cannot be later than 73/4 CE, the date when the stronghold was captured by the Romans, and two medieval manuscripts, discovered in the storeroom (*genizah*) of a synagogue in Cairo in 1896, have preserved about two thirds of the Greek version.

A third category of religious books, the Pseudepigrapha, though very popular in some Jewish circles, failed to attain canonical rank either in Palestine or in the Diaspora. Some of them, previously known in Greek, Latin or Syriac translations, have turned up in their original Hebrew (e.g. the Book of Jubilees) or Aramaic (e.g. the Book of Enoch). A good many further compositions pertaining to this class have also come to light, such as fictional accounts relating among others to Joseph, Amram, Moses, Joshua or Jeremiah, as well as apocryphal psalms, five of which have survived also in Syriac translation, others being revealed for the first time at Qumran.

The sectarian Dead Sea Scrolls, thought to have been composed or revised by the Qumran Community, constitute, with one exception,* a complete novelty. This literature comprises rule books, Bible interpretation of various kinds, religious poetry, Wisdom compositions in prose and in verse, sectarian calendars and liturgical texts, one of them purporting to echo the angelic worship in the heavenly temple. To these are to be added several 'horoscopes' or, more precisely, documents of astrological physiognomy, a literary genre based on the belief that the temper,

* The exception is the Damascus Document, well attested in Caves 4, 5 and 6, but previously known from two incomplete medieval manuscripts found in the Cairo Genizah.

physical features and fate of an individual depend on the configuration of the heavens at the time of the person's birth. Finally,
the Copper Scroll alludes in cryptic language to sixty-four caches
of precious metals and scrolls, including another copy of this
same inventory written without riddles.

After a first few gaffes committed before the excavation of the
site, the palaeographical, archaeological and literary-historical
study of the evidence produced a general consensus among
scholars concerning (a) the age, (b) the provenance and (c) the
significance of the discoveries. Holders of fringe opinions have
recently tended to explain this consensus as tyrannically imposed
from above by Roland de Vaux. The truth, however, is that the
opinio communis has resulted from a natural evolutionary process – from arguments which others found persuasive even when
advanced by single individuals often unconnected with the international team – and not from an almighty establishment forcing
an official view down the throats of weaklings.

Palaeography was the first method employed to establish the age
of the texts. Despite the paucity of comparative material, experts
independently arrived at dates ranging between the second century BCE and the first century CE. By the 1960s, in addition to the
Qumran texts, they could make use also of manuscripts from
Masada (first century CE), as well as from the Murabba'at and
other Judaean desert caves yielding first- and second-century CE
Jewish writings. These conclusions were boosted by archaeological findings and radiocarbon dating. The archaeological thesis,
based *inter alia* on the study of pottery and coins, was formulated
by R. de Vaux. He assigned the occupation of Qumran to the
period between the second half of the second century BCE and
the first war between Jews and Romans (66–70 CE).

Radiocarbon tests were first applied to the cloth wrapping of
one of the scrolls as early as 1951. The date suggested was 33 CE,
but one had to reckon with a 10 per cent margin of error
each way. However, with the improved techniques of the 1990s,
eight Qumran manuscripts were subjected to Accelerator Mass
Spectrometry or AMS. Six of them were found to be definitely
pre-Christian, and only two straddled over the first century
BCE/first century CE dividing line. Most importantly, with a

single exception – the Testament of Qahat being shown to be
about 300 years earlier than expected – the radiocarbon dates
confirm in substance those proposed by the palaeographers.

Unfortunately, the manuscripts tested in 1990 did not include
historically sensitive texts. But in 1994 the Arizona AMS Labora-
tory at the University of Arizona, Tucson analysed thirteen of the
Qumran manuscripts, three of which were 'date-bearing'. While
the margin of error was considerably greater than that appearing
in the 1990 tests, nevertheless Arizona scored on one highly
significant point: the Habakkuk Commentary, chief source of the
history of the Qumran sect, is definitely put in the pre-Christian
era between 120 and 5 BCE. In consequence, fringe scholars who
see in this writing allusions to events described in the New Testament will find they have a problem on their hands. In sum, the
general scholarly view today places the Qumran Scrolls roughly
between 200 BCE and 70 CE, with a small portion of the texts
possibly stretching back to the third century BCE, and the bulk of
the extant material dating to the first century BCE, i.e. late Hasmonaean or early Herodian in the jargon of the palaeographers.

With negligible exceptions, scholarly opinion recognised already
in the 1950s that the Scrolls found in the caves and the nearby
ruined settlement were related. To take the obvious example,
Cave 4 with its 575 (or perhaps 555) documents lies literally
within a stone's throw from the buildings. At the same time, the
Essene identity of the ancient inhabitants of Qumran gained general acceptance.

The mainstream hypothesis, built on archaeology and literary
analysis, sketches the history of the Scrolls Community (or *Essene*
sect) as follows. Its prehistory starts in Palestine – some claim also
Babylonian antecedents – with the rise of the Hasidic movement,
at the beginning of the second century BCE as described in the
first book of the Maccabees (1 Mac. ii, 42–4; vii, 13–17). Essene
history itself originated in a clash between the Wicked Priest or
Priests (Jonathan and/or possibly Simon Maccabaeus) and the
Teacher of Righteousness, the anonymous priest who was the
spiritual leader of the Community. The sect consisted of the survivors of the Hasidim, linked with a group of dissident priests
who, by the mid-second century, came under the leadership of

the sons of Zadok, associates of the Zadokite high priests. This history continues at Qumran, and no doubt in many other Palestinian localities, until the years of the first Jewish rebellion against Rome, when possibly in 68 CE the settlement is believed to have been occupied by Vespasian's soldiers. Whether the legionaries encountered sectarian resistance – such a theory would be consonant with Josephus' reference to an Essene general among the revolutionaries and to a massacre of the Essenes by the Romans – or whether the threatening presence of the contingents of Zealot Sicarii, who had already expelled the Essenes from Qumran, provoked a Roman intervention, are purely speculative matters. One fact is certain, however. No one of the original occupants of Qumran returned to the caves to reclaim their valuable manuscripts.

Today the Essene theory is questioned by some. Most notably Norman Golb of Chicago has launched a forceful attack on the common opinion. His objections, reiterated in a series of papers, culminated in 1995 in a hefty tome. The target of his criticism is the provenance of the scrolls found at Qumran. According to him, the manuscripts originated in a Jerusalem library (or libraries), the contents of which were concealed in desert caves when the capital was besieged between 67 and 70 CE. The chief corollary of the hypothesis is that the Essenes had nothing to do either with the Qumran settlement – a fortress in Golb's opinion* – or with the manuscripts.

The early assumption of Scroll scholars that every non-biblical Dead Sea text was an Essene writing might have justified to some extent Norman Golb's scepticism. But nowadays specialists distinguish between Qumran manuscripts written by members of the Essene sect, and others either predating the Community, or simply brought there from outside. Emanuel Tov, for instance, has drawn a dividing line on scribal grounds between scrolls produced at Qumran and the rest. However, in my view the soft

---

* At the Scrolls Symposium held at the Library of Congress in Washington on 21–2 April 1993, Magen Broshi, Director of the Shrine of the Book at the Israel Museum in Jerusalem, delivered a powerful rebuttal of the Golb conjecture as well as the speculative theory advanced at another conference, held in New York in December 1992, by Pauline Donceel-Voûte, in whose view Qumran was a winter villa built for wealthy inhabitants of Jerusalem and the room which de Vaux identified as a *scriptorium* a dining hall.

underbelly of the Jerusalem hypothesis is revealed – apart from
the patent weakness of the archaeological interpretation, for
Qumran is not a fortress – by the composition of the manuscript
collection itself, definitely pointing towards a *sectarian* library. If
Cave 4 is taken as representative, whereas several biblical books
(Kings, Lamentations, Ezra and Chronicles) are attested only
in *single* copies, and others, as important as Numbers, Joshua,
Judges, Proverbs, Ruth and Ecclesiastes, in *two* copies, we find *ten*
copies of the Community Rule and *nine* of the Damascus Document. Over a *dozen* manuscripts contain sectarian calendars, yet
not one mainstream calendar figures among the 575 (or 555)
compositions found in that cave! So, if the texts discovered at
Qumran came from the capital, can their source have been an
Essene library in Jerusalem?*

Yet, if its intricacies are handled with sophistication, the
Essene thesis is still the best today. Indeed, it accounts best for
such striking peculiarities as common ownership of property and
the lack of reference to women in the Community Rule, the probable coexistence of celibate and married sectaries (in accordance
with Flavius Josephus' account of two kinds of Essenes), and the
remarkable coincidence between the geographical setting of
Qumran and Pliny the Elder's description of an Essene establishment near the Dead Sea between Jericho and Engedi. I admit of
course that the Scrolls and the archaeological data surrounding
them do not always fully agree with the Greek and Latin notices,
and that both the Qumran and the classical accounts need to be
interpreted and adjusted, bearing in mind that the Scrolls represent the views of initiates against those of more or less complete
outsiders. But since none of the competing theories associating
the Qumran group with Pharisees, Sadducees, Zealots, or Jewish-
Christians can withstand critical scrutiny, I remain unrepentant
in upholding my statement formulated in 1977 as still valid today:
'The final verdict must . . . be that of the proposed solutions the
Essene theory is relatively the soundest. It is even safe to say that
it possesses a high degree of intrinsic probability.'†

* It may also be wondered why the librarians of Jerusalem should have chosen
such a distant place to hide their manuscripts when equally inaccessible caves
could have been found closer to home.
† G. Vermes, *An Introduction to the Complete Dead Sea Scrolls*, London, 1999,
126.

2 The Essenes and the Qumran Community

Before the discovery of the scrolls at Qumran, the primary sources concerning the Essenes, a Jewish religious community flourishing during the last two centuries of the Second Temple era (*c.* 150 BCE–70 CE), were furnished by the Greek writings of two Jewish authors, Philo of Alexandria (*That Every Good Man Should be Free*; *Apology for the Jews*, quoted in Eusebius, *Praeparatio evangelica* VIII) and Flavius Josephus (*War* II; *Antiquities* XVIII) and by the Roman geographer and naturalist, Pliny the Elder, who left a short but very important notice in Latin (*Natural History* V).* Despite the apparent importance attributed to it by Philo, Josephus and Pliny, the sect is not explicitly mentioned either in the New Testament or in rabbinic literature. There is no general agreement regarding the meaning of the group's name: *Essaioi* or *Essenoi* in Greek, and *Esseni* in Latin. The designation may signify 'the Pious', or 'the Healers', devoted to the cure of body and soul. If the latter interpretation is adopted, it provides a parallel to the Greek *therapeutai*, the title given by Philo to an Egyptian-Jewish ascetic society akin to the Essenes.

The membership of the Palestinian group exceeded four thousand. Josephus and Philo locate them in Judaean towns; Pliny refers only to a single Essene settlement in the wilderness between Jericho and Engedi.

Individual congregations, directed by superiors, resided in commonly occupied houses. Initiation consisted of one year of probation, and two years of further training, leading to full table-fellowship on swearing an oath of loyalty to the sect. Only adult men qualified according to Philo and Pliny, but Josephus reports that boys were also trained by them. Serious disobedience resulted in expulsion from the order.

One of the principal characteristics of the Essenes was common ownership of property. New members handed over their belongings to the superiors, who collected also the wages earned by every sectary. Agriculture was the main Essene occupation. Having renounced private possessions, the members received all

* For a more detailed account see G. Vermes and Martin Goodman, *The Essenes According to the Classical Sources* (Sheffield, 1989).

that they needed: food, clothes, care. Further peculiarities included the wearing of white garments; ritual bathing before meals which were given only to initiates, and cooked and blessed by priests; the rejection of animal sacrifice and of oaths to support their statements, and, above all, of marriage. Josephus, however, admits that one Essene branch adopted the married state as long as sex was used only for the purpose of procreation.

Theologically, they showed extreme reverence for the Law and were famous for their strictest observance of the Sabbath. Their esoteric teachings were recorded in secret books. Experts in the healing of body and soul, they also excelled in prophecy. They preferred belief in Fate to freedom of the will and, rejecting the notion of bodily resurrection, envisaged a purely spiritual after-life.

The common opinion identifying or closely associating the Qumran sectaries with the Essenes is based on three principal considerations.

1. There is no better site than Qumran to correspond to Pliny's settlement between Jericho and Engedi.
2. Chronologically, Essene activity placed by Josephus in the period between Jonathan Maccabaeus (*c.* 150 BCE) and the first Jewish war (66–70 CE) and the sectarian occupation of the Qumran site coincide perfectly.
3. The similarities of common life, organisation and customs are so fundamental as to render the identification of the two bodies extremely probable as long as some obvious differences can be explained.

A good many contradictions appear in the diverse sources and are not simply due to a lack of harmony between the Scrolls and the Graeco-Latin documents. Thus Qumran attests to both communism and private property; married and unmarried states. Likewise, Josephus speaks of celibate and married Essenes, and the prohibition to 'fornicate' with one's wife remarkably echoes the married Essenes' ban on marital sex when the woman was not in a state to conceive.* Furthermore, the Qumran movement

* The *therapeutai* or Egyptian ascetics of Philo adopted celibacy, but formed separate male and female communities (mature men having left behind family

incorporated two separate branches and the manuscripts reflect an organisational and doctrinal development of some two centuries. It would be unreasonable to expect complete agreement among the sources. It must finally be borne in mind that the sectarian compositions were written by initiates for insiders, whereas Pliny and Philo, and to some extent even Josephus (although he claims to have undergone a partial Essene education), are bound to have reproduced hearsay evidence, unlikely to echo fully the views and beliefs prevalent among members. Hence the identification of Essenism and the Qumran sect remains in my view the likeliest of all proposed solutions.

Since the early 1950s, the information garnered from the Scrolls and from Qumran's archaeological remains has been combined by experts to form a persuasive portrait of the people to which they allude. Yet for all the advances made in knowledge and understanding, the enigma of the sect is by no means definitely solved. After all this time, we are still not certain that we have collated the whole evidence correctly or interpreted it properly. Questions continue to arise in the mind and there is still no way to be sure of the answers.

Our perplexity is mainly due to an absence in the documents, singly or together, of any systematic exposition of the sect's constitution and laws. The Community Rule legislates for a group of ascetics living in a kind of 'monastic' society, the statutes of the Damascus Document for an ordinary lay existence; *Miqsat Ma'ase ha-Torah*, or Some Observances of the Law, probably echoes the prehistory or early history of the sect; and the War Rule and Messianic Rule in their turn, while associated with the Community Rule and the Damascus Document, and no doubt

---

and property, and women being mostly aged virgins; cf. Philo, *Contemplative Life*) whose members met for worship. A badly damaged manuscript from Cave 4, repeatedly mentioning old men and women, has been interpreted by J. M. Baumgarten, in 'Marriage or Golden Age Ritual?', *Journal of Jewish Studies* 34 (1983), as probably alluding to a similar institution. Not a single coherent section of this liturgical composition has survived; however, it is worth noting that a small fragment contains the phrase 'daughter of truth' and an allusion to the examination of women concerning their 'intelligence and understanding'. Josephus states in connection with the marrying Essenes that they trained their women – like their men – for three years.

reflecting to some extent a contemporary state of affairs, first and foremost plan for a future age.

Taken together, however, it is clear from this literature that the sectaries regarded themselves as the true Israel, the repository of the authentic traditions of the religious body, from which they had seceded. Accordingly, they organised their movement so that it corresponded faithfully to that of the Jewish people, dividing it into priests and laity (or Aaron and Israel), and the laity grouped after the biblical model into twelve tribes. This structure is described in the War Scroll's account of reconstituted Temple worship as it was expected to be at the end of time:

The twelve chief Priests shall minister at the daily sacrifice before God . . . Below them . . . shall be the chiefs of the Levites to the number of twelve, one for each tribe . . . Below them shall be the chiefs of the tribes.

Still following the biblical pattern, sectarian society (apart from the tribe of Levi) was further distinguished into units of Thousands, Hundreds, Fifties and Tens. To what extent these figures are symbolical, we do not know, but it is improbable that 'Thousands' amounted to anything more than a figure of speech. Archaeologists have deduced from the fact that the cemetery contained 1,100 graves, dug over the course of roughly 200 years, that the population of Qumran, an establishment of undoubted importance, can never have numbered more than 150 to 200 souls at a time. Also, it should be borne in mind that the total membership of the Essene sect in the first century CE only slightly exceeded 'four thousand' (Josephus, *Antiquities* XVIII).

The 'monastic' brotherhood at Qumran alludes to itself in the Community Rule as 'the men of holiness' and 'the men of perfect holiness', and to the sect as 'the Community' and 'Council of the Community' or 'the men of the Law'. The establishment was devoted exclusively to religion. Work must have formed a necessary part of their existence; it is obvious from the remains discovered at Qumran that they farmed, made pots, cured hides and reproduced manuscripts. But no indication of this appears in the documents. It is said only that they were to 'eat in common and bless in common and deliberate in common', living in such a way as to 'seek God with a whole heart and soul'. Perfectly obedient to

each and every one of the laws of Moses and to all that was commanded by the Prophets, they were to love one another and to
share with one another their 'knowledge, powers and possessions'. They were to be scrupulous in their observance of the times
appointed for prayer, and for every other aspect of a liturgical
existence conducted apart from the Temple of Jerusalem and its
official cult. 'Separate from the habitation of unjust men', they
were to study the Torah in the wilderness and thereby 'atone for
the Land' and its wicked men, for whom they were to nourish an
'everlasting hatred', though this went together with a firm convic-
tion that their fate was in God's hands alone. And the poet proclaims in the Hymn with which the Community Rule ends:

> I will pay to no man the reward of evil;
>   I will pursue him with goodness.
> For judgement of all the living is with God
>   And it is He who will render to man his reward.

They were to be truthful, humble, just, upright, charitable and
modest. They were to

watch in community for a third of every night of the year, to read the
Book and to study the Law and to bless together.

These are, as may be seen, mostly the sort of recommendations to
be expected of men devoting themselves to contemplation. A
point to bear in mind, however, is that the contemplative life is
not a regular feature of Judaism. An additional distinctive trait of
these sectaries is that another qualification was required of them
besides holiness: they were expected to become proficient in the
knowledge of the 'two spirits' in which all men 'walk', the spirits of
truth and falsehood, and to learn how to discriminate between
them. They were taught in the so-called 'instruction concerning
the Two Spirits', the earliest Jewish theological tractate incorporated into the Community Rule, how to recognise a 'son of Light' or
potential 'son of Light', and how to distinguish a 'son of Darkness'
belonging to the lot of Belial.

The hierarchy at Qumran was strict and formal, from the highest level to the lowest. Every sectary was inscribed in 'the order of

his rank' – the term 'order' recurs constantly – and was obliged to keep to it in all the Community meetings and at table, an order that was subject to an annual review on the Feast of the Renewal of the Covenant. But after democratic beginnings, with the 'Congregation' (literally, 'the Many') as such forming the supreme authority, testified to by what seems to be the earliest formulation of the communal constitution, the 'sons of Zadok, the priests', members of the 'Zadokite' high-priestly family, took over the leadership of the sect. Although nothing to this effect is mentioned specifically in the Community Rule, the superior, the so-called *mebaqqer* or Guardian, was undoubtedly one of their number, as was the Bursar of the Congregation entrusted with handling the material affairs of the Community. In their hands lay the ultimate responsibility for decisions on matters of doctrine, discipline, purity and impurity, and in particular everything pertaining to 'justice and property'. It was also a basic rule of the order that a priest was required to be present at any gathering of ten or more members who were meeting for debate, Bible study or prayer. A priest was to recite the grace before the common meals and to pronounce blessings. He was no doubt the man whose duty it was to study the Law continually. One interesting feature of the priesthood at Qumran is that their precedence was absolute. In Judaism as represented by the Mishnah, the priest is superior to the Levite, the Levite to the Israelite, and the Israelite to the 'bastard'. But the priestly precedence is conditional. If the 'bastard' is a man of learning, we are told, and the High Priest an uneducated 'boor', 'the bastard . . . precedes the High Priest'.

The highest office was vested in the person of the Guardian, known also, it would seem, as the 'Master' (*maskil*). The Community was to be taught by him how to live in conformity with the 'Book of the Community Rule', and to be instructed by him in the doctrine of the 'two spirits'. He was to preside over assemblies, giving leave to speak to those wishing to do so. He was to assess, in concert with the brethren, the spiritual progress of the men in his charge and rank them accordingly. And negatively, he was not to dispute with 'the men of the Pit (or Dawn)' and not to transmit to them the sect's teachings. Of the sect's institutions, the most significant appears to have been the Council of the Community, or assembly of the Congregation. From a passage ordering all the members to sit in their correct places – 'The Priests shall sit first, and the elders second, and all the rest of the people according to their rank' – the Council seems to have been a gathering of the whole community, under the priests and men of importance, marshalled by the Levites, and with the Guardian at the head. But in another text, generally held to be an early section, the rule is as follows:

In the Council of the Community there shall be twelve men and three Priests, perfectly versed in all that is revealed of the Law, whose works shall be truth, righteousness, justice, loving-kindness and humility. They shall preserve the faith in the Land with steadfastness and meekness and shall atone for sin by the practice of justice and by suffering the sorrows of affliction. They shall walk with all men according to the standard of truth and the rule of the time.

These three priests and twelve men are referred to also as 'fifteen men' in a hybrid version of the Community Rule and the Damascus Document. Their presence was obviously essential: both documents state that when they 'are in Israel, the Council of the Community shall be established in truth'. But whether they formed the nucleus of the sect as a whole, or the minimum quorum of the leadership of the Community, symbolically portrayed as consisting of the twelve tribes and the three Levitical clans, or a special elite within the Council designated elsewhere 'the Foundations of the Community', must be left open to question. The purpose of the meetings is in any case clear. It was to debate the Law, to discuss their current business, to select or reject newcomers under the guidance of the Guardian, to hear charges against offenders and to conduct a yearly inquiry into the progress of every sectary, promoting or demoting them in rank, again under the Guardian's supervision. During their sessions, order and quiet were to prevail: a person wishing to offer his opinion or ask a question was to crave permission in a prescribed way. He was to rise and tell the Guardian and the Congregation, 'I have something to say to the Congregation' and then wait for their consent before going ahead.

The procedure followed in inquiries into infringements of the Law and the sect's Rule has been preserved, and the list of faults with their corresponding sentences tells us more about the mentality of the Dead Sea ascetics than any isolated exposition of their doctrine and principles can do.

Beginning with the blackest sins: any transgression, by commission or omission, of 'one word of the Law of Moses, on any point whatever' earned outright expulsion. No former companion might from then on associate with the sinner in any way at all. Expulsion followed, secondly, the pronouncement for any reason whatever of the divine Name:

If any man has uttered the *Most* Venerable Name, even though frivolously, or as a result of shock, or for any other reason whatever, while reading the Book or blessing, he shall be dismissed and shall return . . . no more.

Thirdly, a sectary was expelled for slandering the Congregation. Fourthly, he was sent away for rebelling against the 'Foundations' of the Community:

Whoever has murmured against the authority of the Community shall be expelled and shall not return.

Lastly, where a man had been a member of the Council for at least ten years and had then defected to 'walk in the stubbornness of his heart', not only was he to be expelled, but the same judgement was extended to any of his former colleagues who might take pity on him and share with him their food or money.

The remaining offences are of a kind that might be confessed and censured in any Christian religious order of today, though one cannot perhaps say the same of the penances imposed for them.

In a descending order of gravity: a man who 'betrayed the truth and walked in the stubbornness of his heart', or transgressed the Mosaic Law inadvertently, was visited with two years of penance. He was to lose his rank and during the first year be separated from the 'purity' of the Congregation, and during the second year, from its 'drink'. He was then to be re-examined by the Congregation and subsequently returned to his place in the order.

Lying in matters of property, in all probability, the partial concealment of personal possessions, earned exclusion from 'purity' for a year and a cut by one quarter in the food ration. One of the penal code scrolls found in Cave 4 prescribes for deceiving a companion an exclusion for six months and a halving of the guilty person's food portion. Disrespect to a companion of higher rank, rudeness and anger towards a priest, slander and deliberate insult, all earned one year of penance and exclusion from 'purity'. After this, the sentences decrease to six months, three months, thirty days and ten days of penance.

For lying deliberately and similarly deceiving by word or deed, for bearing malice unjustly, for taking revenge, for murmuring against a companion unjustly and also for going 'naked before his companion, without having been obliged to do so' – a curious proviso – the sectary was to atone for six months. For failing to care for a companion and for speaking foolishly: three months. For falling asleep during a meeting of the Council, for leaving the Council while members were standing (in prayer?), for spitting in Council, for 'guffawing foolishly', for being 'so poorly dressed that when drawing his hand from beneath his garment his nakedness has been seen': thirty days. The penal code contained in another of the Cave 4 manuscripts of the Damascus Document mentions also ten days' penance, in addition to the thirty days' expulsion inflicted on someone who has fallen asleep during a meeting! And for leaving an assembly three times without reason, for interrupting another while speaking, for gesticulating with the left hand: ten days. A fascinating fragment has preserved in writing cases of misbehaviour by *named* sectaries: 'Yohanan son of . . .' was 'short-tempered'; 'Hananiah Notos' led astray 'the spirit of the Community' and either pampered himself or showed favouritism to his near kin; and another 'Hananiah son of Simon' 'loved' something no doubt prohibited.

That the common table was of high importance to Qumran daily life is evident from the fact that only the fully professed and the faultless, that is to say those who were 'inscribed . . . for purity' and not subsequently disqualified, were allowed to sit at it. There is no explicit mention of a ritual bath preceding the meals, but from various references to purification by water, as well as the presence of bathing installations at Qumran, it is likely that the sectaries immersed themselves before eating as did the Essenes according to Josephus. But little more is learnt of the meal itself from the Community Rule than that when the table had been 'prepared for eating, and the new wine for drinking', the priest was to be the first to bless the food and drink. The implication would be that after him the others did the same, an inference supported by the Messianic Rule, where a similar meal is described attended by two Messiahs. Some uncertainty surrounds the meaning of 'new wine', but it would seem from the use in the Scrolls (with the exception of the Temple Scroll), of the alternative Hebrew words for wine – *tirosh* and *yayin* – that the latter often has pejorative connotations. More likely than not, the 'wine' drunk by the sectaries, 'the drink of the Congregation', was unfermented grape-juice.

Another topic to be considered under the heading of communal life and institutions is the crucial one of induction into the sect. According to the regime adopted at Qumran, a person desiring to join the Essenes remained on probation, certainly for two years and possibly for three or more. His first move was to appear before the Guardian 'at the head of the Congregation', meaning no doubt during a session of the Congregation, who inquired into his principles to discover if he was a suitable postulant. If they were satisfied, he 'entered the Covenant'. That is to say, he solemnly swore there and then to adhere to the Torah as the sect interpreted it, vowing

by a binding oath to return with all his heart and soul to every commandment of the Law of Moses in accordance with all that has been revealed of it to the sons of Zadok . . . the Keepers of the Covenant.

After a further period of unspecified length, during which he received instruction from the Guardian 'in all the rules of the Community', he appeared once more before the Congregation, who confirmed him as a novice or dismissed him. But although he was now accepted into the Council of the Community, he was nevertheless still not admitted to 'purity' for another full year.

This concept of pure things (*tohorah*, *taharah* or *tohorot*, literally 'purity' or 'purities') needs some comment. It seems to designate here as in rabbinic literature ritually pure food, as well as the vessels and utensils in which it is contained or cooked. It includes also garments. The *tohorot*, moreover, are distinguished by the rabbis from *mashqin*, liquids, the latter being considered much more susceptible to contract impurity than solid comestibles. Hence, in ordering the novice not to touch the pure things of the Congregation, the Community forbade him all contact with its pots, plates, bowls and necessarily the food that they held. He was not, in effect, to attend the common table and had to eat elsewhere. Although the context is very different, a parallel rule figures in the Temple Scroll, in which a Gentile woman married to her Jewish captor is prohibited from touching his *tohorah* for seven years.

During this first year of the novitiate, the newcomer could not share the sect's property. At a third Community inquiry, he was examined for 'his understanding and observance of the Law' and, if his progress was judged to be adequate, he handed over his money and belongings to the 'Bursar of the Congregation', but they were set aside and not yet absorbed into Community ownership. During this second year, furthermore, the ban on touching the pure things was relaxed, but he could still not touch liquids, the 'Drink [*mashqeh*] of the Congregation'. Finally, with the second year over, the novice had once more to undergo an examination, after which, 'according to the judgement of the Congregation', he was at last inscribed among the brethren in the order of his rank 'for the Law, and for justice, and for purity'. Also, his property was amalgamated with theirs and he possessed the right from then on to speak his mind in the Council of the Community.

In sum, this strict and extended curriculum falls into two stages. The postulant is first brought into the Covenant, swearing total fidelity to the Mosaic Law as interpreted by the sect's priestly teachers, and to 'separate from all the men of injustice who walk in the way of wickedness'. He then secondly embarks on a course of training as a preliminary to joining the 'holy Congregation'. In other words, entering the Covenant and entering the Community was not one act, but two.

It has long been debated whether the Qumran sectaries were married or celibate. From the image of their life projected so far on the basis of the Community Rule, few will probably disagree that the idea of the presence of women among them appears incongruous. The impression received is that of a wholly masculine society:

indeed, they were actually enjoined 'to not follow a sinful heart and lustful eyes, committing all manner of evil'. In further support of the argument for celibacy, the word *ishah*, woman, occurs nowhere in the Community Rule. Or rather, to be more exact, it is encountered once in the final Hymn, in the cliché, 'one born of woman'. Moreover, against the Cave 4 Damascus Document regulation which envisages a membership of married people and imposes the penalty of expulsion on anyone murmuring against 'the Fathers' but only a ten-day penance for murmuring against 'the Mothers', the Community Rule speaks only of the crime of murmuring against 'the authority of the Community'. Silence concerning the presence of women seems therefore deliberate. Yet the fact cannot be overlooked that although in the main graveyard itself the twenty-six tombs so far opened at random (out of 1,100) have all contained adult male skeletons, the archaeologists have uncovered on the peripheries of the cemetery the bones of six women and three children too. A more extensive exploration of the cemetery would eliminate most of these uncertainties.

The Damascus Document, the Temple Scroll and the Messianic Rule, among others, are concerned with a style of religious existence quite at variance with that at Qumran. In the 'towns' or 'camps', as the Damascus Document terms them, adherents of the sect lived an urban or village life side by side with, yet apart from, their fellow Jewish and Gentile neighbours. They had wives and reared children, but clearly their sexual morality followed particularly strict rules. A Cave 4 Damascus Document manuscript lays down that 'whoever has approached his wife, not according to the rules, thus fornicating, he shall leave and will not return again'. The married sectaries employed servants, engaged in commerce and trade (even with Gentiles), tended cattle, grew vines and corn in the surrounding fields, discharged their duties to the Temple by way of offerings, but in doing so they were obliged like their brothers in the desert to show absolute obedience to the Law and to observe the sect's 'appointed times'. There is no indication, however, that the continual and intensive study of the Torah played any part in their lives. Nor in their regard is there any mention of instruction in the doctrine of the two spirits, as membership of the group was a birthright and not the outcome of a process of selection and training.

How many of these people, if any, lived in Jerusalem is not known, but they must at least have visited the city from time to time, since a statute forbids them to enter the 'house of worship' (possibly the Temple) in a state of ritual uncleanness, or to 'lie with a woman in the city of the Sanctuary to defile the city of the Sanctuary with their uncleanness'.

Little is revealed in the Damascus Document of how the life span of the individual progressed in the 'towns', and for this we have to turn to the Messianic Rule in the hope that it reflects contemporary actuality as well as the ideal life of an age to come.

According to the latter Rule, members of the Covenant were permitted to marry at the age of twenty, when they were estimated to have reached adulthood and to 'know *good* and evil'. For the subsequent five years they were then allowed to 'assist' (as opposed to taking an active part) at hearings and judgements. At twenty-five, they advanced one grade further and qualified to 'work in the service of the Congregation'. At thirty, they were regarded as at last fully mature and could 'participate' in the affairs of the tribunals and assemblies, taking their place among the higher ranks of the sect, the 'chiefs of the thousands of Israel, the Hundreds, the chiefs of the Fifties and Tens, the judges and the officers of their tribes, in all their families *under the authority* of the sons of *Aaron* the Priests'. As office-holders, they were expected to perform their duties to the best of their ability and were accorded more honour or less in conformity with their 'understanding' and the 'perfection' of their 'way'. As they grew older, so their burdens became lighter.

As at Qumran, supreme authority rested in the hands of the priests, and every group of ten or more was to include a priest 'learned in the Book of Meditation' and to be 'ruled by him'. His precedence, on the other hand, is not represented as absolute in the 'towns'. It is explicitly stated that in the absence of a properly qualified priest, he was to be replaced by a Levite who would perform all the functions of a superior except those specially reserved in the Bible to the priesthood such as applying the laws of leprosy. The Cave 4 manuscripts of the Damascus Document describe at length the diagnosis of the onset and eventual cure of skin disease. Priests with speech defects, those who had been prisoners of war or had settled and been active among Gentiles were disqualified from performing priestly duties or eating 'sacred food'.

As in the Community Rule, the head of the 'camp' is designated in the Damascus Document, as well as in other fragments, as the *mebaqqer* or Guardian. He appears, however, not to be supported by a council. There is reference to the 'company of Israel', on the advice of which it would be licit to attack Gentiles, but this type of war council, mentioned also in the Messianic Rule, can surely have had nothing to do with the assemblies described in the Community Rule. The Guardian of the 'camps', in any case, stands on his own as teacher and helper of his people. He shall love them, writes the author,

as a father loves his children, and shall carry them in all their distress like a shepherd his sheep. He shall loosen all the fetters which bind them that in his Congregation there may be none that are oppressed or broken.

The Guardian was to examine newcomers to his congregation, though not, it should be noted, to determine their 'spirit', and was to serve as the deciding authority on the question of their admission. But an additional task of the *mebaqqer* in the towns was to ensure that no friendly contact occurred between his congregation and everyone outside the sect. Whatever exchanges took place had to be paid for; and even these transactions were to be subject to his consent.

Instead of dealing with offenders in Community courts of inquiry, the towns had their tribunals for hearing cases, equipped moreover with 'judges'. These were to be ten in number, elected for a specific term and drawn from the tribes of Levi, Aaron and Israel: four priests and Levites, and six laymen. They were to be not younger than twenty-five and not older than sixty – in the Messianic Rule, which also speaks of judges, the age-limits are thirty and sixty years – and were to be expert in biblical law and the 'constitutions of the Covenant'. The arrangement would seem, in fact, to be fairly straightforward. Yet it is not entirely so. For example, it is evident that the Guardian was also implicated in legal matters; he had to determine whether a proper case had been made out against a sectary and whether it should be brought before the court, and in certain cases he appears to have imposed penalties on his own. The 'Priest overseeing the Congregation' of one of the Cave 4 fragments of the Damascus Document appears to perform the same single judicial function as the Guardian in the case of an inadvertent sin. We are not told whether the ten judges sat together, whether they were all drawn from the locality in which they lived, or whether they travelled as it were on circuit as nowadays. The code of law they were expected to administer, as laid down in the Damascus Document, differs in content from that of the Community Rule. Furthermore, although, unlike the Qumran code, a sentence is prescribed only rarely, sometimes it is the death penalty. We have here, in addition to matters relating primarily to communal discipline to a large extent identical with the Community Rule, a more detailed sectarian reformulation of scriptural laws regulating Jewish life as such.

The first group of statutes, concerned with vows, opens with the injunction that in order to avoid being put to death for the capital sin of uttering the names of God, the sectary must swear by the Covenant alone. Such an oath would be fully obligatory and might not be cancelled. If he subsequently violated his oath, he would then have only to confess to the priest and make restitution. The sectary is also ordered not to vow to the altar articles acquired unlawfully, or the food of his own house, and not to make any vow 'in the fields' but always before the judges. He is threatened with death if he 'vow another to destruction by the laws of the Gentiles'. As for the right conferred by the Bible on fathers and husbands to annul vows made by their daughters or wives, the Damascus Document limits it to the cancellation of oaths which should have never been made in the first place. It is clearly stated that no accusation is valid without prior warnings before witnesses.

A few ordinances are concerned with witnesses. No one under the age of twenty was to testify before the judges in a capital charge. Also, whereas the normal biblical custom is that two or three witnesses are needed before any sentence can be pronounced, a single witness being quite unacceptable, *unus testis nullus testis*, sectarian law allowed the indictment of a man guilty of repeating the same capital offence on the testimony of single witnesses to the separate occasions on which it was committed, providing they reported it to the Guardian at once and that the Guardian recorded it at once in writing. With regard to capital cases, to which should be added apostasy in a state of demonic possession, the adultery of a betrothed girl, slandering the people of Israel and treason, it is highly unlikely that either the Jewish or the Roman authorities would have granted any rights of execution to the sect. So this is probably part of the sect's vision of the future age, when it as Israel *de jure* would constitute *de facto* the government of the chosen people.

The penal code of the Damascus Document stipulates irrevocable expulsion in the case of a man 'fornicating' with his wife. This may refer to illicit sexual relations with a menstruating woman or, perhaps more likely, with a pregnant or post-menopausal woman since, as Josephus clearly states in connection with married Essenes, sex between spouses was licit only if it could result in conception.

A section devoted to Sabbath laws displays a marked bias towards severity. In time, rabbinic law developed the Sabbath rules in still greater detail than appears here, but the tendency is already manifest.

The sectary was not only to abstain from labour 'on the sixth day from the moment when the sun's orb is distant by its own fullness from the gate wherein it sinks', he was not even to speak about work. Nothing associated with money or gain was to interrupt his Sabbath of rest. No member of the Covenant of God was to go out of his house on business on the Sabbath. In fact, he was not to go out, for any reason, further than 1,000 cubits (about 500 yards), though he could pasture his beast at a distance of 2,000 cubits from his town. He could not cook. He could not pick and eat fruit and other edible things 'lying in the fields'. He could not draw water and carry it away, but must drink where he found it. He could not strike his beast or reprimand his servant. He could not carry a child, wear perfume or sweep up the dust in his house. He could not assist his animals to give birth or help them if they fell into a pit; he could, however, pull a man out of water or fire without the help of a ladder or rope. Interpreting the Bible restrictively (Lev. xxiii, 38), the sect's lawmaker (or makers) commanded him to offer no sacrifice on the Sabbath save the Sabbath burnt-offering, and never to send a gift to the Temple by the hand of one 'smitten with any uncleanness, permitting him thus to defile the altar'. He was also never to have intercourse while in the 'city of the Sanctuary'.

The punishment imposed for profaning the Sabbath and the feasts in any of these ways was not death as in the Bible (Num. xv, 35), nor even expulsion as in the Community Rule. It was seven years' imprisonment.

It shall fall to men to keep him in custody. And if he is healed of his error, they shall keep him in custody for seven years and he shall afterwards approach the Assembly.

In the last group, the ordinances appear to be only loosely connected, though some of them involve relations with the larger Jewish–Gentile world. One such forbids killing or stealing from a non-Jew, 'unless so advised by the company of Israel'. Another proscribes the sale to Gentiles of ritually pure beasts and birds, as well as the produce of granary and wine-press, in case they should blaspheme by offering them in heathen sacrifice. Miqsat Ma'ase Ha-Torah further prohibits acceptance of offerings (wheat or meat) by Gentiles. A ban is similarly laid on selling to Gentiles foreign servants converted to the Jewish faith. But in addition to these regulations affecting contacts with non-Jews, a few are concerned with dietary restrictions. Thus:

No man shall defile himself by eating any live creature or creeping thing, from the larvae of bees to all creatures which creep in water.

Others deal with the laws of purity and purification and with uncleanness resulting from various sexual discharges and childbirth. Outside the Damascus Document, other scrolls provide ample information on purity matters, including the law relative to the burning of the 'red heifer' whose ashes were a necessary ingredient for the making of the 'water for removing uncleanness'.

Two types of meeting are provided for, with equal laconism: the 'assembly of the camp' presided over by a priest or a Levite and the 'assembly of all the camps'. Presumably the latter was the general convention of the whole sect held on the Feast of the Renewal of the Covenant, the annual great festival when both the 'men of holiness' and the 'men of the Covenant' confessed their former errors and committed themselves once more to perfect obedience to the Law and the sect's teachings. According to the available texts, the sectaries were to be mustered and inscribed in their rank by name, the priests first, the Levites second, the Israelites third. A fourth group of proselytes is unique to the 'towns', but as has been observed these were Gentile slaves converted to Judaism. A further remark that in this order the sect's members were to 'be questioned on all matters' leads one to suppose that the allusion must be to the yearly inquiry into their spiritual progress mentioned in the Community Rule.

Two Cave 4 manuscripts of the Damascus Document describe the expulsion ceremony of an unfaithful member. He was cursed and dismissed by the Priest overseeing the Congregation and cursed also by all the inhabitants of the camps. Should the latter maintain contact with the renegade, they would forfeit their own membership of the sect.

Apart from these familiar directions, we learn only that the priest who mustered the gathering was to be between thirty and sixty years old and, needless to say, 'learned in the Book of Meditation'. The 'Guardian of all the camps', in his turn, was to be between thirty and fifty, and to have 'mastered all the secrets of men and the language of all their clans'. He was to decide who was to be admitted, and anything connected with a 'suit or judgement' was to be brought to him.

As for the initiation of new members, the statutes appear to legislate for young men reaching their majority within the brotherhood and for recruits from outside. This is not entirely clear, but the instruction that an aspirant was not to be informed of the sect's rules until he had stood before the Guardian can hardly have applied to a person brought up within its close circle.

Of the sect's own young men the Damascus Document writes merely:

And all those who have entered the Covenant, granted to all Israel for ever, shall make their children who have reached the age of enrolment, swear with the oath of the Covenant.

The Messianic Rule is more discursive. There, enrolment into the sect is represented as the climax of a childhood and youth spent in study. Teaching of the Bible and in the 'precepts of the Covenant' began long before the age of ten, at which age a boy embarked on a further ten years of instruction in the statutes. It was not until after all this that he was finally ready.

From *his* youth they shall instruct him in the Book of Meditation and shall teach him, according to his age, the precepts of the Covenant. They *shall be* educated in their statutes for ten years . . . At the age of twenty years *he shall be* enrolled, that he may enter upon his allotted duties in the midst of his family and be joined to the holy congregation.

The newcomer from outside who repented of his 'corrupted way' was to be enrolled 'with the oath of the Covenant' on the day that he spoke to the Guardian, but no sectarian statute was to be divulged to him 'lest when examining him the Guardian be deceived by him'. Nevertheless, if he broke that oath, 'retribution' would be exacted of him.

It should be added here that one big difference between the organisation of the brethren in the towns and those of the 'monastic' settlement is that new members were not required to surrender their property. There was none of the voluntary communism found at Qumran. On the other hand, where the desert sectaries practised common ownership, those of the towns contributed to the assistance of their fellows in need. Every man able to do so was ordered to hand over a minimum of two days' wages a month to a charitable fund, and from it the Guardian and the judges distributed help to the orphans, the poor, the old and sick, to unmarried women without support and to prisoners held in foreign hands and in need of redemption.

When the two varieties of sectarian life are compared, we find many similarities, but some of the differences still remain striking. In the desert of Qumran men lived together in seclusion; in the towns they were grouped in families, surrounded by non-members with whom they were in inevitable though exiguous contact. The desert brotherhood was to keep apart from the Temple in Jerusalem until the restoration of the true cult in the seventh year of the eschatological war; the town sectaries participated in worship there. The judges of the towns had no

counterparts at Qumran. The Qumran Guardian was supported
by a Council; the town Guardians acted independently. Unfaithful
desert sectaries were sentenced to irrevocable excommunication,
or to temporary exclusion from the common life, or to suffer
lighter penances; the penal code concerned with the towns envisages also the death penalty (whether actually executed or not) as
well as corrective custody. The common table and the 'purity'
associated with it played an essential role at Qumran; in connection with the towns the common meal, but not the pure food, goes
unmentioned. Furthermore, at Qumran all the new recruits came
from outside; in the towns, some were converts but others were
the sons of sectaries. The desert novices underwent two years of
training and were instructed in the doctrine of the 'two spirits';
the towns' converts were subjected to neither experience. In the
desert, property was owned in common; in the towns, it was not.
And last but not least, the desert community appears to have
practised celibacy, whereas the town sectaries patently did not.

Yet despite the dissimilarities, at the basic level of doctrine,
aims and principles, a perceptible bond links the brethren of the
desert with those of the towns. They both claim to represent the
true Israel. They both are led by priests. Both form units of Thousands, Hundreds, Fifties and Tens, both insist on a wholehearted
return to the Mosaic Law in accordance with their own particular
interpretation of it. They are both governed by priests (or Levites). The principal superior, teacher and administrator of both is
known by the unusual title of *mebaqqer*. In both cases, initiation
into the sect is preceded by entry into the Covenant, sworn by
oath. Both groups convene yearly to review the order of precedence of their members after an inquiry into the conduct of each
man during the previous twelve months. Above all, both embrace
the same 'unorthodox' liturgical calendar that sets them apart
from the rest of Jewry.

There can be only one logical conclusion: this was a single religious movement with two branches. It does not, however, answer
all our questions. It does not tell us in particular whether the dif-
ferentiation resulted from a relaxation or from a hardening of the
original ascetic rules. Neither are we told whether the sectaries of
desert and towns maintained regular contact among themselves.
After all, the history of religions furnishes scores of examples of

1a A view of the caves at Qumran, where the first scrolls were discovered in 1947. 1b *Right*, the interior of Cave 4 at Qumran where in 1952 fragments of over 550 documents were found

2a Muhammad edh-Dhib (right), the Bedouin shepherd who found the first cave containing Dead Sea Scrolls. 2b *Below*, Khalil Iskandar Sahin (Kando), the antiques dealer and cobbler (left), who acted as middle man between the Bedouin discoverers of the first scroll fragments and Roland de Vaux

3a Professor E. L. Sukenik at work on scroll fragments. 3b *Below left*, the Thanksgiving Hymns manuscript, which was one of the first scrolls to be found at Qumran. 3c *Below right*, pottery jars which contained some of the scrolls. The discovery at both the Qumran settlement and in the caves of these cylindrical and lidded vessels, of a type unknown elsewhere, is strong evidence of a link between the two

4 The 'Scrollery' at the Rockefeller Museum, Jerusalem

5a Excavation of a cache of pottery vessels at the Qumran settlement.
5b *Below*, Father Roland de Vaux, J. T. Milik and G. Lankester Harding
at the excavation site

6a The Copper Scroll, found in Cave 3 in 1952. The treasures it lists may have belonged to the Temple in Jerusalem. 6b *Below*, Professor H. Wright Baker of the Manchester College of Science and Technology cutting the Copper Scroll into sections prior to its translation

7 The ruins of the fortified tower at Khirbet Qumran

8 The graveyard at Qumran, located slightly to the east of the settlement. The graves are aligned north–south, contrary to the normal Jewish practice.

sister sects which turned into mortal enemies. Did the Qumran and towns fellowships profess and practise unity? A few vital clues suggest that they did.

One indication of a living relationship between the two groups derives from the Qumran library itself. In it were discovered no less than ten copies of the Damascus Document and other writings reflecting the same form of life. It seems hardly likely that they would have figured so prominently among the Qumran literary treasures if they had been the rule books of some rival institution. Another pointer towards unity appears in the passage of the Damascus Document outlining the procedure for the 'assembly of all the camps' and prescribing that the members were to be 'inscribed by name' in hierarchical rank. This clause corresponds exactly to the statute in the Community Rule ordaining a yearly ranking of the sectaries, with a solemn ritual for the Renewal of the Covenant. This leads us to suppose that the Feast of the Covenant, when the desert brethren held their annual spiritual survey, was also the occasion for that of the towns. Can we go further still and establish that the two ceremonies took place, not only at the same time, but at the same place? In effect, the literary and archaeological evidence tends to support the theory that the 'assembly of all the camps', identical with the yearly assembly of the Qumran branch, gathered at Qumran.

The first clue turns on the qualifications of the *mebaqqer* of the Community Rule and the Damascus Document respectively. As may be remembered, the superior at Qumran was required to be expert in recognising 'the nature of all the children of men according to the kind of spirit which they possess', while the *mebaqqer* of the towns was to be concerned rather more with a man's 'deeds', 'possessions', 'ability', etc., than with his inner spirit. When, however, the Damascus Document describes the attributes needed of the 'Guardian of all the camps', what do we find but a reformulation of those accredited to the superior of the desert community, that he should know 'all the secrets of men and all the languages of their clans'? It would emerge from this, therefore, that the Guardian of all the camps and the Guardian at Qumran were one and the same person. The next hint comes from the fact that the Damascus Document is directed to both desert and town sectaries. As an example, the passage from the Exhortation advising

men to choose whatever is pleasing to God and to reject whatever
he hates, 'that you may walk perfectly in all his ways and not follow
after thoughts of the guilty inclination and after eyes of lust',
seems to be addressed to celibates. Yet in this very same document
we later come upon injunctions aimed explicitly at non-celibates:

And if they live in camps according to the rule of the Land, marrying
and begetting children, they shall walk according to the Law and according to the statute concerning binding vows, according to the rule of the
Law which says, *Between a man and his wife and between a father and
his son* (Num. xxx, 17).

The Exhortation would seem in short to be a sermon intended for
delivery on a certain occasion to married and unmarried members of the sect; and as its theme is perseverance in the Covenant,
the appropriate setting would be the Feast of the Renewal of the
Covenant in the third month, i.e. the Feast of Weeks or Pentecost,
and the venue, Qumran.

These literary pointers are supported by two archaeological
finds. First, the twenty-six deposits of animal bones buried on the
Qumran site – goats, sheep, lambs, calves, cows or oxen – have for
long intrigued scholars. Can J. T. Milik be correct in identifying
them as the remains of meals served to large groups of pilgrims in
the Qumran mother-house of the sect (*Ten Years of Discovery in
the Wilderness of Judaea*)? Naturally, he too connects the gathering with the Covenant festival.

The second archaeological clue also is concerned with bones.
The skeletons of four women and one child, and possibly of two
further female bodies and those of two children, were found in the
extension of the Qumran cemetery. Now, if the Renewal of the
Covenant was attended by sectaries from the towns and their families, this may well account for the presence of dead women and
children among the otherwise male skeletons of the graveyard
proper.

Drawing the threads of these various arguments together,
there would seem to be little doubt not only that the desert and
town sectaries were united in doctrine and organisation, but that
they remained in actual and regular touch with each other, under
the ultimate administrative and spiritual authority of the shad-

owy figure of the Priest, of whom we hear so little, and his dominant partner, the Qumran Guardian, Guardian of all the camps. Qumran, it seems, was the seat of the sect's hierarchy and also the centre to which all those turned who professed allegiance to the Council of the Covenant.

3 The Wider World: The Essenes in Jewish History, 200 BCE–70 CE

The absence from the Dead Sea Scrolls of historical texts proper should not surprise us. Neither in the inter-Testamental period, nor in earlier biblical times, was the recording of history as we understand it a strong point among the Jews. Chroniclers are concerned not with factual information about bygone events, but with their religious significance. In Scripture, the 'secular' past is viewed and interpreted by the prophets as revealing God's pleasure or displeasure. Victory or defeat in war, peace or social unrest, abundance of harvest or famine, serve to demonstrate the virtue or sinfulness of the nation and to forecast its future destiny. And when prophecy declined in the fifth century BCE, it was still not succeeded by a growth of historiography: it was followed instead by eschatological speculation, by apocalyptic visions of the end of time, with their awe-inspiring beasts and battles, and by announcements of the ultimate triumph of truth and justice in a future Kingdom of God.

In the Scrolls, the apocalyptic compositions form part of this later tradition. The Qumran writers, while meditating on the words of the Old Testament prophets, sought to discover in them allusions to their own past, present and future. Convinced that they were living in the last days, they read the happenings of their times as the fulfilment of biblical predictions.

For an understanding of the sect's past as it developed within the larger framework of late Second Temple Jewish history, we have to rely principally on Flavius Josephus, the Palestinian Jew who became a Greek man of letters, and on other Jewish Hellenists, such as the authors of the Books of the Maccabees, and Philo of Alexandria, all of whom inherited the Greek predilection for recording and interpreting the past and set out to depict the life of the Jews of Palestine in itself, and as part of the Graeco-Roman world, from the early second century B C E to the first anti-Roman war in 66–70 C E. It is only with the help of the wider canvas painted by these ancient writers that places can be found for the often cryptic historical allusions contained in the Scrolls.

At the beginning of the second century B C E, Palestinian Jewry passed through a state of crisis. Alexander the Great had conquered the Holy Land in 332 B C E and, after the early uncertainties which followed his death, it became part of the empire of the Greeks of Egypt, known as the Ptolemies. During the third century, the Ptolemies avoided, as much as possible, interfering with the internal life of the Jewish nation and, while taxes were required to be paid, it remained under the rule of the High Priest and his council. Important changes in the patterns of population nevertheless took place during this time. Hellenistic cities were built along the Mediterranean coast, such as Gaza, Ascalon (Ashkelon), Joppa (Jaffa), Dor and Acco, re-named Ptolemais. Inland also, to the south of the Lake of Tiberias, the ancient town of Beth Shean was reborn as the Greek city of Scythopolis; Samaria, the capital city of the Samaritans, was Hellenised as Sebaste; and in Transjordan, Rabbath-Ammon (Amman) was re-founded as Philadelphia. In other words, Greeks, Macedonians and Hellenised Phoenicians took up permanent residence on Palestinian soil and the further spread of Greek civilisation and culture was merely a matter of time.

With the conquest of the Holy Land by the Seleucids, or Syrian Greeks, in 200 B C E, the first signs appeared of Jews succumbing to a foreign cultural influence. In the apocryphal Book of Ecclesiasticus, dated to the beginning of the second century B C E, its author, Jesus ben Sira, a sage from Jerusalem, rages against those 'ungodly men' who have 'forsaken the Law of the Most High God' (xli, 8). But the real trouble started when Antiochus IV Epiphanes (175–164 B C E) officially promoted a Hellenising programme in Judaea that was embraced with eagerness by the Jewish elite. The leader of the modernist faction was the brother of the High Priest Onias III. Known as Jesus among his compatriots, he adopted the Greek name of Jason, and set about transforming Jerusalem into a Hellenistic city, by building a gymnasium there and persuading the Jewish youth to participate in athletic games. As 2 Maccabees describes the situation:

So Hellenism reached a high point with the introduction of foreign customs through the boundless wickedness of the impious Jason, no true
High Priest. As a result, the priests no longer had any enthusiasm for
their duties at the altar, but despised the temple and neglected the sacrifices; and in defiance of the law they eagerly contributed to the expenses
of the wrestling-school whenever the opening gong called them. They
placed no value on their hereditary dignities, but cared above everything
for Hellenic honours.

Jason was succeeded by two other High Priests with the same
Greek sympathies, Menelaus and Alcimus. In 169 BCE Antiochus
IV visited Jerusalem and looted the Temple. But when in 167 he
actually prohibited the practice of Judaism under pain of death
and rededicated the Jerusalem Sanctuary to Olympian Zeus, the
'abomination of desolation', the opponents of the Hellenisers
finally rose up in violent resistance. An armed revolt was insti-
gated by the priest Mattathias and his sons the Maccabee brothers, supported by all the traditionalist Jews, and in particular by
the company of the Pious, the Asidaeans or Hasidim, 'stalwarts of
Israel, every one of them a volunteer in the cause of the Law' (1
Mac. ii, 42–3). Led by Judas Maccabaeus and, after his death on
the battlefield, by his brothers Jonathan and Simon, the fierce
defenders of Judaism were able not only to restore Jewish worship in Jerusalem, but against all expectations even managed to
eject the ruling Seleucids and to liberate Judaea.

The Maccabaean triumph was, however, not simply a straightforward victory of godliness and justice over idolatry and tyranny;
it was accompanied by serious social and religious upheavals.
There was first a change in the pontifical succession. With the
murder in 171 BCE of Onias III and the deposition of the usurper,
his brother Jason, the Zadokite family, from which the incum-
bents of the High Priest's office traditionally came, lost the mono-
poly which it had held for centuries. Furthermore, when Onias IV,
the son of Onias III, was prevented from taking over the High
Priesthood from Menelaus, he emigrated to Egypt and in direct
breach of biblical law, which authorises only a single sanctuary
in Jerusalem, erected a Jewish temple in Leontopolis with the

blessing of King Ptolemy Philometor (182–146 BCE). His inaug-
uration of Israelite worship outside Zion, with the connivance of
some priests and Levites, must have scandalised every Palestinian
conservative, especially other priests who belonged, or were allied,
to the Zadokite dynasty.

There was trouble also within the ranks of the Maccabees
themselves. The Hasidim – or part of their group – defected when
Alcimus, whom they trusted, was appointed High Priest in 162
BCE. This move on their part turned out to be naïve; Alcimus' Syrian allies massacred sixty of them in one day (1 Mac. vii, 2–20).

Lastly, a major political change came about when Jonathan
Maccabaeus, himself a priest but not a Zadokite, accepted in
153–152 BCE pontifical office from Alexander Balas, a usurper of
the Seleucid throne. Alexander was anxious for Jewish support
and was not mistaken in thinking that an offer of the High Priesthood would be irresistible. For the conservatives this was an
illegal seizure of power. But they were even more scandalised by
the appointment in 140 BCE, following Jonathan's execution in
143–142 by the Syrian general Tryphon, of Simon Maccabee as
High Priest and hereditary leader of the people by means of a
decree passed by a Jewish national assembly.

From then on, until Pompey's transformation of the independent Jewish state into a Roman province in 63 BCE, Judaea was
ruled by a new dynasty of High Priests, later Priest-Kings, known
as the Hasmonaeans after the grandfather of the Maccabees,
Hasmon, or Asamonaeus according to Josephus. During the in-
tervening years, all Simon's successors, but especially John Hyrcanus I (134–104 BCE) and Alexander Jannaeus (103–76 BCE),
for whom their political role took precedence over their office of
High Priest, occupied one by one the Hellenistic cities of Palestine and conquered the neighbouring territories of Idumaea in
the south, Samaria in the centre and Ituraea in the north.

Throughout this period of territorial expansion, the Hasmonaean rulers enjoyed the support of the Sadducees, one of the three
religious parties first mentioned under Jonathan Maccabaeus and
regular allies of the government. They were opposed by the Pharisees, an essentially lay group formed from one of the branches of
the Hasidim of the Maccabaean age. Already in the days of John
Hyrcanus I there was Pharisaic objection to his usurpation of the

High Priesthood, though they were willing to recognise him as national leader, but on one other occasion, at least, their opposition was overcome by force. Accused of plotting against Alexander Jannaeus in 88 BCE in collusion with the Syrian Seleucid king Demetrius III Eucaerus, 800 Pharisees were condemned by Jannaeus to die on the cross.

After Pompey's seizure of Jerusalem, the Hasmonaean High Priesthood continued for another three decades, but the political power formerly belonging to them passed to the Judaised Idumaean, Herod the Great, when he was promoted to the throne of Jerusalem by Rome in 37 BCE. It is to the last year or two of his reign – he died in 4 BCE – that the Gospels of Matthew and Luke date the birth of Jesus of Nazareth (Matth. ii, 1; Lk. i, 5).

After the ephemeral rule of the successor to Herod the Great, Herod Archelaus (4 BCE–6 CE), who was deposed by Augustus for his misgovernment of Jews and Samaritans alike, Galilee continued in semi-autonomy under the Herodian princes Antipas (4 BCE–39 CE) and Agrippa (39–41 CE), but Judaea was placed under the direct administration of Roman authority. In 6 CE, Coponius, the first Roman prefect of Judaea, arrived to take up his duties there. This prefectorial regime, whose most notorious representative was Pontius Pilate (26–36 CE), lasted for thirty-five years until 41, when the emperor Claudius appointed Agrippa I as king. He died, however, three years later, and in 44 CE the government of the province once more reverted to Roman officials, this time with the title of procurator. Their corrupt and unwise handling of Jewish affairs was one of the chief causes of the war of 66 which led to the destruction of Jerusalem in 70 CE, and to the subsequent decline of the Sadducees, the extinction of the Zealots in Masada in 74, the disappearance of the Essenes, and the survival and uncontested domination of the Pharisees and their rabbinic successors.

It is into this general course of events that the history of Qumran has to be inserted.

The search for clues to the origins and story of the Essene movement begins with the Damascus Document because it is a writing particularly rich in such hints. Here, the birth of the Community is said to have occurred in the 'age of wrath', 390 years after the

destruction of Jerusalem by Nebuchadnezzar, king of Babylon. At
that time, a 'root' sprang 'from Israel and Aaron', i.e. a group of
pious Jews, laymen and priests, and came into being in a situation
of general ungodliness. These people 'groped for the way' for
twenty years, and then God sent them a 'Teacher of Righteousness' to guide them 'in the way of His heart'. The Teacher did not
meet with unanimous approval within the congregation, and a
faction described as 'seekers of smooth things', 'removers of the
bounds' and 'builders of the wall', all metaphors seeming to point
to religious laxity and infidelity, turned against him and his followers. The leader of the breakaway party, though accorded a
number of unflattering sobriquets, such as 'Scoffer', 'Liar' or
'Spouter of Lies', seems to be one and the same person. His associates erred in matters of ritual cleanness, justice, chastity, the dates
of festivals and Temple worship; they were lovers of money and
enemies of peace. In the ensuing fratricidal struggle, the Teacher
and those who remained faithful to him went into exile in the
'land of Damascus' where they entered into a 'new Covenant'.
There, the Teacher of Righteousness was 'gathered in', meaning
that he died. In the meantime, the wicked dominated over Jerusalem and the Temple, though not without experiencing God's
vengeance at the hands of the 'Chief of the Kings of Greece'.

A similar picture emerges from the Habakkuk Commentary
with its explicit mention of desertion by disciples of the Teacher
of Righteousness to the Liar, but also by members unfaithful to
the 'new Covenant'. The allusions to the protagonists of the conflict are sharper in this work than in the Damascus Document. We
learn that the villain, known in this Scroll as the 'Wicked Priest' as
well as the 'Liar' and 'Spouter of Lies', was 'called by the name of
truth' before he became Israel's ruler and was corrupted by wealth
and power – the implication being that for a time he had met with
the sect's approval. Subsequently, however, he defiled Jerusalem
and the Temple. He also sinned against the Teacher of Righteousness and his disciples, chastising him while the 'House of
Absalom' looked silently on, and confronting him in his place of
exile on the sect's Day of Atonement. He 'vilified and outraged the
elect of God', 'plotted to destroy the Poor', i.e. the Community,
and stole their riches. As a punishment, God delivered him 'into
the hand of his enemies', who 'took vengeance on his body of

flesh'. At the last judgement, predicts the Commentary, the Wicked Priest will empty 'the cup of wrath of God'. His successors, the 'last Priests of Jerusalem', are also charged with amassing 'money and wealth by plundering the peoples', i.e. foreigners. But, so the commentator asserts, all their riches and booty will be snatched from them by the Kittim, the conquerors of the world commissioned by God to pay them their just deserts.

The Nahum Commentary moves on to an age following that of the Teacher of Righteousness and the Wicked Priest, as neither of them is mentioned. The principal character here is the 'furious young lion', a Jewish ruler of Jerusalem. He is said to have taken revenge on the 'seekers of smooth things', whom he reproached for having invited 'Demetrius' the king of Greece to Jerusalem. The attempt failed; no foreigner entered the city 'from the time of Antiochus until the coming of the rulers of the Kittim'. The enemies of the 'furious young lion' were 'hanged alive on the tree', a familiar Hebrew circumlocution for crucifixion.

The chronological setting of Qumran history may be reconstructed from archaeological and literary evidence. The excavations of 1951–6 date the beginning, the *terminus a quo*, of the sectarian establishment to 150–140 BCE and its end, the *terminus ad quem*, to the middle of the first war against Rome, 68 CE. The literary allusions, particularly the identifiable historical names, confirm this general finding. It goes without saying, however, that the initial phases of the Community's existence must have preceded by some years or decades the actual establishment of the sect at Qumran. The Nahum Commentary, for example, implies that a king by the name of Antiochus was alive at the beginning of the period with which the documents are concerned. This Antiochus, although one among several so called, can only have been Antiochus IV Epiphanes, notorious for his looting of Jerusalem and the profanation of the Temple in 169–168 BCE.

More significant as a chronological pointer is the dating, in the Damascus Document, of the sect's beginnings to the 'age of wrath', 390 years after the conquest of Jerusalem by Nebuchadnezzar in 586 BCE. This should bring us to 196 BCE but, as is well known, Jewish historians are not very reliable in their time-reckoning for the post-exilic era. Yet even if the literal figure of

390 is rejected, there are still compelling reasons for placing the 'age of wrath' in the opening decades of the second pre-Christian century. Only the Hellenistic crisis which occurred at that time, and which is recalled in various Jewish literary sources from the last two centuries BCE, provides a fitting context for the historical allusions made in the sectarian writings, for example, Enoch and Jubilees.

As for the *terminus ad quem* of Qumran history, as this is linked to the appearance of the Kittim, we have to determine who these people were. In its primitive sense, the word 'Kittim' described the inhabitants of Kition, a Phoenician colony in Cyprus. Later the name tended to be applied indiscriminately to those living in 'all islands and most maritime countries';* but from the second century BCE, Jewish writers also used 'Kittim' more precisely to denote the greatest world power of the day. In 1 Maccabees (i, 1; viii, 5) they are Greeks; Alexander the Great and Perseus are called kings of the 'Kittim'. In Daniel (xi, 30), on the other hand, the 'Kittim' are Romans; it was the ambassador of the Roman senate, Poppilius Laenas, brought to Alexandria by 'ships of Kittim', i.e. the Roman fleet, who instructed the 'king of the North', the Seleucid monarch Antiochus Epiphanes, to withdraw at once from Egypt. None of these texts is critical of the 'Kittim'. They are seen as the ruling force of the time, but not as hostile to Israel. In fact, in Daniel they humiliate the enemy of the Jews. It is not till a later stage, especially after 70 CE, that they come to symbolise oppression and tyranny.

Since the identification of the 'Kittim' as Romans is nowadays generally accepted, it will suffice to cite a single, but very striking, feature in the Habakkuk Commentary, where, in an interpretation referring to the 'Kittim', the commentator writes: 'This means that they sacrifice to their standards and worship their weapons of war.' Now this custom of worshipping the *signa* was a characteristic of the religion of the Roman armies both in republican and in imperial times, as Josephus testifies in his report of the capture of the Temple of Jerusalem by the legionaries of Titus in 70.

The Romans, now that the rebels had fled to the city, and the Sanctuary itself and all around it were in flames, carried their standards into the

* Josephus, *Antiquities* I.

Temple court, and setting them up opposite the eastern gate, there sacrificed to them.

In sum, therefore, the time-limits of the sect's history appear to be at one extreme, the beginning of the second century BCE, and at the other, some moment during the Roman imperial epoch, i.e. after 27 BCE. And this latter date is determined by Qumran archaeology as coinciding with the first Jewish war, and even more precisely, with the arrival of the armies of Vespasian and Titus in the neighbourhood of the Dead Sea in June 68 CE.

The 'age of wrath' having been identified as that of the Hellenistic crisis of the beginning of the second century BCE, the 'root' as the Hasidim of the pre-Maccabaean age, and the 'Kittim' as the Romans, the next major problem is to discover who was, or were, the principal Jewish enemy or enemies of the sect at the time of the ministry of the Teacher of Righteousness variously known as the 'Scoffer', the 'Liar', the 'Spouter of Lies' and the 'Wicked Priest'.

It is not unreasonable to conclude that all these insults are directed at the same individual. It would appear from the Damascus Document that the 'Scoffer' and the 'Liar' were one and the same ('when the Scoffer arose who shed over Israel the waters of lies'); and we read in Habakkuk of the 'Wicked Priest' that he was called 'by the name of truth' at the outset of his career, the inference being that later he changed into a 'Liar'.

The evidence points to a man who exercised both political and secular power and enjoyed a good reputation before he assumed office. He 'ruled over Israel'. He 'robbed . . . the riches of the men of violence who rebelled against God'. He built 'his city of vanity with blood', committed 'abominable deeds in Jerusalem and defiled the Temple of God'. He was victorious over his adversaries at home and abroad. He rebuilt Jerusalem. And he was eventually captured and put to death by a foreign rival.

The chronological guidelines established in the preceding section locate the period in which this individual flourished between the reign of Antiochus Epiphanes (175–164 BCE) and the probable date of the foundation at Qumran (150–140 BCE). During that time, five men held the office of High Priest. Three of them were pro-Greek: Jason, Menelaus and Alcimus. The remaining two were the Maccabee brothers, Jonathan and Simon. All the Helenisers can be eliminated as candidates for the role of 'Wicked Priest' since none can be said to have enjoyed anything like good repute at the beginning of their ministry. Jason and Alcimus fail also because neither was killed by an enemy, as implied in the Habakkuk Scroll. Jason died in exile (2 Mac. v, 7–9) and Alcimus in office (1 Mac. ix, 54–6). The Maccabee brothers, by contrast, meet all the conditions. The careers of both men fall easily into two stages, marked, in the case of Jonathan, by his acceptance of the High Priesthood from Alexander Balas, and in the case of Simon by his willingness to become a hereditary High Priest. Both were also 'instruments of violence' and both died by violence. Jonathan is nevertheless to be chosen rather than Simon because he alone suffered the vengeance of the 'Chief of the Kings of Greece' and died at the hands of the 'violent of the nations', whereas Simon was murdered by his son-in-law (1 Mac. xvi, 14–16). A gallant defender of Jewish religion and independence, Jonathan succeeded the heroic Judas in 161 BCE when the latter fell in battle. But he qualified for the epithet 'Wicked Priest' when he accepted in 153–152 BCE from Alexander Balas, a heathen usurper of the Seleucid throne who had no right to grant them, the pontifical vestments which Jonathan was not entitled to wear. Captured later by a former general of Alexander Balas, Tryphon, he was killed by him at Bascama in Transjordan (1 Mac. xiii, 23).

Concerning the identity of the 'last Priests of Jerusalem', the passion for conquest, wealth and plunder for which they are reproached points to the Hasmonaean priestly rulers, from Simon's son, John Hyrcanus I (134–104 BCE), to Judas Aristobulus II (67–63 BCE). There can in particular be little doubt that the 'furious young lion', designated also as 'the last Priest' in a badly damaged Commentary on Hosea, was one of them, namely Alexander Jannaeus. The application to him of the words of Nahum, 'who chokes prey for its lionesses', and the report that the 'young lion' executed the 'seekers of smooth things' by 'hanging men alive', accord perfectly with the known story that Jannaeus crucified 800 Pharisees whilst feasting with his concubines.

From this it follows that 'Ephraim', equated in the Commentary on Nahum with the 'seekers of smooth things', symbolises the Pharisees, and that if so, 'Manasseh' and his dignitaries must refer to the Sadducees. In other words, the political and doctrinal opponents of the Essene community were the Sadducees and the Pharisees.

This division of Jewish society into three opposing groups corresponds to the conformation described by Josephus as existing from the time of Jonathan Maccabaeus, but the new insight provided by the Scrolls suggests that the united resistance to Hellenism first fell apart when the Maccabees, and more precisely Jonathan, refused to acknowledge the spiritual leadership of the Teacher of Righteousness, the priestly head of the Hasidim. From then on, the sect saw its defectors as 'Ephraim' and 'Manasseh', these being the names of the sons of Joseph, associated in biblical history with the apostate Northern kingdom, and referred to itself as the 'House of Judah', the faithful South.

Unfortunately, on the most vital topic of all, the question of the identity of the Teacher of Righteousness, we can be nothing like as clear. If the 'Wicked Priest' was Jonathan Maccabaeus, the Teacher would, of course, have been one of his contemporaries. Yet all we know of him is that he was a priest, no doubt of Zadokite affiliation. He founded or re-founded the Community. He transmitted to them his own distinctive interpretation of the Prophets and, if we can rely at least indirectly on the Hymns, of the laws relating to the celebration of festivals. The 'Liar' and his sympathisers in the congregation of the Hasidim disagreed with him; and after a violent confrontation between the two factions in which the 'Liar' gained the upper hand, the Teacher and his remaining followers fled to a place of refuge called 'the land of Damascus': it has been suggested that this is a cryptic designation of Babylonia, the original birthplace of the group, or else that 'Damascus' is a symbolical name for Qumran. The 'House of Absalom' gave the Teacher of Righteousness no help against the 'Liar', writes the Habakkuk commentator, the implication being that this was support on which he might have relied.

Even in his 'place of exile' the Teacher continued to be harassed and persecuted by the Wicked Priest. In this connection, the most important and painful episode appears to have been the Priest's pursuit of the Teacher to his settlement with the purpose of pouring on him 'his venomous fury'. Appearing before the sectaries on 'their Sabbath of repose', at the 'time appointed for rest, for the

Day of Atonement', his intention was to cause them 'to stumble on the Day of Fasting'. It is impossible to say, from the evidence so far available, precisely what happened on this portentous occasion, or whether it was then or later that the Wicked Priest 'laid hands' on the Teacher 'that he might put him to death'. The wording is equivocal.

So, we neither know who the founder of the Essenes was, nor how, nor where, nor when he died. Only writers upholding the most unlikely Christian identification of the Community claim to be better informed, but disagree among themselves as to whether the Teacher was Jesus, John the Baptist or James the Just. Only the sensation-seeking media have been taken in by their theories.

It has been suggested that this inability to identify the Teacher of Righteousness in the context of the Maccabaean period undermines the credibility of the reconstruction as a whole. Is it conceivable, it is asked, that a figure of the stature of the Teacher should have left no trace in the literature relating to that time? The answer to this objection is that such writings are to all intents and purposes restricted to the Books of the Maccabees, sources politically biased in favour of their heroes and virtually oblivious of the very existence of opposition movements. Josephus himself relies largely on 1 Maccabees and cannot therefore be regarded as an independent witness. But even were this not so, and he had additional material at his disposition, his silence vis-à-vis the Teacher of Righteousness would still not call for particular comment since he also makes no mention of the founder of the Pharisees. And incidentally, not a few historians hold that he has nothing to say either of Jesus of Nazareth. The so-called Testimonium Flavianum (*Antiquities* xviii), they maintain, is a Christian interpolation into the genuine text of *Antiquities* (though others, myself included, think that part of the text is authentic). Be this as it may, not a word is breathed by him about Hillel, the greatest of the Pharisee masters, or about Yohanan ben Zakkai, who reorganised Judaism after the destruction of the Temple, although both of these men lived in Josephus' own century and Yohanan was definitely his contemporary.

Admittedly, the various fragments of information gleaned from the Dead Sea Scrolls result in an unavoidably patchy story, but it is fundamentally sound, and the continuing anonymity of the

Teacher does nothing to impair it. For the present synthesis to be complete it remains now to turn to Josephus for his occasional historical references to individual Essenes and to Essenism.

To begin with it should be pointed out that four members of the Community are actually mentioned by the Jewish historian, three of them associated with prophecy, one of the distinctive interests of the Teacher of Righteousness himself. The first, called Judas, is encountered in Jerusalem surrounded by a group of pupils taking instruction in 'foretelling the future', which probably means how to identify prophetic pointers to future events. Josephus writes of him that he had 'never been known to speak falsely in his prophecies', and that he predicted the death of Antigonus, the brother of Aristobulus I (104–103 BCE). A second Essene prophet, Menahem, apparently foretold that Herod would rule over the Jews. Herod showed his gratitude to him by dispensing the Essenes, who were opposed to all oaths except their own oath of the Covenant, from taking the vow of loyalty imposed on all his Jewish subjects. A third Essene named Simon interpreted a dream of Archelaus, ethnarch of Judaea (4 BCE–6 CE), in 4 BCE to mean that his rule would last for ten years. John the Essene, the last sectary to be referred to by Josephus, was not a prophet, but the commander or *strategos* of the district of Thamna in northwestern Judaea, and of the cities of Lydda (Lod), Joppa and Emmaus at the beginning of the first revolution. A man of 'first-rate prowess and ability', he fell in battle at Ascalon.

Finally, Josephus depicts in vivid language the bravery of the Essenes subjected to torture by the Romans.

The war with the Romans tried their souls through and through by every variety of test. Racked and twisted, burned and broken, and made to pass through every instrument of torture in order to induce them to blaspheme their lawgiver or to eat some forbidden thing, they refused to yield to either demand, nor ever once did they cringe to their persecutors or shed a tear. Smiling in their agonies and mildly deriding their tormentors, they cheerfully resigned their souls, confident that they would receive them back again.

Since it would appear from this passage that the Romans were persecuting not individuals, but a group, it is tempting, bearing in mind the archaeologists' claim that the Qumran settlement was destroyed by the Romans, to associate it with the story of Essenes captured by the Dead Sea. If such a surmise is correct, the sect's disappearance from history may well have been brought about in the lethal blow suffered by its central establishment during the fateful summer of 68 CE. The fact that no attempt was made to recover nearly 800 manuscripts from the caves confirms, it would seem, such a reconstruction of the end of Qumran and, with the annihilation of its central establishment, of the whole Essene movement.

Essenism is dead. The brittle structure of its stiff and exclusive brotherhood was unable to withstand the national catastrophe which struck Palestinian Judaism in 70 CE. Animated by the loftiest of ideals and devoted to the observance of 'perfect holiness', it yet lacked the pliant strength and the elasticity of thought and depth of spiritual vision which enabled rabbinic Judaism to survive and flourish. And although the Teacher of Righteousness clearly sensed the deeper obligations implicit in the Mosaic Law, he was without the genius of Jesus the Jew who succeeded in uncovering the essence of religion as an existential relationship between man and man and man and God.

However, the collection of writings which the members of this vanished community bequeathed to us has enriched to a considerable extent our understanding of the history of the literature and religious ideas of Palestinian Judaism around the turn of the era (150 BCE – 70 CE) and of their impact on the rise of Christianity.

As far as the books of the Old Testament are concerned, the Qumran caves have allowed us to trace back the history of the Hebrew Bible for more than a millennium. Prior to Qumran the oldest complete manuscript of the Old Testament dated to the beginning of the eleventh century CE, but now we possess documents which go back as far as the second century BCE. The Dead Sea biblical texts basically agree with the traditional form of Scripture, but at the same time display a substantial amount of variation in vocabulary, style, word order, longer and shorter formulation and other details.

The Qumran Scrolls have also restored, in their original languages (Hebrew and Aramaic), a whole body of writings some of which were previously available only in translation (Greek, Latin, Syriac, etc.), others completely unknown. They had disappeared from circulation in their Semitic version because the rabbis of the early Christian centuries showed no interest in them on account of ideas which they thought clashed with later Jewish orthodoxy.

These compositions are nevertheless of great significance for the study of pre-Rabbinic Judaism and shed also fresh light on the New Testament and the literature, organisation and customs of the primitive Christian Church. They display similarities in terminology (e.g. 'sons of light'), ideology (both Essenes and first Christians envisaged an imminent coming of the messianic kingdom of God as taught by their respective masters, the Teacher of Righteousness and Jesus of Nazareth) and their outlook on the Bible (they both claimed the scriptural prophecies aimed at and were fulfilled in the persons and events of their own community). A comparative study of Qumran and primitive Christianity cannot fail to improve our understanding of both.

GEZA VERMES

Chronology

197 BCE Judaea became a province of the Seleucid Empire ruled by the Syrian successors of ALEXANDER THE GREAT.

187–175 SELEUCUS IV. Beginning of Hellenistic infiltration, resisted by the Zadokite High Priest ONIAS III.

175–164 ANTIOCHUS IV (EPIPHANES). ONIAS deposed and replaced by his Hellenophile brother JASON.

172 JASON expelled from office in favour of MENELAUS, Hellenising High Priest from 172 to 162 BCE.

171 ONIAS III murdered at the instigation of MENELAUS. Forced Hellenisation.

169 ANTIOCHUS led by MENELAUS profaned and plundered the Temple of Jerusalem.

168 ANTIOCHUS thwarted by the Romans in his second campaign against Egypt.

167 Persecution of those Jews who opposed the unification of the Seleucid Empire on the basis of Greek culture and religion. Official abolition of Jewish religion and practice under threat of death. The Temple transformed into a sanctuary of Olympian Zeus.

166 Rising of the Maccabees supported by all the traditional parties under the leadership of JUDAS MACCABEE.

164 Truce. Cleansing of the Temple, still held by MENELAUS.

162–150 DEMETRIUS I. MENELAUS executed by the Syrians. ALCIMUS appointed High Priest by the king.

161 JUDAS killed in battle. JONATHAN assumed leadership of the rebels (161–152 BCE).

160 ALCIMUS, the last Hellenising High Priest, died of a stroke. End of Syrian military intervention.

152–145 ALEXANDER BALAS usurped the Seleucid throne and appointed JONATHAN High Priest (152–143/2 BCE).

145–142 ANTIOCHUS VI, son of ALEXANDER, raised to the throne by TRYPHON, his father's general. JONATHAN named governor of Syria. SIMON, his brother, made

	military governor of the Palestinian littoral.
143	JONATHAN arrested by TRYPHON.
143/2–135/4	SIMON High Priest and ethnarch.
142	JONATHAN executed in prison.
140	SIMON's titles confirmed as hereditary. Foundation of the Maccabaean, or Hasmonaean, dynasty.
135/4	SIMON murdered by his son-in-law.
135/4–104	JOHN HYRCANUS I High Priest and ethnarch. Opposed by the Pharisees.
104–103	ARISTOBULUS I High Priest and king.
103–76	ALEXANDER JANNAEUS High Priest, king, and conqueror. Resisted by the Pharisees.
76–67	ALEXANDRA, widow of JANNAEUS, queen. Friend of the Pharisees. HYRCANUS II High Priest.
67	HYRCANUS II king and High Priest. Deposed by his brother ARISTOBULUS.
67–63	ARISTOBULUS II king and High Priest. Taken prisoner by POMPEY in 63 BCE after the fall of Jerusalem. Judaea became a Roman province.
63–40	HYRCANUS II reinstated as High Priest without the royal title.
40–37	ANTIGONUS, son of ARISTOBULUS II, occupied the throne and pontificate with Parthian support. HYRCANUS maimed and exiled.
37–4 BCE	HEROD THE GREAT. End of Hasmonaean dynasty. HYRCANUS executed in 30 BCE.
27 BCE–14 CE	AUGUSTUS emperor.
6 BCE (?)	Birth of JESUS OF NAZARETH.
4 BCE–6 CE	ARCHELAUS ethnarch of Judaea and Samaria.
14–37 CE	TIBERIUS emperor.
26–36	PONTIUS PILATE prefect of Judaea.
30 (?)	Crucifixion of JESUS.
66–70	First Jewish War ending with the capture of Jerusalem and the destruction of the Temple by TITUS.
73/4	Fall of Masada.

'You will understand the end of the ages and you will gaze at ancient things . . .'

THE RULES

∙∙

The Community Rule

The Community Rule is probably one of the oldest documents of the sect. Its composition may have originated around 100 BCE, and the eleven relatively well-preserved columns of the Cave 1 manuscript itself are said to have been produced during the quarter of a century following that date. It seems to have been intended for the Community's teachers, for its Masters or Guardians, and contains extracts from liturgical ceremonies, an outline of a tractate on the spirits of truth and falsehood, statutes concerned with initiation into the sect and with its common life, organisation and discipline, a penal code, and finally a poetic dissertation on the fundamental religious duties of the Master and his disciples, and on the sacred seasons proper to the Community.

There are, to my knowledge, no writings in ancient Jewish sources parallel to the Community Rule, but a similar type of literature flourished among Christians between the second and fourth centuries, the so-called 'Church Orders' represented by works such as the Didache, the Didascalia, the Apostolic Constitution.

The contents of the manuscript may be divided into three main sections:

1. Entry into the Covenant, followed by an instruction on the two spirits (I–IV).
2. Statutes relating to the Council of the Community (V–IX).
3. Directives addressed to the Master, and the Master's Hymn (IX–XI).

I *The Master shall teach the* saints to live according to the Book of the Community *Rule*, that they may seek God with a whole heart and soul, and do what is good and right before Him as He commanded by the hand of Moses and all His servants the Prophets; that they may love all that He has chosen and hate all that he has rejected; that they may abstain from all evil and hold fast to all good; that they may practise truth, righteousness, and justice upon earth and no longer stubbornly follow a sinful heart and lustful eyes, committing all manner of evil. He shall admit into the Covenant of Grace all those who have freely devoted themselves to the observance of God's precepts, that they may be joined to the counsel of God and may live perfectly before Him in accordance with all that has been revealed concerning their appointed times, and that they may love all the sons of light, each according to his lot in God's design, and hate all the sons of darkness, each according to his guilt in God's vengeance.

All those who freely devote themselves to His truth shall bring all their knowledge, powers and possessions into the Community of God, that they may purify their knowledge in the truth of God's precepts and order their powers according to His ways of perfection and all their possessions according to His righteous counsel. They shall not depart from any command of God concerning their times; they shall be neither early nor late for any of their appointed times, they shall stray neither to the right nor to the left of any of His true precepts. All those who embrace the Community Rule shall enter into the Covenant before God to obey all His commandments so that they may not abandon Him during the dominion of Belial because of fear or terror or affliction.

On entering the Covenant, the Priests and Levites shall bless the God of salvation and all His faithfulness, and all those entering the Covenant shall say after them, 'Amen, Amen!'

Then the Priests shall recite the favours of God manifested in His mighty deeds and shall declare all His merciful grace to Israel, and the Levites shall recite the iniquities of the children of Israel, all their guilty rebellions and sins during the dominion of Belial. And after them, all those entering the Covenant shall confess and say: 'We have strayed! We have *disobeyed!* We and our fathers before us have sinned and done wickedly in walking *counter to the precepts* of truth and righteousness. *And God has* judged us and our fathers also;   **II** but He has bestowed His bountiful mercy on us from everlasting to everlasting.' And the Priests shall bless all the men of the lot of God who walk perfectly in all His ways, saying: 'May He bless you with all good and preserve you from all evil! May He lighten your heart with life-giving wisdom and grant you eternal knowledge! May He raise His merciful face towards you for everlasting bliss!'

And the Levites shall curse all the men of the lot of Belial, saying: 'Be cursed because of all your guilty wickedness! May He deliver you up for torture at the hands of the vengeful Avengers! May He visit you with destruction by the hand of all the Wreakers of Revenge! Be cursed without mercy because of the darkness of your deeds! Be damned in the shadowy place of everlasting fire! May God not heed when you call on Him, nor pardon you by blotting out your sin! May He raise His angry face towards you for vengeance! May there be no "Peace" for you in the mouth of those who hold fast to the Fathers!' And after the blessing and the cursing, all those entering the Covenant shall say, 'Amen, Amen!'

And the Priests and Levites shall continue, saying: 'Cursed be the man who enters this Covenant while walking among the idols of his heart, who sets up before himself his stumbling-block of sin so that he may backslide! Hearing the words of this Covenant, he blesses himself in his heart and says, "Peace be with me, even though I walk in the stubbornness of my heart" (Deut. xxix, 18–19), whereas his spirit, parched for lack of truth and watered with lies, shall be destroyed without pardon. God's wrath and His zeal for His precepts shall consume him in everlasting destruction. All the curses of the Covenant shall cling to him and God will set him apart for evil. He shall be cut off from the midst of all the sons of light, and because he has turned aside from God on account of his idols and his stumbling-block of sin, his lot shall be among those who are cursed for ever.' And after them, all those entering the Covenant shall answer and say, 'Amen, Amen!'

Thus shall they do, year by year, for as long as the dominion of Belial endures. The Priests shall enter first, ranked one after another according to the perfection of their spirit; then the Levites; and thirdly, all the people one after another in their Thousands, Hundreds, Fifties, and Tens, that every Israelite may know his place in the Community of God according to the everlasting design. No man shall move down from his place nor move up from his allotted position. For according to the holy design, they shall all of them be in a Community of truth and virtuous humility, of loving-kindness and good intent one towards the other, and they shall all of them be sons of the everlasting Company.

No man *shall be in the* Community of His truth who refuses to enter *the Covenant of* God so that he may walk in the stubbornness of his heart, for **III** his soul detests the wise teaching of just laws. He shall not be counted among the upright for he has not persisted in the conversion of his life. His knowledge, powers, and possessions shall not enter the Council of the Community, for whoever ploughs the mud of wickedness returns defiled. He shall not be justified by that which his stubborn heart declares lawful, for seeking the ways of light he looks towards darkness. He shall not be reckoned among the perfect; he shall neither be purified by atonement, nor cleansed by purifying waters, nor sanctified by seas and rivers, nor washed clean with any ablution. Unclean, unclean shall he be. For as long as he despises the precepts of God he shall receive no instruction in the Community of His counsel.

For it is through the spirit of true counsel concerning the ways of man that all his sins shall be expiated, that he may contemplate the light of life. He shall be cleansed from all his sins by the spirit of holiness uniting him to His truth, and his iniquity shall be expiated by the spirit of uprightness and humility. And when his flesh is sprinkled with purifying water and sanctified by cleansing water, it shall be made clean by the humble submission of his soul to all the precepts of God. Let him then order his steps to walk perfectly in all the ways commanded by God concerning the times appointed for him, straying neither to the right nor to the left and transgressing none of His words, and he shall be accepted by virtue of a pleasing atonement before God and it shall be to him a Covenant of the everlasting Community.

The Master shall instruct all the sons of light and shall teach them the nature of all the children of men according to the kind of spirit which they possess, the signs identifying their works during their lifetime, their visitation for chastisement, and the time of their reward.

From the God of Knowledge comes all that is and shall be. Before ever they existed He established their whole design, and when, as ordained for them, they come into being, it is in accord with His glorious design that they accomplish their task without change. The laws of all things are in His hand and He provides them with all their needs.

He has created man to govern the world, and has appointed for him two spirits in which to walk until the time of His visitation: the spirits of truth and injustice. Those born of truth spring from a fountain of light, but those born of injustice spring from a source of darkness. All the children of righteousness are ruled by the Prince of Light and walk in the ways of light, but all the children of injustice are ruled by the Angel of Darkness and walk in the ways of darkness. The Angel of Darkness leads all the children of righteousness astray, and until his end, all their sin, iniquities, wickedness, and all their unlawful deeds are caused by his dominion in accordance with the mysteries of God. Every one of their chastisements, and every one of the seasons of their distress, shall be brought about by the rule of his persecution; for all his allotted spirits seek the overthrow of the sons of light.

But the God of Israel and His Angel of Truth will succour all the sons of light. For it is He who created the spirits of Light and Darkness and founded every action upon them and established every deed *upon* their *ways*. And He loves the one   **IV** everlastingly and delights in its works for ever; but the counsel of the other He loathes and for ever hates its ways.

These are their ways in the world for the enlightenment of the heart of man, and so that all the paths of true righteousness may be made straight before him, and so that the fear of the laws of God may be instilled in his heart: a spirit of humility, patience, abundant charity, unending goodness, understanding, and intelligence; a spirit of mighty wisdom which trusts in all the deeds of God and leans on His great loving-kindness; a spirit of discernment in every purpose, of zeal for just laws, of holy intent with steadfastness of heart, of great charity towards all the sons of truth, of admirable purity which detests all unclean idols, of humble conduct sprung from an understanding of all things, and of faithful concealment of the mysteries of truth. These are the counsels of the spirit to the sons of truth in this world.

And as for the visitation of all who walk in this spirit, it shall be healing, great peace in a long life, and fruitfulness, together with every everlasting blessing and eternal joy in life without end, a crown of glory and a garment of majesty in unending light.

But the ways of the spirit of falsehood are these: greed, and slackness in the search for righteousness, wickedness and lies, haughtiness and pride, falseness and deceit, cruelty and abundant evil, ill-temper and much folly and brazen insolence, abominable deeds committed in a spirit of lust, and ways of lewdness in the service of uncleanness, a blaspheming tongue, blindness of eye and dullness of ear, stiffness of neck and heaviness of heart, so that man walks in all the ways of darkness and guile.

And the visitation of all who walk in this spirit shall be a multitude of plagues by the hand of all the destroying angels, everlasting damnation by the avenging wrath of the fury of God, eternal torment and endless disgrace together with shameful extinction in the fire of the dark regions. The times of all their generations shall be spent in sorrowful mourning and in bitter misery and in calamities of darkness until they are destroyed without remnant or survivor.

The nature of all the children of men is ruled by these two spirits, and during their life all the hosts of men have a portion of their divisions and walk in both their ways. And the whole reward for their deeds shall be, for everlasting ages, according to whether each man's portion in their two divisions is great or small. For God has established the spirits in equal measure until the final age, and has set everlasting hatred between their divisions. Truth abhors the works of injustice, and injustice hates all the ways of truth. And their struggle is fierce in all their arguments for they do not walk together. But in the mysteries of His understanding, and in His glorious wisdom, God has ordained an end for injustice, and at the time of the visitation He will destroy it for ever. Then truth, which has wallowed in the ways of wickedness during the dominion of injustice until the appointed time of judgement, shall arise in the world for ever. God will then purify every deed of man with His truth; He will refine for Himself the human frame by rooting out all spirit of injustice from the bounds of his flesh. He will cleanse him of all wicked deeds with the spirit of holiness; like purifying waters He will shed upon him the spirit of truth to cleanse him of all abomination and injustice. And he shall be plunged into the spirit of purification, that he may instruct the upright in the knowledge of the Most High and teach the wisdom of the sons of heaven to the perfect of way. For God has chosen them for an everlasting Covenant and all the glory of Adam shall be theirs. There shall be no more lies and all the works of injustice shall be put to shame.

Until now the spirits of truth and injustice struggle in the hearts of men and they walk in both wisdom and folly. According to his portion of truth so does a man hate injustice, and according to his inheritance in the realm of injustice so is he wicked and so hates truth. For God has established the two spirits in equal measure until the determined end, and until the Renewal, and He knows the reward of their deeds from all eternity. He has allotted them to the children of men that they may know good *and evil, and* that the destiny of all the living may be according to the spirit within *them at the time* of the visitation.

V *And this is the Rule for the men of the Community who have freely pledged themselves to be converted from all evil and to cling to all His commandments according to His will*

They shall separate from the congregation of the men of injustice and shall unite, with respect to the Law and possessions, under the authority of the sons of Zadok, the Priests who keep the Covenant, and of the multitude of the men of the Community who hold fast to the Covenant. Every decision concerning doctrine, property, and justice shall be determined by them.

They shall practise truth and humility in common, and justice and uprightness and charity and modesty in all their ways. No man shall walk in the stubbornness of his heart so that he strays after his heart and eyes and evil inclination, but he shall circumcise in the Community the foreskin of evil inclination and of stiffness of neck that they may lay a foundation of truth for Israel, for the Community of the everlasting Covenant. They shall atone for all those in Aaron who have freely pledged themselves to holiness, and for those in Israel who have freely pledged themselves to the House of Truth, and for those who join them to live in community and to take part in the trial and judgement and condemnation of all those who transgress the precepts.

On joining the Community, this shall be their code of behaviour with respect to all these precepts.

Whoever approaches the Council of the Community shall enter the Covenant of God in the presence of all who have freely pledged themselves. He shall undertake by a binding oath to return with all his heart and soul to every commandment of the Law of Moses in accordance with all that has been revealed of it to the sons of

Zadok, the Priests, Keepers of the Covenant and Seekers of His will, and to the multitude of the men of their Covenant who together have freely pledged themselves to His truth and to walking in the way of His delight. And he shall undertake by the Covenant to separate from all the men of injustice who walk in the way of wickedness.

For they are not reckoned in His Covenant. They have neither inquired nor sought after Him concerning His laws that they might know the hidden things in which they have sinfully erred; and matters revealed they have treated with insolence. Therefore Wrath shall rise up to condemn, and Vengeance shall be executed by the curses of the Covenant, and great chastisements of eternal destruction shall be visited on them, leaving no remnant. They shall not enter the water to partake of the pure Meal of the men of holiness, for they shall not be cleansed unless they turn from their wickedness: for all who transgress His word are unclean. Likewise, no man shall consort with him in regard to his work or property lest he be burdened with the guilt of his sin. He shall indeed keep away from him in all things: as it is written, *Keep away from all that is false* (Exod. xxiii, 7). No member of the Community shall follow them in matters of doctrine and justice, or eat or drink anything of theirs, or take anything from them except for a price; as it is written, *Keep away from the man in whose nostrils is breath, for wherein is he counted?* (Isa. ii, 22). For all those not reckoned in His Covenant are to be set apart, together with all that is theirs. None of the men of holiness shall lean upon works of vanity: for they are all vanity who know not His Covenant, and He will blot from the world all them that despise His word. All their deeds are defilement before Him, and all their property unclean.

But when a man enters the Covenant to walk according to all these precepts that he may be joined to the holy Congregation, they shall examine his spirit in community with respect to his understanding and practice of the Law, under the authority of the sons of Aaron who have freely pledged themselves in the Community to restore His Covenant and to heed all the precepts commanded by Him, and of the multitude of Israel who have freely pledged themselves in the Community to return to His Covenant. They shall inscribe them in order, one after another, according to their understanding and their deeds, that every one may obey his companion, the man of lesser rank obeying his superior. And they shall examine their spirit and deeds yearly, so that each man may be advanced in accordance with his understanding and perfection of way, or moved down in accordance with his distortions. They shall rebuke one another in truth, humility, and charity. Let no man address his companion with anger, or ill-temper, or obduracy, *or with envy prompted by* the spirit of wickedness. Let him not hate him *because of his uncircumcised* heart, but let him rebuke him on the very same day lest **VI** he incur guilt because of him. And furthermore, let no man accuse his companion before the Congregation without having admonished him in the presence of witnesses.

These are the ways in which all of them shall walk, each man with his companion, wherever they dwell. The man of lesser rank shall obey the greater in matters of work and money. They shall eat in common and bless in common and deliberate in common.

Wherever there are ten men of the Council of the Community there shall not lack a Priest among them. And they shall all sit before him according to their rank and shall be asked their counsel in all things in that order. And when the table has been prepared for eating, and the new wine for drinking, the Priest shall be the first to stretch out his hand to bless the firstfruits of the bread and new wine.

And where the ten are, there shall never lack a man among them who shall study the Law continually, day and night, concerning the right conduct of a man with his companion. And the Congregation shall watch in community for a third of every night of the year, to read the Book and to study the Law and to bless together.

This is the Rule for an Assembly of the Congregation

Each man shall sit in his place: the Priests shall sit first, and the elders second, and all the rest of the people according to their rank. And thus shall they be questioned concerning the Law, and concerning any counsel or matter coming before the Congregation, each man bringing his knowledge to the Council of the Community.

No man shall interrupt a companion before his speech has ended, nor speak before a man of higher rank; each man shall speak in his turn. And in an Assembly of the Congregation no man shall speak without the consent of the Congregation, nor indeed of the Guardian of the Congregation. Should any man wish to speak to the Congregation, yet not be in a position to question the Council of the Community, let him rise to his feet and say: 'I have something to say to the Congregation.' If they command him to speak, he shall speak.

Every man, born of Israel, who freely pledges himself to join the Council of the Community shall be examined by the Guardian at the head of the Congregation concerning his understanding and his deeds. If he is fitted to the discipline, he shall admit him into the Covenant that he may be converted to the truth and depart from all injustice; and he shall instruct him in all the rules of the Community. And later, when he comes to stand before the Congregation, they shall all deliberate his case, and according to the decision of the Council of the Congregation he shall either enter or depart. After he has entered the Council of the Community he shall not touch the pure Meal of the Congregation until one full year is completed, and until he has been examined concerning his spirit and deeds; nor shall he have any share of the property of the Congregation. Then when he has completed one year within the Community, the Congregation shall deliberate his case with regard to his understanding and observance of the Law. And if it be his destiny, according to the judgement of the Priests and the multitude of the men of their Covenant, to enter the company of the Community, his property and earnings shall be handed over to the Bursar of the Congregation who shall register it to his account and shall not spend it for the Congregation. He shall not touch the Drink of the Congregation until he has completed a second year among the men of the Community. But when the second year has passed, he shall be examined, and if it be his destiny, according to the judgement of the Congregation, to enter the Community, then he shall be inscribed among his brethren in the order of his rank for the Law, and for justice, and for the pure Meal; his property shall be merged and he shall offer his counsel and judgement to the Community.

These are the Rules by which they shall judge at a Community Court of Inquiry according to the cases

If one of them has lied deliberately in matters of property, he shall be excluded from the pure Meal of the Congregation for one year and shall do penance with respect to one quarter of his food.

Whoever has answered his companion with obstinacy, or has addressed him impatiently, going so far as to take no account of the dignity of his fellow by disobeying the order of a brother inscribed before him, he has taken the law into his own hand; therefore he shall do penance for one year *and shall be excluded.*

If any man has uttered the *Most* Venerable Name **VII** even though frivolously, or as a result of shock or for any other reason whatever, while reading the Book or blessing, he shall be dismissed and shall return to the Council of the Community no more.

If he has spoken in anger against one of the Priests inscribed in the Book, he shall do penance for one year and shall be excluded for his soul's sake from the pure Meal of the Congregation. But if he has spoken unwittingly, he shall do penance for six months.

Whoever has deliberately lied shall do penance for six months.

Whoever has deliberately insulted his companion unjustly shall do penance for one year and shall be excluded.

Whoever has deliberately deceived his companion by word or by deed shall do penance for six months.

If he has failed to care for his companion, he shall do penance for three months. But if he has failed to care for the property of the Community, thereby causing its loss, he shall restore it in full. And if he be unable to restore it, he shall do penance for sixty days.

Whoever has borne malice against his companion unjustly shall do penance for six months/one year; and likewise, whoever has taken revenge in any matter whatever.

Whoever has spoken foolishly: three months.

Whoever has interrupted his companion whilst speaking: ten days.

Whoever has lain down to sleep during an Assembly of the Congregation: thirty days. And likewise, whoever has left, without reason, an Assembly of the Congregation as many as three times during one Assembly, shall do penance for ten days. But if he has departed whilst they were standing he shall do penance for thirty days.

Whoever has gone naked before his companion, without having been obliged to do so, he shall do penance for six months.

Whoever has spat in an Assembly of the Congregation shall do penance for thirty days.

Whoever has been so poorly dressed that when drawing his hand from beneath his garment his nakedness has been seen, he shall do penance for thirty days.

Whoever has guffawed foolishly shall do penance for thirty days.

Whoever has drawn out his left hand to gesticulate with it shall do penance for ten days.

Whoever has gone about slandering his companion shall be excluded from the pure Meal of the Congregation for one year and shall do penance. But whoever has slandered the Congregation shall be expelled from among them and shall return no more.

Whoever has murmured against the authority of the Community shall be expelled and shall not return. But if he has murmured against his companion unjustly, he shall do penance for six months.

Should a man return whose spirit has so trembled before the authority of the Community that he has betrayed the truth and walked in the stubbornness of his heart, he shall do penance for two years. During the first year he shall not touch the pure Meal of the Congregation, and during the second year he shall not touch the Drink of the Congregation and shall sit below all the men of the Community. Then when his two years are completed, the Congregation shall consider his case, and if he is admitted he shall be inscribed in his rank and may then question concerning the Law.

If, after being in the Council of the Community for ten full years, the spirit of any man has failed, so that he has betrayed the Community and departed from the Congregation to walk in the stubbornness of his heart, he shall return no more to the Council of the Community. Moreover, if any member of the Community has shared with him his food or property which . . . of the Congregation, his sentence shall be the same; he shall be *expelled*.

VIII In the Council of the Community there shall be twelve men and three Priests, perfectly versed in all that is revealed of the Law, whose works shall be truth, righteousness, justice, loving-kindness and humility. They shall preserve the faith in the Land with steadfastness and meekness and shall atone for sin by the practice of justice and by suffering the sorrows of affliction. They shall walk with all men according to the standard of truth and the rule of the time.

When these are in Israel, the Council of the Community shall be established in truth. It shall be an Everlasting Plantation, a House of Holiness for Israel, an Assembly of Supreme Holiness for Aaron. They shall be witnesses to the truth at the Judgement, and shall be the elect of Goodwill who shall atone for the Land and pay to the wicked their reward. It shall be that tried wall, that *precious corner-stone*, whose foundations shall neither rock nor sway in their place (Isa. xxviii, 16). It shall be a Most Holy Dwelling for Aaron, with everlasting knowledge of the Covenant of justice, and shall offer up sweet fragrance. It shall be a House of Perfection and Truth in Israel that they may establish a Covenant according to the everlasting precepts. And they shall be an agreeable offering, atoning for the Land and determining the judgement of wickedness, and there shall be no more iniquity. When they have been confirmed for two years in perfection of way in the Foundation of the Community, they shall be set apart as holy within the Council of the men of the Community. And the Interpreter shall not conceal from them, out of fear of the spirit of apostasy, any of those things hidden from Israel which have been discovered by him.

And when these become members of the Community in Israel according to all these rules, they shall separate from the habitation of unjust men and shall go into the wilderness to prepare there the way of Him; as it is written, *Prepare in the wilderness the way of . . . make straight in the desert a path for our God* (Isa. xl, 3). This path is the study of the Law which He commanded by the hand of Moses, that they may do according to all that has been revealed from age to age, and as the Prophets have revealed by His Holy Spirit.

And no man among the members of the Covenant of the Community who deliberately, on any point whatever, turns aside from all that is commanded, shall touch the pure Meal of the men of holiness or know anything of their counsel until his deeds are purified from all injustice and he walks in perfection of way. And then, according to the judgement of the Congregation, he shall be admitted to the Council and shall be inscribed in his rank. This rule shall apply to whoever enters the Community.

And these are the rules which the men of perfect holiness shall fol-
low in their commerce with one another

Every man who enters the Council of Holiness, the Council of those who walk in the way of perfection as commanded by God, and who deliberately or through negligence transgresses one word of the Law of Moses, on any point whatever, shall be expelled from the Council of the Community and shall return no more; no man of holiness shall be associated in his property or counsel in any matter at all. But if he has acted inadvertently, he shall be excluded from the pure Meal and the Council and they shall interpret the rule as follows. For two years he shall take no part in judgement or ask for counsel; but if, during that time, his way becomes perfect, then he shall return to the Court of Inquiry and the Council, in accordance with the judgement of the Congregation, provided that he commit no further inadvertent sin during two full years.   **IX** For one sin of inadvertence alone he shall do penance for two years. But as for him who has sinned deliberately, he shall never return; only the man who has sinned inadvertently shall be tried for two years, that his way and counsel may be made perfect according to the judgement of the Congregation. And afterwards, he shall be inscribed in his rank in the Community of Holiness.

When these become members of the Community in Israel according to all these rules, they shall establish the spirit of holiness according to everlasting truth. They shall atone for guilty rebellion and for sins of unfaithfulness, that they may obtain loving-kindness for the Land without the flesh of holocausts and the fat of sacrifice. And prayer rightly offered shall be as an acceptable fragrance of righteousness, and perfection of way as a delectable free-will offering. At that time, the men of the Community shall set apart a House of Holiness in order that it may be united to the most holy things and a House of Community for Israel, for those who walk in perfection. The sons of Aaron alone shall command in matters of justice and property, and every rule concerning the men of the Community shall be determined according to their word.

As for the property of the men of holiness who walk in perfection, it shall not be merged with that of the men of injustice who have not purified their life by separating themselves from iniquity and walking in the way of perfection. They shall depart from none of the counsels of the Law to walk in all the stubbornness of their hearts, but shall be ruled by the primitive precepts in which the men of the Community were first instructed until there shall come the Prophet and the Messiahs of Aaron and Israel.

These are the precepts in which the Master shall walk in His commerce with all the living, according to the rule proper to every season and according to the worth of every man

He shall do the will of God according to all that has been revealed from age to age.

He shall measure out all knowledge discovered throughout the ages, together with the Precept of the age.

He shall separate and weigh the sons of righteousness according to their spirit.

He shall hold firmly to the elect of the time according to His will, as He has commanded.

He shall judge every man according to his spirit. He shall admit him in accordance with the cleanness of his hands and advance him in accordance with his understanding. And he shall love and hate likewise.

He shall not rebuke the men of the Pit nor dispute with them.

He shall conceal the teaching of the Law from men of injustice, but shall impart true knowledge and righteous judgement to those who have chosen the Way. He shall guide them all in knowledge according to the spirit of each and according to the rule of the age, and shall thus instruct them in the mysteries of marvellous truth, so that in the midst of the men of the Community they may walk perfectly together in all that has been revealed to them. This is the time for the preparation of the way into the wilderness, and he shall teach them to do all that is required at that time and to separate from all those who have not turned aside from all injustice.

These are the rules of conduct for the Master in those times with respect to His loving and hating

Everlasting hatred in a spirit of secrecy for the men of perdition! He shall leave to them wealth and earnings like a slave to his lord and like a poor man to his master.

He shall be a man zealous for the Precept whose time is for the Day of Revenge. He shall perform the will of God in all his deeds, and in all his dominion as He has commanded. He shall freely delight in all that befalls him and nothing shall please him save God's will. He shall delight in all the words of His mouth and shall desire nothing except His command. He shall watch always *for* the judgement of God, and shall bless his Maker *for all His goodness* and declare *His mercies* in all that befalls.

He shall bless Him *with the offering* of the lips　**X** at the times ordained by Him: at the beginning of the dominion of light, and at its end when it retires to its appointed place; at the beginning of the watches of darkness when He unlocks their storehouse and spreads them out, and also at their end when they retire before the light; when the heavenly lights shine out from the dwelling-place of Holiness, and also when they retire to the place of Glory; at the entry of the monthly seasons on the days of the new moon, and also at their end when they succeed to one another. Their renewal is a great day for the Holy of Holies, and a sign for the unlocking of everlasting mercies at the beginning of seasons in all times to come.

> At the beginning of the months of the yearly seasons
> 　　and on the holy days appointed for remembrance,
> in their seasons I will bless Him
> 　　with the offering of the lips
> 　　according to the Precept engraved for ever:
> at the beginning of the years
> 　　and at the end of their seasons
> 　　when their appointed law is fulfilled,
> on the day decreed by Him
> 　　that they should pass from one to the other –
> the season of early harvest to the summer time,
> the season of sowing to the season of grass,
> the seasons of years to their weeks of years –
> and at the beginning of their weeks
> 　　for the season of Jubilee.
> All my life the engraved Precept shall be on my tongue
> 　　as the fruit of praise
> 　　and the portion of my lips.

I will sing with knowledge and all my music
    shall be for the glory of God.
My lyre and my harp shall sound
    for His holy order
and I will tune the pipe of my lips
    to His right measure.
With the coming of day and night
    I will enter the Covenant of God,
and when evening and morning depart
    I will recite His decrees.
I will place in them my bounds without return.
I will declare His judgement concerning my sins,
    and my transgressions shall be before my eyes
    as an engraved Precept.
I will say to God, 'My Righteousness'
    and 'Author of my Goodness' to the Most High,
'Fountain of Knowledge' and 'Source of Holiness',
    'Summit of Glory' and 'Almighty Eternal Majesty'.
I will choose that which He teaches me
    and will delight in His judgement of me.

Before I move my hands and feet
    I will bless His Name.
I will praise Him before I go out or enter,
    or sit or rise,
    and whilst I lie on the couch of my bed.
I will bless Him with the offering
    of that which proceeds from my lips
    from the midst of the ranks of men,
and before I lift my hands to eat
    of the pleasant fruits of the earth.
I will bless Him for His exceeding wonderful deeds
    at the beginning of fear and dread
    and in the abode of distress and desolation.
I will meditate on His power
    and will lean on His mercies all day long.
I know that judgement of all the living
    is in His hand,
    and that all His deeds are truth.

I will praise Him when distress is unleashed
    and will magnify Him also because of His salvation.

I will pay to no man the reward of evil;
    I will pursue him with goodness.
For judgement of all the living is with God
    and it is He who will render to man his reward.
I will not envy in a spirit of wickedness,
    my soul shall not desire the riches of violence.
I will not grapple with the men of perdition
    until the Day of Revenge,
but my wrath shall not turn from the men of falsehood
    and I will not rejoice until judgement is made.
I will bear no rancour
    against them that turn from transgression,
but will have no pity
    on all who depart from the way.
I will offer no comfort to the smitten
    until their way becomes perfect.

I will not keep Belial within my heart,
and in my mouth shall be heard
    no folly or sinful deceit,
    no cunning or lies shall be found on my lips.
The fruit of holiness shall be on my tongue
    and no abominations shall be found upon it.
I will open my mouth
    in songs of thanksgiving,
and my tongue shall always proclaim
    the goodness of God and the sin of men
    until their transgression ends.
I will cause vanities
    to cease from my lips,
uncleanness and crookedness
    from the knowledge of my heart.

I will impart/conceal knowledge with discretion
    and will prudently hedge it within a firm bound
to preserve faith and strong judgement

in accordance with the justice of God.
I will distribute the Precept
    by the measuring-cord of the times,
and . . . righteousness
    and loving-kindness towards the oppressed,
encouragement to the troubled heart
    XI and discernment to the erring spirit,
teaching understanding to them that murmur
    that they may answer meekly
    before the haughty of spirit
and humbly before men of injustice
    who point the finger and speak of iniquity
    and who are zealous for wealth.
As for me,
    my justification is with God.
In His hand are the perfection of my way
    and the uprightness of my heart.
He will wipe out my transgression
    through His righteousness.

For my light has sprung
    from the source of His knowledge;
my eyes have beheld His marvellous deeds,
    and the light of my heart, the mystery to come.
He that is everlasting
    is the support of my right hand;
the way of my steps is over stout rock
    which nothing shall shake;
for the rock of my steps is the truth of God
    and His might is the support of my right hand.

From the source of His righteousness
    is my justification,
and from His marvellous mysteries
    is the light in my heart.
My eyes have gazed
    on that which is eternal,
on wisdom concealed from men,
    on knowledge and wise design

hidden from the sons of men;
on a fountain of righteousness
    and on a storehouse of power,
on a spring of glory
    hidden from the assembly of flesh.
God has given them to His chosen ones
    as an everlasting possession,
and has caused them to inherit
    the lot of the Holy Ones.
He has joined their assembly
    to the Sons of Heaven
to be a Council of the Community,
a foundation of the Building of Holiness,
and eternal Plantation throughout all ages to come.

As for me,
    I belong to wicked mankind,
    to the company of unjust flesh.
My iniquities, rebellions, and sins,
    together with the perversity of my heart,
belong to the company of worms
    and to those who walk in darkness.
For mankind has no way,
    and man is unable to establish his steps
since justification is with God
    and perfection of way is out of His hand.
All things come to pass by His knowledge;
He establishes all things by His design
    and without Him nothing is done.

As for me,
    if I stumble, the mercies of God
    shall be my eternal salvation.
If I stagger because of the sin of flesh,
    my justification shall be
    by the righteousness of God which endures for ever.
When my distress is unleashed
    He will deliver my soul from the Pit
    and will direct my steps to the way.

He will draw me near by His grace,
    and by His mercy will He bring my justification.
He will judge me in the righteousness of His truth
    and in the greatness of His goodness
    He will pardon all my sins.
Through His righteousness he will cleanse me
    of the uncleanness of man
    and of the sins of the children of men,
that I may confess to God His righteousness,
    and His majesty to the Most High.

Blessed art Thou, my God,
    who openest the heart of Thy servant to knowledge!
Establish all his deeds in righteousness,
and as it pleases Thee to do for the elect of mankind,
    grant that the son of Thy handmaid
    may stand before Thee for ever.
For without Thee no way is perfect,
    and without Thy will nothing is done.
It is Thou who hast taught all knowledge
    and all things come to pass by Thy will.
There is none beside Thee to dispute Thy counsel
    or to understand all Thy holy design,
or to contemplate the depth of Thy mysteries
    and the power of Thy might.

Who can endure Thy glory,
    and what is the son of man
    in the midst of Thy wonderful deeds?
What shall one born of woman
    be accounted before Thee?
Kneaded from the dust,
    his abode is the nourishment of worms.
He is but a shape, but moulded clay,
    and inclines towards dust.
What shall hand-moulded clay reply?
    What counsel shall it understand?

Community Rule Manuscripts from Cave 4

This is the best preserved of the ten Community Rule manuscripts from Cave 4.

I Teaching for the Master concerning the men of the Law who have freely pledged themselves to convert from all evil and hold fast to all that He has commanded. And they shall separate from the congregation of the men of injustice and shall unite with respect to doctrine and property, and they shall be under the authority of the Congregation concerning all matters of doctrine and property. They shall practise humility and righteousness and justice and loving-*kindness* and modesty in all their ways. And no man shall walk in the stubbornness of his heart so as to stray. He is rather to lay *a foundation* of truth for Israel for the Community, for all those who have freely pledged themselves to Holiness in Aaron and to a House of Truth in Israel and for those who join them for a Community. Whoever enters the Council *of the Community* shall undertake by binding oath to *return* to the Law of Moses with all his heart and soul, to all that has been revealed from the *Law*.

And whoever enters the Council of the men of the Community *shall separate from all the men* of injustice . . . He shall not touch the purity of the men *of holiness* and shall not eat with them *in community. And no* one of the men of the Community *shall follow* their decision in any *doctrine* and judgement . . . *And* they shall not lean upon *works* of vanity, for they are all vanity who *do not know His Covenant and all who despise* His word He will blot them out from the world. All their deeds are defilement *before Him and all their property unclean . . . But when a man enters the Covenant according to all these precepts, that he may be joined to the* holy *Congregation, they shall examine their spirit in community, among themselves concerning their understanding* **II** and their practice of the Law under the authority of the sons of Aaron who have freely pledged themselves to restore His

Covenant and heed to all the precepts commanded by Him to be practised by the multitude of Israel who have freely pledged themselves to return in common. They shall be inscribed in the order, one after another, each according to his understanding and his deeds in the Law, that all may obey one another, the man of lesser rank the greater. And they shall examine their spirit and their deeds in the Law yearly so that each man may be advanced in accordance with *his understanding* or moved down in accordance with his aberrations. They shall rebuke one another in loving-kindness. Let no man address his companion with anger or ill-temper or wicked envy. Also let no man accuse his companion before the Congregation without having rebuked him before witnesses. These are the ways in which all of them shall walk, each man with his companion, wherever they dwell. *The man of lesser rank* shall obey the greater in matters of work and *property. And they shall* eat *in common* and bless in common and deliberate in common. *And wherever there are ten* **III** men of *the Council of the Community, there shall not lack* a priest *from* among them. *And* they *shall sit, each* man according to his rank, *before him and shall be asked their counsel in all things in that order.* And when *the table has been prepared for eating or the* new wine *for drinking, the* priest shall *be first to stretch out his hand to bless the firstfruit of the bread* and of the wine. *And where the ten are, there shall never lack a man among them who shall study the Law day and night. And the Congregation shall* watch *for one third of every night of the year, to read the Book* . . . **VI** . . . *It shall be a tried wall, that precious corner-stone whose foundations shall not* rock nor sway *from* their place; it shall be a most holy dwelling-place *for Aaron, with the knowledge of them all of a covenant of justice and of the offering of fragrance; it shall be a house of perfection and truth for Israel* to establish a covenant according to the everlasting precepts.

They shall be an acceptance to atone for the land and to determine the judgement of wickedness with no injustice any more. When these have been confirmed in the foundation of the Community for two years, *in perfection of way, they shall be separated as holy within the council of the men* of the Community. *And anything hidden from* Israel but discovered by the man *who interprets, he shall not conceal it from them for fear of the spirit of apostasy.* And when these become part of the Community/in Israel, they shall separate from *the midst of the habitation* of the men *of injustice to go into the wilderness to prepare there the way of HIM. This is the study of the Law* which He has commanded by the hand *of Moses, to* practise all *that has been revealed from age to age, and as the prophets have revealed by His holy spirit. And no man* from the men of the covenant of the *Community who turns aside from any commandment* deliberately shall touch the purity of the men of holiness, nor shall he know any of their counsel until his deeds are purified from all injustice so that he walks in perfection of way. And they shall admit him to the council by the decision of the Congregation and afterwards he shall be inscribed in his rank. And this rule shall apply to everyone who attaches himself to the Community.

VII . . . For one sin of inadvertence he shall do penance for two years, and for a deliberately committed sin he shall return no more. But he shall be tried for two years concerning the perfection of his way and for his counsel according to the decision of the Congregation and he shall be inscribed in his rank in the Community of holiness. *When* these *become part* of the Community in Israel according to these rules, they shall establish the spirit of holiness as eternal truth. They shall atone for guilty rebellion *and the sin of unfaithfulness* and shall gain divine acceptance for the land *without the flesh* of holocausts and the fat of sacrifices and offerings. And the correct free-will gift of the lips shall be like a fragrance *of righteousness and the perfection* of the way like the free-will offering *of* agreeable *tribute.* And at that time they shall separate a house of Aaron for holiness for all . . . of God *and a house of Community for* Israel who walk in perfection. *Only the sons of* Aaron *shall command in matters of* justice and property. And the property *of the men of holiness who* walk in perfection, let *their property* not be merged *with* the property *of the men of falsehood* who have not confirmed *their way to separate from all evil things* so as to walk in *the way of perfection. Let them not depart from any counsel of the Law* and they shall be judged by the *primitive precepts in which the men of the Community began to be instructed. He shall perform the judgement of every man according to his spirit and he shall admit him according to the* *cleanness of his hands* **VIII** and shall advance him according to his understanding, and so shall be his love and his hatred. Furthermore he shall not rebuke a man and shall not dispute with the men of the pit. He shall conceal his counsel among the men of injustice, but he shall impart true knowledge and righteous judgement to those who have chosen the way, to each according to his spirit and according to the rule of the age, *guiding them* with knowledge. And thus shall he instruct them in the mysteries of marvel and truth among the men of the Community that they may walk in perfection each man with *his fellow in all that has been* revealed to them. This is the time for the preparation of the way into the wilderness. He shall instruct them in all that is to be done in that time.

And he shall separate from every man who has not turned away from all injustice. And these are the rules of conduct for the Master in *those times with respect to his loving and* hating. Everlasting hatred for the men of the pit in a spirit of secrecy. He shall leave to them property and gain *and the earnings of toil like a slave to* his lord and the poor man to his master. Each shall be zealous for the precept and his time shall become a day *of revenge.* He shall *perform the will of God in all his actions and in all* his dominion as *He has commanded. And* all that befalls him, he shall enjoy as a free gift and without the will *of GOD he shall not enjoy anything. He shall delight in all the words of His mouth and shall desire nothing that He has not commanded. And* he shall watch *always for the judgement* of GOD . . . and he shall bless his Maker and in all that befalls he shall declare . . . and with the offering of the lips he shall bless Him at *the times which He has decreed. At the beginning of the dominion of light* and the *completion of its circuit when it* retires to *its* appointed dwelling at the beginning *of the watches' darkness. When He opens its storehouse and spreads it out and at the completion of its circuit when it retires* before the light. When *the heavenly lights* shine out *from the* abode *of His holiness together with their withdrawal to the dwelling of glory. At the entry of seasons according to the new moon as well as their completion of their circuit when one succeeds to the other;* **IX** at their renewal there is a great day for the Holy of Holies and a sign for the opening of the everlasting mercies at the beginning of the seasons for all ages to come. At the beginning of the months for their seasons and on the holy days according to their rules for remembrance in *their* seasons, I will bless Him *with the offering of the* lips according to the precept engraved for ever. At the beginning of the years and at the completion of the circuit *of their seasons, when they* fulfil their determined precept on the day decreed for one to follow another, the season *of early harvest the summer, and the season of* sowing the season of grass, the seasons of the years their weeks *and at the beginning of* their weeks the seasons of jubilee. And during all my existence the engraved precept shall be on *my tongue as a fruit* of praise and a *portion* of my lips. I will sing with knowledge and all my music is for the glory of GOD. *And I will* strike my lyre to the order *of His holiness and the pipe of my lips I will* tune to *His* right measure. *At the coming* of the day *and the* night I will enter the covenant *of GOD* and at the departure of evening and morning I will recite His precepts. And in them will I re-establish *my boundaries without return. I will declare His judgement correct concerning* my transgression *and* my *rebellion* shall be before my eyes *as an engraved precept. And I say to GOD, 'My righteousness' and to the Most High,* 'Author of my goodness', 'Fountain *of Knowledge' and 'Source of Holiness', 'Summit of Glory' and 'Almighty Eternal Majesty'. I will choose*   **X**   that which He teaches *me and I will delight in His judgement of me. Before I move my hands* and feet I will bless *His name and before I lift my hand to grow fat from* the pleasant *produce of the world. At the beginning of fear and dread and in the abode of distress and desolation, I will confess His marvel and I will meditate on His might and on His mercies* I will lean *all day long. I know that in His hand is the judgement of all the living and all His deeds are truth. When distress starts I will praise Him and I will exalt Him for His salvation. And I will not pay an evil reward to a man; I will pursue him with goodness. For the judgement of all the living is with GOD, and He* will repay *man his reward* . . .   **XIII**   . . . *He will* atone *for all* my sins. Through His righteousness He will cleanse me of the uncleanness of man and from the sins of the children of men *that I may confess to God* His righteousness . . .

The Damascus Document

Extensive fragments of the Damascus Document have been recovered from three of the Qumran caves but two incomplete medieval copies of this document had been found already many years earlier, in 1896–7, amongst a mass of discarded manuscripts in a store-room (*genizah*) of an old Cairo synagogue. Dating from the tenth and twelfth centuries respectively, the Cairo manuscripts – Manuscript A and Manuscript B – raise a certain number of textual problems in that they present two different versions of the original composition. I have settled the difficulty as satisfactorily as I can by following Manuscript A, to which the cave fragments correspond, and by inserting the Manuscript B variants where appropriate. At a certain point, Manuscript A comes to an end and we then have to rely entirely on Manuscript B.

The title 'Damascus Document' derives from the references in the Exhortation to the 'New Covenant' made 'in the land of Damascus'. The chronological data included in the manuscript suggests that the document was written in about 100 BCE and this hypothesis is indirectly supported by the absence of any mention in the historical passages of the Kittim (Romans) whose invasion of the Orient did not take place until after 70 BCE.

The work is divided into an Exhortation and a list of Statutes. In the Exhortation, the preacher – probably a Guardian of the Community – addresses his 'sons' on the themes of the sect's teaching, many of which appear also in the Community Rule. His aim is to encourage the sectaries to remain faithful, and with this end in view he sets out to demonstrate from the history of Israel and the Community that fidelity is always rewarded and apostasy chastised.

During the course of his argument, the author of the Damascus Document frequently interprets biblical passages in a most unexpected way. For example, there is another intricate exposition of Amos v, 26–7 on p. 105 which may not be easy to understand. In the Bible these verses convey a divine threat: the Israelites were to take themselves and their idols into exile: 'You shall take up Sakkuth your king and Kaiwan your star-god, your images which you made for yourselves, for I will take you into exile beyond Damascus.' But the Damascus Document transforms this threat into a promise of salvation; by changing certain words in the

biblical text and omitting others its version reads: 'I will exile the tabernacle of your king and the bases of your statues from my tent to
Damascus.'

In this new text, the three key phrases are interpreted symbolically as
follows: 'tabernacle' = 'Books of the Law'; 'king' = 'congregation'; 'bases
of statues' = 'Books of the Prophets'. Thus: 'The Books of the Law are the
tabernacle of the king; as God said, *I will raise up the tabernacle of
David which is fallen* (Amos ix, 11). The *king* is the congregation; and
the *bases of the statues* are the Books of the Prophets whose sayings
Israel despised.'

The omission of any reference to the 'star-god' is made good by intro-
ducing a very different 'Star', the messianic 'Interpreter of the Law' with
his companion the 'Prince of the congregation'. 'The star is the Interpreter of the Law who shall come to Damascus; as it is written, *A star
shall come forth out of Jacob and a sceptre shall rise out of Israel* (Num.
xxiv, 17). The sceptre is the Prince of the whole congregation . . .'

The second part of the Damascus Document, the Statutes, consists of
a collection of laws which mostly reflect a sectarian reinterpretation of
the biblical commandments relative to vows and oaths, tribunals, purification, the Sabbath and the distinction between ritual purity and
impurity. They are followed by rules concerned with the institutions and
organisation of the Community. Some of the particular laws of the Damascus Rule appear also in the Temple Scroll (cf. p. 141–2).

Whereas the Exhortation represents a literary *genre* adopted by both
Jewish and Christian religious teachers (e.g. the Letter to the Hebrews),
the methodical grouping of the Statutes prefigures that of the Mishnah,
the oldest extant Jewish code.

The Statutes as they appear in the Qumran fragments include the
form of the ritual for the Feast of the Renewal of the Covenant, so it may
be assumed that the entire Damascus Document was originally connected with that festival.

The Exhortation

I Listen now all you who know righteousness, and consider the
works of God; for He has a dispute with all flesh and will condemn
all those who despise Him.

For when they were unfaithful and forsook Him, He hid His
face from Israel and His Sanctuary and delivered them up to the

sword. But remembering the Covenant of the forefathers, He left a remnant to Israel and did not deliver it up to be destroyed. And in the age of wrath, three hundred and ninety years after He had given them into the hand of King Nebuchadnezzar of Babylon, He visited them, and He caused a plant root to spring from Israel and Aaron to inherit His Land and to prosper on the good things of His earth. And they perceived their iniquity and recognised that they were guilty men, yet for twenty years they were like blind men groping for the way.

And God observed their deeds, that they sought Him with a whole heart, and He raised for them a Teacher of Righteousness to guide them in the way of His heart. And he made known to the latter generations that which God had done to the latter generation, the congregation of traitors, to those who departed from the way. This was the time of which it is written, *Like a stubborn heifer thus was Israel stubborn* (Hos. iv, 16), when the Scoffer arose who shed over Israel the waters of lies. He caused them to wander in a pathless wilderness, laying low the everlasting heights, abolishing the ways of righteousness and removing the boundary with which the forefathers had marked out their inheritance, that he might call down on them the curses of His Covenant and deliver them up to the avenging sword of the Covenant. For they sought smooth things and preferred illusions (Isa. xxx, 10) and they watched for breaks (Isa. xxx, 13) and chose the fair neck; and they justified the wicked and condemned the just, and they transgressed the Covenant and violated the Precept. They banded together against the life of the righteous (Ps. xciv, 21) and loathed all who walked in perfection; they pursued them with the sword and exulted in the strife of the people. And the anger of God was kindled against **II** their congregation so that He ravaged all their multitude; and their deeds were defilement before Him.

Hear now, all you who enter the Covenant, and I will unstop your ears concerning the ways of the wicked.

God loves knowledge. Wisdom and understanding He has set before Him, and prudence and knowledge serve Him. Patience and much forgiveness are with Him towards those who turn from transgression; but power, might, and great flaming wrath by the hand of all the Angels of Destruction towards those who depart from the way and abhor the Precept. They shall have no remnant or survivor. For from the beginning God chose them not; He knew their deeds before ever they were created and He hated their generations, and He hid His face from the Land until they were consumed. For He knew the years of their coming and the length and exact duration of their times for all ages to come and throughout eternity. He knew the happenings of their times throughout all the everlasting years. And in all of them He raised for Himself men called by name that a remnant might be left to the Land, and that the face of the earth might be filled with their seed. And He made known His Holy Spirit to them by the hand of His anointed ones, and He proclaimed the truth to them. But those whom He hated He led astray.

Hear now, my sons, and I will uncover your eyes that you may see and understand the works of God, that you may choose that which pleases Him and reject that which He hates, that you may walk perfectly in all His ways and not follow after thoughts of the guilty inclination and after eyes of lust. For through them, great men have gone astray and mighty heroes have stumbled from former times till now. Because they walked in the stubbornness of their heart the Heavenly Watchers fell; they were caught because they did not keep the commandments of God. And their sons also fell who were tall as cedar trees and whose bodies were like mountains. All flesh on dry land perished; they were as though they had never been because they did their own will and did not keep the commandment of their Maker so that His wrath was kindled against them.   **III** Through it, the children of Noah went astray, together with their kin, and were cut off. Abraham did not walk in it, and he was accounted a friend of God because he kept the commandments of God and did not choose his own will. And he handed them down to Isaac and Jacob, who kept them, and were recorded as friends of God and party to the Covenant for ever. The children of Jacob strayed through them and were punished in accordance with their error. And their sons in Egypt walked in the stubbornness of their hearts, conspiring against the commandments of God and each of them doing that which seemed right in his own eyes. They ate blood, and He cut off their males in the wilderness. And at Kadesh He said to them, *Go up and possess the land* (Deut. ix, 23). But they chose their own will and did not heed the voice of their Maker, the commands of their Teacher, but murmured in their tents; and the anger of God was kindled against their congregation. Through it their sons perished, and through it their kings were cut off; through it their mighty heroes perished and through it their land was ravaged. Through it the first members of the Covenant sinned and were delivered up to the sword, because they forsook the Covenant of God and chose their own will and walked in the stubbornness of their hearts, each of them doing his own will.

But with the remnant which held fast to the commandments of God He made His Covenant with Israel for ever, revealing to them the hidden things in which all Israel had gone astray. He unfolded before them His holy Sabbaths and his glorious feasts, the testimonies of His righteousness and the ways of His truth, and the desires of His will which a man must do in order to live. And they dug a well rich in water; and he who despises it shall not live. Yet they wallowed in the sin of man and in ways of uncleanness, and they said, 'This is our way.' But God, in His wonderful mysteries, forgave them their sin and pardoned their wickedness; and He built them a sure house in Israel whose like has never existed from former times till now. Those who hold fast to it are destined to live for ever and all the glory of Adam shall be theirs. As God ordained for them by the hand of the Prophet Ezekiel, saying, *The Priests, the Levites, and the sons*   **IV** *of Zadok who kept the charge of my sanctuary when the children of Israel strayed from me, they shall offer me fat and blood* (Ezek. xliv, 15).

The *Priests* are the converts of Israel who departed from the land of Judah, and the *Levites* are those who joined them. The *sons of Zadok* are the elect of Israel, the men called by name who shall stand at the end of days. Behold the exact list of their names according to their generations, and the time when they lived, and the number of their trials, and the years of their sojourn, and the exact list of their deeds . . .

They were the first men of holiness whom God forgave, and who justified the righteous and condemned the wicked. And until the age is completed, according to the number of those years, all who enter after them shall do according to that interpretation of the Law in which the first men were instructed. According to the Covenant which God made with the forefathers, forgiving their sins, so shall He forgive their sins also. But when the age is completed, according to the number of those years, there shall be no more joining the house of Judah, but each man shall stand on his watch-tower: *The wall is built, the boundary far removed* (Mic. vii, 11).

During all those years Belial shall be unleashed against Israel, as He spoke by the hand of Isaiah, son of Amoz, saying, *Terror and the pit and the snare are upon you, O inhabitant of the land* (Isa. xxiv, 17). Interpreted, these are the three nets of Belial with which Levi son of Jacob said that he catches Israel by setting them up as three kinds of righteousness. The first is fornication, the second is riches, and the third is profanation of the Temple. Whoever escapes the first is caught in the second, and whoever saves himself from the second is caught in the third (Isa. xxiv, 18).

The 'builders of the wall' (Ezek. xiii, 10) who have followed after 'Precept' – 'Precept' was a spouter of whom it is written, *They shall surely spout* (Mic. ii, 6) – shall be caught in fornication twice by taking a second wife while the first is alive, whereas the principle of creation is, *Male and female created He them* (Gen. i, 27). **V** Also, those who entered the Ark went in two by two. And concerning the prince it is written, *He shall not multiply wives to himself* (Deut. xvii, 17); but David had not read the sealed book of the Law which was in the ark of the Covenant, for it was not opened in Israel from the death of Eleazar and Joshua, and the elders who worshipped Ashtoreth. It was hidden and was not revealed until the coming of Zadok. And the deeds of David rose up, except for the murder of Uriah, and God left them to him.

Moreover, they profane the Temple because they do not observe the distinction between clean and unclean in accordance with the Law, but lie with a woman who sees her bloody discharge.

And each man marries the daughter of his brother or sister, whereas Moses said, *You shall not approach your mother's sister; she is your mother's near kin* (Lev. xviii, 13). But although the laws against incest are written for men, they also apply to women. When, therefore, a brother's daughter uncovers the nakedness of her father's brother, she is also his near kin.

Furthermore, they defile their holy spirit and open their mouth with a blaspheming tongue against the laws of the Covenant of God saying, 'They are not sure.' They speak abominations concerning them; *they are all kindlers of fire and lighters of brands*

(Isa. i, 11), *their webs are spiders' webs and their eggs are vipers' eggs* (Isa. lix, 5). No man that approaches them shall be free from guilt; the more he does so, the guiltier shall he be, unless he is pressed. For already in ancient times God visited their deeds and His anger was kindled against their works; *for it is a people of no discernment* (Isa. xxvii, 11), *it is a nation void of counsel inasmuch as there is no discernment in them* (Deut. xxxii, 28). For in ancient times, Moses and Aaron arose by the hand of the Prince of Lights and Belial in his cunning raised up Jannes and his brother when Israel was first delivered.

And at the time of the desolation of the land there arose removers of the bound who led Israel astray. And the land was ravaged because they preached rebellion against the command-ments of God given by the hand of Moses and   **VI** of His holy anointed ones, and because they prophesied lies to turn Israel away from following God. But God remembered the Covenant with the forefathers, and he raised from Aaron men of discern-ment and from Israel men of wisdom, and He caused them to hear. And they dug the Well: *the well which the princes dug, which the nobles of the people delved with the stave* (Num. xxi, 18).

The *Well* is the Law, and those who dug it were the converts of Israel who went out of the land of Judah to sojourn in the land of Damascus. God called them all *princes* because they sought Him, and their renown was disputed by no man. The *Stave* is the Inter-preter of the Law of whom Isaiah said, *He makes a tool for His work* (Isa. liv, 16); and the *nobles of the people* are those who come to dig the *Well* with the staves with which the *Stave* ordained that they should walk in all the age of wickedness – and without them they shall find nothing – until he comes who shall teach right-eousness at the end of days.

None of those brought into the Covenant shall enter the Temple to light His altar in vain. They shall bar the door, foras-much as God said, *Who among you will bar its door?* And, *You shall not light my altar in vain* (Mal. i, 10). They shall take care to act according to the exact interpretation of the Law during the age of wickedness. They shall separate from the sons of the Pit, and shall keep away from the unclean riches of wickedness acquired by vow or anathema or from the Temple treasure; they shall not rob the poor of His people, to make of widows their prey and of the fatherless their victim (Isa. x, 2). They shall distinguish between clean and unclean, and shall proclaim the difference between holy and profane. They shall keep the Sabbath day according to its exact interpretation, and the feasts and the Day of Fasting according to the finding of the members of the New Covenant in the land of Damascus. They shall set aside the holy things according to the exact teaching concerning them. They shall love each man his brother as himself; they shall succour the poor, the needy, and the stranger.

A man shall seek his brother's well-being **VII** and shall not sin against his near kin. They shall keep from fornication according to the statute. They shall rebuke each man his brother according to the commandment and shall bear no rancour from one day to the next. They shall keep apart from every uncleanness according to the statutes relating to each one, and no man shall defile his holy spirit since God has set them apart. For all who walk in these precepts in perfect holiness, according to all the teaching of God, the Covenant of God shall be an assurance that they shall live for thousands of generations as it is written, *Keeping the Covenant and grace with those who love me and keep my commandments, to a thousand generations* (Deut. vii, 9).

And if they live in camps according to the rule of the Land as it was from ancient times, marrying according to the custom of the Law and begetting children, they shall walk according to the Law and according to the statute concerning binding vows, according to the rule of the Law which says, *Between a man and his wife and between a father and his son* (Num. xxx, 17). And all those who despise the commandments and the statutes shall be rewarded with the retribution of the wicked when God shall visit the Land, when the saying shall come to pass which is written* among the words of the Prophet Isaiah son of Amoz: *He will bring upon you,*

---

* MS. B continues: by the hand of the prophet Zechariah: *Awake, O Sword, against my shepherd, against my companion, says God. Strike the shepherd that the flock may be scattered and I will stretch my hand over the little ones* (Zech. xiii, 7). The humble of the flock are those who watch for Him. They shall be saved at the time of the Visitation whereas the others shall be delivered up to the sword when the Anointed of Aaron and Israel shall come, as it came to pass at the time of the former Visitation concerning which God said by the hand of Ezekiel: *They shall put a mark on the foreheads of those who sigh and groan* (Ezek. ix, 4). But the others were delivered up to the avenging sword of the Covenant.

and upon your people, and upon your father's house, days such as have not come since the day that Ephraim departed from Judah (Isa. vii, 17). When the two houses of Israel were divided, Ephraim departed from Judah. And all the apostates were given up to the sword, but those who held fast escaped to the land of the north; as God said, *I will exile the tabernacle of your king and the bases of your statues from my tent to Damascus* (Amos v, 26–7).

The Books of the Law are the *tabernacle* of the king; as God said, *I will raise up the tabernacle of David which is fallen* (Amos ix, 11). The *king* is the congregation; and the *bases of the statues* are the Books of the Prophets whose sayings Israel despised. The *star* is the Interpreter of the Law who shall come to Damascus; as it is written, *A star shall come forth out of Jacob and a sceptre shall rise out of Israel* (Num. xxiv, 17). The *sceptre* is the Prince of the whole congregation, and when he comes *he shall smite all the children of Seth* (Num. xxiv, 17).

At the time of the former Visitation they were saved, whereas the apostates **VIII** were given up to the sword; and so shall it be for all the members of His Covenant who do not hold steadfastly to the curse of the precepts. They shall be visited for destruction by the hand of Belial. That shall be the day when God will visit. As He said, *The princes of Judah have become like those who remove the bound; wrath shall be poured upon them* (Hos. v, 10). For they shall hope for healing but He will crush them. They are all of them rebels, for they have not turned from the way of traitors but have wallowed in the ways of whoredom and wicked wealth. They have taken revenge and borne malice, every man against his brother, and every man has hated his fellow, and every man has sinned against his near kin, and has approached for unchastity, and has acted arrogantly for the sake of riches and gain. And every man has done that which seemed right in his eyes and has chosen the stubbornness of his heart. They have not kept apart from the people and their sin and have wilfully rebelled by walking in the ways of the wicked of whom God said, *Their wine is the venom of serpents, the cruel poison of asps* (Deut. xxxii, 33).

The *serpents* are the kings of the peoples and their *wine* is their ways. And the *head of asps* is the chief of the kings of Greece who came to wreak vengeance upon them. But all these things the *builders of the wall and those who daub it with plaster* (Ezek. xiii, 10) have not understood because a follower of the wind, one who raised storms and rained down lies, had preached to them (Mic. ii, 11), against all of whose assembly the anger of God was kindled.

And as for that which Moses said, *You enter to possess these nations not because of your righteousness or the uprightness of your hearts* (Deut. ix, 5) *but because God loved your fathers and kept the oath* (Deut. vii, 8), thus shall it be with the converts of Israel who depart from the way of the people. Because God loved the first men who testified in His favour, so will He love those who come after them, for the Covenant of the fathers is theirs. But He hated the *builders of the wall* and His anger was kindled against them and against all those who followed them; and so shall it be for all who reject the commandments of God and abandon them for the stubbornness of their hearts. This is the word which Jeremiah spoke to Baruch son of Neriah, and which Elisha spoke to his servant Gehazi.

None of the men who enter the New Covenant in the land of Damascus, and who again betray it and depart from the fountain of living waters, shall be reckoned with the Council of the people or inscribed in its Book from the day of the gathering in of the Teacher of the Community until the coming of the Messiah out of Aaron and Israel.

And thus shall it be for every man who enters the congregation of men of perfect holiness but faints in performing the duties of the upright. He is a man who has melted in the furnace (Ezek. xxii, 22); when his deeds are revealed he shall be expelled from the congregation as though his lot had never fallen among the disciples of God. The men of knowledge shall rebuke him in accordance with his sin against the time when he shall stand again before the Assembly of the men of perfect holiness. But when his deeds are revealed, according to the interpretation of the Law in which the men of perfect holiness walk, let no man defer to him with regard to money or work, for all the Holy Ones of the Most High have cursed him.

And thus shall it be for all among the first and the last who reject the precepts, who set idols upon their hearts and walk in the stubbornness of their hearts; they shall have no share in the house

of the Law. They shall be judged in the same manner as their companions were judged who deserted to the Scoffer. For they have
spoken wrongly against the precepts of righteousness, and have
despised the Covenant and the Pact – the New Covenant – which
they made in the land of Damascus. Neither they nor their kin
shall have any part in the house of the Law.

From the day of the gathering in of the Teacher of the Community until the end of all the men of war who deserted to the Liar
there shall pass about forty years (Deut. ii, 14). And during that
age the wrath of God shall be kindled against Israel; as He said,
*There shall be no king, no prince, no judge, no man to rebuke with
justice* (Hos. iii, 4). But those who turn from the sin of Jacob, who
keep the Covenant of God, shall then speak each man to his fellow, to justify each man his brother, that their step may take the
way of God. And God will heed their words and will hear, and a
Book of Reminder shall be written before Him of them that fear
God and worship His Name, against the time when salvation and
righteousness shall be revealed to them that fear God. *And then
shall you distinguish once more between the just and the wicked,
between one that serves God and one that serves Him not* (Mal. iii,
18); *and He will show loving-kindness to thousands, to them that
love Him and watch for Him, for a thousand generations* (Exod.
xx, 6).

And every member of the House of Separation who went out of
the Holy City and leaned on God at the time when Israel sinned
and defiled the Temple, but returned again to the way of the
people in small matters, shall be judged according to his spirit in
the Council of Holiness. But when the glory of God is made manifest to Israel, all those members of the Covenant who have
breached the bound of the Law shall be cut off from the midst of
the camp, and with them all those who condemned Judah in the
days of its trials.

But all those who hold fast to these precepts, going and coming
in accordance with the Law, who heed the voice of the Teacher
and confess before God, saying, 'Truly we have sinned, we and our
fathers, by walking counter to the precepts of the Covenant, Thy
judgements upon us are justice and truth'; who do not lift their
hand against His holy precepts or His righteous statutes or His
true testimonies; who have learned from the former judgements

by which the members of the Community were judged; who have listened to the voice of the Teacher of Righteousness and have not despised the precepts of righteousness when they heard them; they shall rejoice and their hearts shall be strong, and they shall prevail over all the sons of the earth. God will forgive them and they shall see His salvation because they took refuge in His holy Name.*

The Statutes

. . . He shall not **XV** swear by the Name, nor by *Aleph* and *Lamed* (Elohim), nor by *Aleph* and *Daleth* (Adonai), but a binding oath by the curses of the Covenant.

He shall not mention the Law of Moses for . . . were he to swear and then break his oath he would profane the Name.

But if he has sworn an oath by the curses of the Covenant before the judges and has transgressed it, then he is guilty and shall confess and make restitution; but he shall not be burdened with a capital sin.

And all those who have entered the Covenant, granted to all Israel for ever, shall make their children who have reached the age of enrolment, swear with the oath of the Covenant. And thus shall it be during all the age of wickedness for every man who repents of his corrupted way. On the day that he speaks to the Guardian of the congregation, they shall enrol him with the oath of the Covenant which Moses made with Israel, the Covenant to return to the Law of Moses with a whole heart and soul, to whatever is found should be done at that time. No man shall make known the statutes to him until he has stood before the Guardian, lest when examining him the Guardian be deceived by him. But if he transgresses after swearing to return to the Law of Moses with a whole heart and soul, the members shall be innocent should he transgress. And should he err in any matter that is revealed of the Law to the multitude of the camp, the Guardian shall instruct him and shall issue directions concerning him: he should study for a full year. And according to the Guardian's knowledge, no mad-

* The end of the Exhortation in the Cairo document is followed in the Cave document by a badly preserved allusion to the Messiah: 'God *will set up* a shepherd *for His people* and He will feed *them* in *pastures* . . .'

man, or lunatic shall enter, no simpleton, or fool, no blind man, or maimed, or lame, or deaf man, and no minor, none of these shall enter into the Community, for the Angels of Holiness are *in their midst.*

For God made **XVI** a Covenant with you and all Israel; therefore a man shall bind himself by oath to return to the Law of Moses, for in it all things are strictly defined.

As for the exact determination of their times to which Israel turns a blind eye, behold it is strictly defined in the *Book of the Divisions of the Times into their Jubilees and Weeks.* And on the day that a man swears to return to the Law of Moses, the Angel of Persecution shall cease to follow him provided that he fulfils his word: for this reason Abraham circumcised himself on the day that he knew.

And concerning the saying, *You shall keep your vow by fulfilling it* (Deut. xxiii, 24), let no man, even at the price of death, annul any binding oath by which he has sworn to keep a commandment of the Law.

But even at the price of death, a man shall fulfil no vow by which he has sworn to depart from the Law.

Concerning the oath of a woman

Inasmuch as He said, *It is for her husband to cancel her oath* (Num. xxx, 9), no husband shall cancel an oath without knowing whether it should be kept or not. Should it be such as to lead to transgression of the Covenant, he shall cancel it and shall not let it be kept. The rule for her father is likewise.

Concerning the statute for freewill-offerings

No man shall vow to the altar anything unlawfully acquired. Also, no Priest shall take from Israel anything unlawfully acquired. And no man shall consecrate the food of his house to God, for it is as he said, *Each hunts his brother with a net* (or *votive-offering*) (Mic. vii, 2) . . .

IX Every vow by which a man vows another to destruction (cf. Lev. xxvii, 29) by the laws of the Gentiles shall himself be put to death. And concerning the saying, *You shall not take vengeance on the children of your people, nor bear any rancour against them*

(Lev. xix, 18), if any member of the Covenant accuses his companion without first rebuking him before witnesses; if he denounces him in the heat of his anger or reports him to his elders to make him look contemptible, he is one that takes vengeance and bears rancour, although it is expressly written, *He takes vengeance upon His adversaries and bears rancour against His enemies* (Nah. i, 2). If he holds his peace towards him from one day to another and thereafter speaks of him in the heat of his anger, he testifies against himself concerning a capital matter because he has not fulfilled the commandment of God which tells him: *You shall rebuke your companion and not be burdened with sin because of him* (Lev. xix, 17).

Concerning the oath with reference to that which He said, You shall not take the law into your own hands (1 Sam. xxv, 26)

Whoever causes another to swear in the field instead of before the Judges, or at their decree, takes the law into his own hands. When anything is lost, and it is not known who has stolen it from the property of the camp in which it was stolen, its owner shall pronounce a curse, and any man who, on hearing it, knows but does not tell, shall himself be guilty.

When anything is returned which is without an owner, whoever returns it shall confess to the Priest, and apart from the ram of the sin-offering, it shall be his.

And likewise, everything which is found but has no owner shall go to the Priests, for the finder is ignorant of the rule concerning it. If no owners are discovered they shall keep it.

Every sin which a man commits against the Law, and which his companion witnesses, he being alone, if it is a capital matter he shall report it to the Guardian, rebuking him in his presence, and the Guardian shall record it against him in case he should commit it again before one man and he should report it to the Guardian once more. Should he repeat it and be caught in the act before one man, his case shall be complete.

And if there are two witnesses, each testifying to a different matter, the man shall be excluded from the pure Meal provided that they are trustworthy and that each informs the Guardian on the day that they witnessed the offence. In matters of property, they shall accept two trustworthy witnesses and shall exclude the culprit from the pure Meal on the word of one witness alone.

No   **X** Judge shall pass sentence of death on the testimony of a witness who has not yet attained the age of enrolment and who is not God-fearing.

No man who has wilfully transgressed any commandment shall be declared a trustworthy witness against his companion until he is purified and able to return.

And this is the Rule for the Judges of the Congregation

Ten shall be elected from the congregation for a definite time, four from the tribe of Levi and Aaron, and six from Israel. They shall be learned in the Book of Meditation and in the constitutions of the Covenant, and aged between twenty-five and sixty years. No man over the age of sixty shall hold office as Judge of the Congregation, for 'because man sinned his days have been shortened, and in the heat of His anger against the inhabitants of the earth God ordained that their understanding should depart even before their days are completed' (Jubilees, xxiii, 11).

Concerning purification by water

No man shall bathe in dirty water or in an amount too shallow to cover a man. He shall not purify himself with water contained in a vessel. And as for the water of every rock-pool too shallow to cover a man, if an unclean man touches it he renders its water as unclean as water contained in a vessel.

Concerning the Sabbath to observe it according to its law

No man shall work on the sixth day from the moment when the sun's orb is distant by its own fullness from the gate wherein it sinks; for this is what He said, *Observe the Sabbath day to keep it holy* (Deut. v, 12). No man shall speak any vain or idle word on the Sabbath day. He shall make no loan to his companion. He shall make no decision in matters of money and gain. He shall say nothing about work or labour to be done on the morrow.

No man shall walk in the field to do business on the Sabbath. He shall not walk more than one thousand cubits beyond his town.

No man shall eat on the Sabbath day except that which is already prepared. He shall eat nothing lying in the fields. He shall not drink except in the camp.   **XI** If he is on a journey and goes down to bathe, he shall drink where he stands, but he shall not draw water into a vessel. He shall send out no stranger on his business on the Sabbath day. No man shall wear soiled garments, or garments brought to the store, unless they have been washed with water or rubbed with incense. No man shall willingly mingle with others on the Sabbath.

No man shall walk more than two thousand cubits after a beast to pasture it outside his town. He shall not raise his hand to strike it with his fist. If it is stubborn he shall not take it out of his house.

No man shall take anything out of the house or bring anything in. And if he is in a booth, let him neither take anything out nor bring anything in. He shall not open a sealed vessel on the Sabbath.

No man shall carry perfumes on himself whilst going and coming on the Sabbath. He shall lift neither stone nor dust in his dwelling.

No man minding a child shall carry it whilst going and coming on the Sabbath.

No man shall chide his manservant or maidservant or labourer on the Sabbath. No man shall assist a beast to give birth on the Sabbath day. And if it should fall into a cistern or pit, he shall not lift it out on the Sabbath.

No man shall spend the Sabbath in a place near to Gentiles on the Sabbath.

No man shall profane the Sabbath for the sake of riches or gain on the Sabbath day. But should any man fall into water or fire, let him not be pulled out with the aid of a ladder or rope or some such utensil.

No man on the Sabbath shall offer anything on the altar except the Sabbath burnt-offering; for it is written thus: *Except your Sabbath offerings* (Lev. xxiii, 38).

No man shall send to the altar any burnt-offering, or cereal offering, or incense, or wood, by the hand of one smitten with any uncleanness, permitting him thus to defile the altar. For it is written, *The sacrifice of the wicked is an abomination, but the prayer of the just is as an agreeable offering* (Prov. xv, 8).

No man entering the house of worship shall come unclean and

in need of washing. And at the sounding of the trumpets for assembly, he shall go there before or after the meeting, and shall not cause the whole service to stop,   **XII** for it is a holy service.

No man shall lie with a woman in the city of the Sanctuary, to defile the city of the Sanctuary with their uncleanness.

Every man who preaches apostasy under the dominion of the spirits of Belial shall be judged according to the law relating to those possessed by a ghost or familiar spirit (Lev. xx, 27). But no man who strays so as to profane the Sabbath and the feasts shall be put to death; it shall fall to men to keep him in custody. And if he is healed of his error, they shall keep him in custody for seven years and he shall afterwards approach the Assembly.

No man shall stretch out his hand to shed the blood of a Gentile for the sake of riches and gain. Nor shall he carry off anything of theirs, lest they blaspheme, unless so advised by the company of Israel.

No man shall sell clean beasts or birds to the Gentiles lest they offer them in sacrifice. He shall refuse, with all his power, to sell them anything from his granary or wine-press, and he shall not sell them his manservant or maidservant inasmuch as they have been brought by him into the Covenant of Abraham.

No man shall defile himself by eating any live creature or creeping thing, from the larvae of bees to all creatures which creep in water. They shall eat no fish unless split alive and their blood poured out. And as for locusts, according to their various kinds they shall plunge them alive into fire or water, for this is what their nature requires.

All wood and stones and dust defiled by the impurity of a man shall be reckoned like men having defilement of oil on them; whoever touches them shall be defiled by their defilement. And every nail or peg in the wall of a house in which a dead man lies shall become unclean as any working tool becomes unclean (Lev. xi, 32).

The Rule for the assembly of the towns of Israel shall be according to these precepts that they may distinguish between unclean and clean, and discriminate between the holy and the profane.

And these are the precepts in which the Master shall walk in his commerce with all the living in accordance with the statute proper to every age. And in accordance with this statute shall the seed of Israel walk and they shall not be cursed.

This is the Rule for the assembly of the camps

Those who follow these statutes in the age of wickedness until the coming of the Messiah of Aaron   **XIII**   and Israel shall form groups of at least ten men, by *Thousands, Hundreds, Fifties, and Tens* (Exod. xviii, 25). And where the ten are, there shall never be lacking a Priest learned in the Book of Meditation; they shall all be ruled by him.

But should he not be experienced in these matters, whereas one of the Levites is experienced in them, then it shall be determined that all the members of the camp shall go and come according to the latter's word.

But should there be a case of applying the law of leprosy to a man, then the Priest shall come and shall stand in the camp and the Guardian shall instruct him in the exact interpretation of the Law.

Even if the Priest is a simpleton, it is he who shall lock up the leper; for theirs is the judgement.

This is the Rule for the Guardian of the camp

He shall instruct the Congregation in the works of God. He shall cause them to consider His mighty deeds and shall recount all the happenings of eternity to them *according to* their explanation. He shall love them as a father loves his children, and shall carry them in all their distress like a shepherd his sheep. He shall loosen all the fetters which bind them that in his Congregation there may be none that are oppressed or broken. He shall examine every man entering his Congregation with regard to his deeds, understanding, strength, ability and possessions, and shall inscribe him in his place according to his rank in the lot of *Light*.

No member of the camp shall have authority to admit a man to the Congregation against the decision of the Guardian of the camp.

No member of the Covenant of God shall give or receive anything from the sons of Dawn (*shahar*)* except for payment.

No man shall form any association for buying and selling with-

* or: of the Pit (*shahat*).

out informing the Guardian of the camp and shall act on his advice and they shall not go astray. Likewise he who marries a woman . . . advice. Likewise he who divorces his wife. And the Guardian shall instruct their sons *and their daughters in a spirit* of humility and in loving-kindness and shall not keep anger towards them . . .

This is the Rule for the assembly of the camps during all *the age of wickedness, and whoever does not hold fast to* these statutes shall not be fit to dwell in the Land *when the Messiah of Aaron and Israel shall come at the end of days.*

And these are the *precepts* in which the Master *shall walk in his commerce with all the living until God shall visit the earth. As He said, There shall come upon you, and upon your people, and upon your father's house days*   **XIV**   *such as have not come since Ephraim departed from Judah* (Isa. vii, 17); but for whoever shall walk in these precepts, the Covenant of God shall stand firm to save him from all the snares of the Pit, whereas the foolish shall be punished.

The Rule for the assembly of all the camps

They shall all be enrolled by name: first the Priests, second the Levites, third the Israelites, and fourth the proselytes. And they shall be inscribed by name, one after the other: the Priests first, the Levites second, the Israelites third, and the proselytes fourth. And thus shall they sit and thus be questioned on all matters. And the Priest who is appointed to head the Congregation shall be from thirty to sixty years old, learned in the Book of Meditation and in all the judgements of the Law so as to pronounce them correctly.

The Guardian of all the camps shall be from thirty to fifty years old, one who has mastered all the secrets of men and the languages of all their clans. Whoever enters the Congregation shall do so according to his word, each in his rank. And whoever has anything to say with regard to any suit or judgement, let him say it to the Guardian.

This is the Rule for the Congregation by which it shall provide for all its needs

They shall place the earnings of at least two days out of every month into the hands of the Guardian and the Judges, and from it they shall give to the fatherless, and from it they shall succour the poor and the needy, the aged sick and the man who is stricken with disease, the captive taken by a foreign people, the virgin with no near kin, and the maid *for* whom no man cares . . .

And this is the exact statement of the assembly . . .

The Messianic Rule

The Messianic Rule was originally included in the same Scroll as the Community Rule. This short but complete work, which dates from the mid-first century BCE, presents the translator with great difficulties owing to its bad state of preservation and to the carelessness of the scribe.

I have named it the Messianic Rule for the following reasons: (1) it was intended for 'all the congregation in the *last days*'; (2) it is a Rule for a Community adapted to the requirements of the messianic war against the nations; (3) it refers to the presence of the Priest and the Messiah of Israel at the Council, and at the Meal described in column 11.

I *This is the Rule for all the congregation of Israel in the last days, when they shall join the Community to walk according to the law of the sons of Zadok the Priests and of the men of their Covenant who have turned aside from the way of the people, the men of His Council who keep His Covenant in the midst of iniquity, offering expiation for the Land*

When they come, they shall summon them all, the little children and the women also, and they shall read into their *ears* all the precepts of the Covenant and shall expound to them all their statutes that they may no longer stray in their *errors.*

And this is the Rule for all the hosts of the congregation, for every man born in Israel

From *his* youth they shall instruct him in the Book of Meditation and shall teach him, according to his age, the precepts of the Covenant. They *shall be* educated in their statutes for ten years . . .

At the age of twenty years *he shall be* enrolled, that he may enter upon his allotted duties in the midst of his family and be joined to the holy congregation. He shall not *approach* a woman to know her by lying with her before he is fully twenty years old, when he shall know *good* and evil. And thereafter, he shall be accepted when he calls to witness the judgements of the Law, and shall be allowed to assist at the hearing of judgements.

At the age of twenty-five years he may take his place among the foundations [i.e. the officials] of the holy congregation to work in the service of the congregation.

At the age of thirty years he may approach to participate in law-suits and judgements, and may take his place among the chiefs of the Thousands of Israel, the chiefs of the Hundreds, Fifties, and Tens, the Judges and the officers of their tribes, in all their families, *under the authority* of the sons of *Aaron* the Priests. And every head of family in the congregation who is chosen to hold office, *to go* and come before the congregation, shall strengthen his loins that he may perform his tasks among his brethren in accordance with his understanding and the perfection of his way. According to whether this is great or little, so shall one man be honoured more than another.

When a man is advanced in years, he shall be given a duty in the service of the congregation in proportion to his strength.

No simpleton shall be chosen to hold office in the congregation of Israel with regard to lawsuits or judgement, nor carry any responsibility in the congregation. Nor shall he hold any office in the war destined to vanquish the nations; his family shall merely inscribe him in the army register and he shall do his service in task-work in proportion to his capacity.

The sons of Levi shall hold office, each in his place, under the authority of the sons of Aaron. They shall cause all the congregation to go and come, each man in his rank, under the direction of the heads of family of the congregation – the leaders, Judges, and officers, according to the number of all their hosts – under the authority of the sons of Zadok the Priests, *and* under the direction *of all the* heads of family of the congregation. And when the whole assembly is summoned for judgement, or for a Council of the Community, or for war, they shall sanctify them for three days that every one of its members may be prepared.

These are the men who shall be called to the Council of the Community . . .

All the wise *men* of the congregation, the learned and the intelligent, men whose way is perfect and men of ability, together with the tribal chiefs and all the Judges and officers, and the chiefs of the Thousands, *Hundreds,*   **II** Fifties, and Tens, and the Levites, each man in the *class* of his duty; these are the men of renown, the members of the assembly summoned to the Council of the Community in Israel before the sons of Zadok the Priests.

And no man smitten with any human uncleanness shall enter the assembly of God; no man smitten with any of them shall be confirmed in his office in the congregation. No man smitten in his flesh, or paralysed in his feet or hands, or lame, or blind, or deaf, or dumb, or smitten in his flesh with a visible blemish; no old and tottery man unable to stay still in the midst of the congregation; none of these shall come to hold office among the congregation of the men of renown, for the Angels of Holiness are *with* their *congregation*. Should *one* of them have something to say to the Council of Holiness, let *him* be questioned privately; but let him not enter among *the congregation* for he is smitten.

This shall be the assembly of the men of renown called to the meeting of the Council of the Community
When God engenders* the Priest-Messiah, he shall come with them *at* the head of the whole congregation of Israel with all *his brethren, the sons* of Aaron the Priests, *those called* to the assembly, the men of renown; and they shall sit *before him, each man* in the order of his dignity. And then *the Messiah* of Israel shall *come*, and the chiefs of the *clans of Israel* shall sit before him, *each* in the order of his dignity, according to *his place* in their camps and marches. And before them shall sit all the heads of *family of the congregation*, and the wise men of *the holy congregation*, each in the order of his dignity.

And *when* they shall gather for the common *table*, to eat and *to drink* new wine, when the common table shall be set for eating and the new wine *poured* for drinking, let no man extend his hand over the firstfruits of bread and wine before the Priest; for *it is he* who shall bless the firstfruits of bread and wine, and shall be the first *to extend* his hand over the bread. Thereafter, the Messiah of Israel shall extend his hand over the bread, *and* all the congregation of the Community *shall utter a* blessing, *each man in the order* of his dignity.

It is according to this statute that they shall proceed at every meal *at which* at least ten men are gathered together.

* This reading (*yolid*), which has been queried by many, including myself, seems to be confirmed by computer image enhancement.

The War Scroll

The nineteen badly mutilated columns of this manuscript from Cave 1 first appeared in 1954 in a posthumous work by E. L. Sukenik, and were re-edited in 1955, with an English introduction, under the title *The Dead Sea Scrolls of the Hebrew University* (Jerusalem).

The contents of the War Rule are as follows:
    Proclamation of war against the Kittim (I)
    Reorganisation of Temple worship (II)
    Programme of the forty years' war (II)
    The trumpets (III)
    The standards (III–IV)
    Disposition and weapons of the front formations (V)
    Movements of the attacking infantry (VI)
    Disposition and movements of the cavalry (VI)
    Age of the soldiers (VI–VII)
    The camp (VII)
    Duties of the Priests and Levites:
    Exhortation, trumpet signals (VII–IX)
    Addresses and prayers of the battle liturgy (X–XII)
    Prayer recited at the moment of victory (XIII)
    Thanksgiving ceremony (XIV)
    Battle against the Kittim (XV–XIX)

Since the five last columns are more or less repetitious, there has been some doubt concerning the unity of the composition as a whole. Those who consider all nineteen columns to be the work of one writer find in column I an introduction, in columns II–XIV general rules, and in columns XV–XIX a 'prophetic' description of the final battle fought according to those rules. Other experts explain that columns XV–XIX are a Rule annexe dependent on the principal Rule (II–XIV).

I am myself inclined to follow the theory first advanced by J. van der Ploeg (*Le Rouleau de la guerre*, Leiden, 1959, 11–22). The primitive work, represented in the present composition by columns I and XV–XIX, draws its inspiration from Daniel xi, 40–xii, 3, and describes the final battle against the Kittim. This account was later combined with the concept of a holy forty years' war against the entire Gentile world, and was extended by the addition of a long series of Rules concerned with the military and religious preparation and with the conduct of the fighting (columns 11–xiv). This appears to me to offer a more satisfactory explanation of the literary complexities of the manuscript than do the previous hypotheses. The text of the manuscripts from Cave 4 indicates that diverse redactions of the War Rule coexisted in the Qumran library.

The only certain pointer to the date of the compilation of the War Rule is that, since the author made use of the Book of Daniel written shortly after 164 BCE, his own work must have been started after that time. But a more accurate dating may be attempted by studying the military strategy and tactics described in the Scroll. Scholars are divided in their opinion as to whether the sons of light modelled them on Greek or Roman custom, or whether they merely drew their ideas from the Bible. Scripture doubtless exercised a definite influence on the author of this Rule, but there is nevertheless a great deal of material completely foreign to it, and he must have possessed, in addition, at least some acquaintance with contemporary warfare.

With Y. Yadin and other archaeologists and historians, I believe that both the weapons and the tactics of the War Rule correspond to the art of war practised by the Roman legion rather than by the Greek phalanx. In particular, the square shield (*scutum*) of the foot-soldier, and the buckler of the horseman (*parma* or *clipeus*), the battle array of three lines (*acies triplex*), the 'gates of war' or openings between the units (*intervalla*), seem to be characteristically Roman. In addition, only the cavalry were to wear greaves – a custom introduced into the Roman army during the time of Julius Caesar in the middle of the first century BCE. This and similar details, as well as the general representation of the Kittim as masters of the world, lead one to conclude that the War Rule was written some time after the middle of the first century BCE, and since the reference to the 'king' of the Kittim points to the Imperial epoch (after 27 BCE), the date of its composition should probably be placed in the last decades of the first century BCE or at the beginning of the first century CE.

This work should not be mistaken for a manual of military warfare pure and simple. It is a theological writing, and the war of which it treats symbolises the eternal struggle between the spirits of Light and Darkness. The phases of its battle are fixed in advance, its plan established and its duration predetermined. The opposing forces are equally matched and only by the intervention of 'the mighty hand of God' is the balance between them to be disturbed when He deals an 'everlasting blow' to 'Belial and all the host of his kingdom'.

I *For the Master. The Rule of War on the unleashing of the attack of the sons of light against the company of the sons of darkness, the army of Belial: against the band of Edom, Moab, and the sons of Ammon, and against the army of the sons of the East and the Philistines, and against the bands of the Kittim of Assyria and their allies the ungodly of the Covenant*

The sons of Levi, Judah, and Benjamin, the exiles in the desert, shall battle against them in . . . all their bands when the exiled sons of light return from the Desert of the Peoples to camp in the Desert of Jerusalem; and after the battle they shall go up from there to Jerusalem.

The king of the Kittim *shall enter* into Egypt, and in his time he shall set out in great wrath to wage war against the kings of the north, that his fury may destroy and cut the horn of *Israel*. This shall be a time of salvation for the people of God, an age of dominion for all the members of His company, and of everlasting destruction for all the company of Belial. The confusion of the sons of Japheth shall be *great* and Assyria shall fall unsuccoured. The dominion of the Kittim shall come to an end and iniquity shall be vanquished, leaving no remnant; *for the sons* of darkness there shall be no escape. *The sons of righteousness* shall shine over all the ends of the earth; they shall go on shining until all the seasons of darkness are consumed and, at the season appointed by God, His exalted greatness shall shine eternally to the peace, blessing, glory, joy, and long life of all the sons of light.

On the day when the Kittim fall, there shall be battle and terrible carnage before the God of Israel, for that shall be the day appointed from ancient times for the battle of destruction of the sons of darkness. At that time, the assembly of gods and the hosts of men shall battle, causing great carnage; on the day of calamity, the sons of light shall battle with the company of darkness amid the shouts of a mighty multitude and the clamour of gods and men to make manifest the might of God. And it shall be a time of *great* tribulation for the people which God shall redeem; of all its afflictions none shall be as this, from its sudden beginning until its end in eternal redemption.

On the day of their battle against the Kittim *they shall set out for* carnage. In three lots shall the sons of light brace themselves in battle to strike down iniquity, and in three lots shall Belial's host gird itself to thrust back the company *of God. And when the hearts of the detachments* of foot-soldiers faint, then shall the might of God fortify *the hearts of the sons of light*. And with the seventh lot, the mighty hand of God shall bring down *the army of Belial, and all* the angels of his kingdom, and all the members *of his company in everlasting destruction* . . .

II . . . They shall rank the chief Priests below the High Priest and his vicar. And the twelve chief Priests shall minister at the daily sacrifice before God, whereas the twenty-six leaders of the priestly divisions shall minister in their divisions.

Below them, in perpetual ministry, shall be the chiefs of the Levites to the number of twelve, one for each tribe. The leaders of their divisions shall minister each in his place.

Below them shall be the chiefs of the tribes together with the heads of family of the congregation. They shall attend daily at the gates of the Sanctuary, whereas the leaders of their divisions, with their numbered men, shall attend at their appointed times, on new moons and on Sabbaths and on all the days of the year, their age being fifty years and over.

These are the men who shall attend at holocausts and sacrifices to prepare sweet-smelling incense for the good pleasure of God, to atone for all His congregation, and to satisfy themselves perpetually before Him at the table of glory. They shall arrange all these things during the season of the year of Release.

During the remaining thirty-three years of the war, the men of renown, those summoned to the Assembly, together with all the heads of family of the congregation, shall choose for themselves fighting-men for all the lands of the nations. They shall arm for themselves warriors from all the tribes of Israel to enter the army year by year when they are summoned to war. But they shall arm no man for entry into the army during the years of Release, for they are Sabbaths of rest for Israel. In the thirty-five years of service, the war shall be fought during six; the whole congregation shall fight it together. And during the remaining twenty-nine years the war shall be divided. During the first year they shall fight against Aram-Naharaim; during the second, against the sons of Lud; during the third, against the remnant of the sons of Aram, against Uz and Hul and Togar and Mesha beyond the Euphrates; during the fourth and fifth, they shall fight against the sons of Arpachshad; during the sixth and seventh, against all the sons of Assyria and Persia and the East as far as the Great Desert; during the eighth year they shall fight against the sons of Elam; during the ninth, against the sons of Ishmael and Keturah. In the ten years which follow, the war shall be divided against all the sons of Ham according to *their clans and in their* habitations; and during the ten years which remain, the war shall be divided against all *the sons of Japheth in* their habitations.

The Rule for the trumpets of Summons and the trumpets of Alarm according to all their duties
    . . . *the trumpets of Summons shall sound for disposal in* **III** battle formations and to summon the foot-soldiers to advance when the gates of war shall open; and the trumpets of Alarm shall sound for massacre, and for ambush, and for pursuit when the enemy shall be smitten, and for retreat from battle.
    On the trumpets calling the congregation they shall write, *The Called of God.*
    On the trumpets calling the chiefs they shall write, *The Princes of God.*
    On the trumpets of the levies they shall write, *The Army of God.*
    On the trumpets of the men of renown and of the heads of family of the congregation gathered in the house of Assembly they shall write, *Summoned by God to the Council of Holiness.*
    On the trumpets of the camps they shall write, *The Peace of God in the Camps of His Saints.*
    And on the trumpets for breaking camp they shall write, *The mighty Deeds of God shall Crush the Enemy, Putting to Flight all those who Hate Righteousness and bringing Shame on those who Hate Him.*
    On the trumpets for battle formations they shall write, *Formations of the Divisions of God for the Vengeance of His Wrath on the Sons of Darkness.*

On the trumpets summoning the foot-soldiers to advance towards the enemy formations when the gates of war are opened they shall write, *Reminder of Vengeance in God's Appointed Time.*

On the trumpets of massacre they shall write, *The Mighty Hand of God in War shall Cause all the Ungodly Slain to Fall.*

On the trumpets of ambush they shall write, *The Mysteries of God shall Undo Wickedness.*

On the trumpets of pursuit they shall write, *God has Smitten All the Sons of Darkness; His Fury shall not End until They are Utterly Consumed.*

On the trumpets of retreat, when they retreat from battle to the formation, they shall write, *God has Reassembled.*

On the trumpets of return from battle against the enemy when they journey to the congregation in Jerusalem they shall write, *Rejoicings of God in the Peaceful Return.*

The Rule for the standards of the whole congregation according to their levies

On the great standard at the head of the people they shall write, *The People of God*, together with the names of Israel and Aaron, and the names of the twelve *tribes of Israel* according to the order of their precedence . . .

IV On the standard of Merari they shall write, *The Votive-Offering of God*, together with the name of the chief of Merari and the names of the leaders of its Thousands.

On the standard of the Thousand they shall write, *The Wrath of God is Kindled against Belial and against the Men of his Company, Leaving no Remnant*, together with the name of the chief of the Thousand and the names of the leaders of its Hundreds.

On the standard of the Hundred they shall write, *From God comes the Might of War against All Sinful Flesh*, together with the name of the chief of the Hundred and the names of the leaders of its Fifties.

On the standard of the Fifty they shall write, *The Stand of the Ungodly is Ended by the Power of God*, together with the name of the chief of the Fifty and the names of the leaders of its Tens.

On the standard of the Ten they shall write, *Praised be God on the Ten-stringed Harp*, together with the name of the chief of the Ten and the names of the nine men under his command.

*

When they march out to battle they shall write on their standards, *Truth of God, Justice of God, Glory of God, Judgement of God*, followed by the whole ordered list of their names.

When they approach for battle they shall write on their standards, *Right Hand of God, Appointed Time of God, Tumult of God, Slain of God*, followed by the whole list of their names.

When they return from battle they shall write on their standards, *Honour of God, Majesty of God, Splendour of God, Glory of God*, together with the whole list of their names.

The Rule for the standards of the congregation
When they set out for battle they shall write on the first standard *Congregation of God*, on the second standard *Camps of God*, on the third standard *Tribes of God*, on the fourth standard *Clans of God*, on the fifth standard *Divisions of God*, on the sixth standard *Assembly of God*, on the seventh standard *The Called of God*, on the eighth standard *Hosts of God*; and they shall write the list of their names with all their order.

When they approach for battle they shall write on their standards, *War of God, Vengeance of God, Trial of God, Reward of God, Power of God, Retributions of God, Might of God, Extermination of God for all the Nations of Vanity*; and they shall write on them the whole list of their names.

When they return from battle they shall write on their standards, *Salvation of God, Victory of God, Help of God, Support of God, Joy of God, Thanksgivings of God, Praise of God, Peace of God* . . .

The measurements of the standards. The standard of the whole congregation shall be fourteen cubits long; the standard *of the three tribes*, thirteen cubits long; *the standard of the tribe*, twelve cubits; *the standard of the Myriad*, eleven cubits; *the standard of the Thousand, ten cubits; the standard of the Hundred*, nine cubits; *the standard of the Fifty, eight* cubits; the standard of the Ten, *seven cubits* . . .

V And on the *shield of* the Prince of all the congregation they shall write his name, together with the names of Israel, Levi and Aaron, the names of the twelve tribes of Israel according to the order of their precedence, with the names of their twelve chiefs.

*

The Rule for the ordering of the battle divisions to complete a front formation when their host has reached its full number

The formation shall consist of one thousand men ranked seven lines deep, each man standing behind the other.

They shall all hold shields of bronze burnished like mirrors. The shield shall be edged with an interlaced border and with inlaid ornament, a work of art in pure gold and silver and bronze and precious stones, a many-coloured design worked by a craftsman. The length of the shield shall be two and a half cubits and its width one and a half cubits.

In their hands they shall hold a spear and a sword. The length of the spear shall be seven cubits, of which the socket and spike shall measure half a cubit. The socket shall be edged with three embossed interlaced rings of pure gold and silver and bronze, a work of art. The inlaid ornaments on both edges of the ring shall be bordered with precious stones – patterned bands worked by a craftsman – and embossed with ears of corn. Between the rings, the socket shall be embossed with artistry like a pillar. The spike shall be made of brilliant white iron, the work of a craftsman; in its centre, pointing towards the tip, shall be ears of corn in pure gold.

The swords shall be made of pure iron refined by the smelter and blanched to resemble a mirror, the work of a craftsman; on both sides of their blades pointing towards the tip, figured ears of corn shall be embossed in pure gold, and they shall have two straight borders on each side. The length of the sword shall be one and a half cubits and its width four fingers. The width of the scabbard shall be four thumbs. There shall be four palms to the scabbard from the girdle, and it shall be attached to the girdle on both sides for a length of five palms. The hilt of the sword shall be of pure horn worked by a craftsman, with patterned bands in gold and silver and precious stones . . .

VI . . . And after them, three divisions of foot-soldiers shall advance and shall station themselves between the formations, and the first division shall hurl seven javelins of war towards the enemy formation. On the point of the javelins they shall write, *Shining Javelin of the Power of God*; and on the darts of the second division they shall write, *Bloody Spikes to Bring Down the Slain by the Wrath of God*; and on the javelins of the third division they shall write, *Flaming Blade to Devour the Wicked Struck Down by the Judgement of God.* All these shall hurl their javelins seven times and shall afterwards return to their positions.

Then two divisions of foot-soldiers shall advance and shall station themselves between the two formations. The first division shall be armed with a spear and a shield, and the second with a shield and a sword, to bring down the slain by the judgement of God, and to bend the enemy formation by the power of God, to pay the reward of their wickedness to all the nations of vanity. And sovereignty shall be to the God of Israel, and He shall accomplish mighty deeds by the saints of His people.

Seven troops of horsemen shall also station themselves to the right and to the left of the formation; their troops shall stand on this side and on that, seven hundred horsemen on one flank and seven hundred horsemen on the other. Two hundred horsemen shall advance with the thousand men of the formation of foot-soldiers; and they shall likewise station themselves on both *flanks* of the camp. Altogether there shall be four thousand six hundred men, and one thousand cavalrymen with the men of the army formations, fifty to each formation. The horsemen, together with the cavalry of the army, shall number six thousand: five hundred to each tribe.

The horses advancing into battle with the foot-soldiers shall all be stallions; they shall be swift, sensitive of mouth, and sound of wind, and of the required age, trained for war, and accustomed to noise and to every kind of sight. Their riders shall be gallant fighting men and skilled horsemen, and their age shall be from thirty to forty-five years. The horsemen of the army shall be from forty to fifty years old. They *and their mounts shall wear breast-plates,* helmets, and greaves; they shall carry in their hands bucklers, and a spear *eight cubits* long. *The horsemen advancing with the foot-soldiers shall carry* bows and arrows and javelins of war. They shall all hold themselves prepared . . . of God and to spill the blood of the wicked . . .

VII The men of the army shall be from forty to fifty years old. The inspectors of the camps shall be from fifty to sixty years old. The officers shall be from forty to fifty years old. The despoilers of the slain, the plunderers of booty, the cleansers of the land, the keepers of the baggage, and those who furnish the provisions shall be from twenty-five to thirty years old.

No boy or woman shall enter their camps, from the time they leave Jerusalem and march out to war until they return. No man who is lame, or blind, or crippled, or afflicted with a lasting bodily blemish, or smitten with a bodily impurity, none of these shall march out to war with them. They shall all be freely enlisted for war, perfect in spirit and body and prepared for the Day of Vengeance. And no man shall go down with them on the day of battle who is impure because of his 'fount', for the holy angels shall be with their hosts. And there shall be a space of about two thousand cubits between all their camps for the place serving as a latrine, so that no indecent nakedness may be seen in the surroundings of their camps.

When the battle formations are marshalled facing the enemy, formation facing formation, seven Priests of the sons of Aaron shall advance from the middle gates to the place between the formations. They shall be clothed in vestments of white cloth of flax, in a fine linen tunic and fine linen breeches; and they shall be girdled with fine cloth of flax embroidered with blue, purple, and scarlet thread, a many-coloured design worked by a craftsman. And on their heads they shall wear mitred turbans. These shall be battle raiment; they shall not take them into the Sanctuary.

The first Priest shall advance before the men of the formation to strengthen their hand for battle, and the six other Priests shall hold in their hands the trumpets of Summons, and the trumpets of the Reminder, and the trumpets of Alarm for massacre, and the trumpets of Pursuit, and the trumpets of Retreat. And when the Priests advance to the place between the formations, seven Levites shall accompany them bearing in their hands seven rams' horns; and three officers of the Levites shall walk before the Priests and Levites. The Priests shall sound the two trumpets of *Summons for the gates of* war to open fifty shields wide and the foot-soldiers shall advance, fifty from one gate *and fifty from the other. With them shall advance* the officers of the Levites, and they shall advance with every formation according to all this *Rule.*

*The Priests shall sound the trumpets, and two divisions of foot-*soldiers *shall advance* from the gate *and shall* station *themselves*

between the two *formations* . . .   **VIII**   the trumpets shall sound
to direct the slingers until they have cast seven times. Afterwards,
the Priests shall sound for them the trumpets of Retreat and they
shall return to the flank of the first formation to take up their
position.

Then the Priests shall sound the trumpets of Summons and
three divisions of foot-soldiers shall advance from the gates and
shall station themselves between the formations; the horsemen
shall be on their flanks, to the right and to the left. The Priests shall
sound a sustained blast on the trumpets for battle array, and the
columns shall move to their battle array, each man to his place.
And when they have taken up their stand in three arrays, the
Priests shall sound a second signal, soft and sustained, for them to
advance until they are close to the enemy formation. They shall
seize their weapons, and the Priests shall then blow a shrill staccato blast on the six trumpets of Massacre to direct the battle, and
the Levites and all the blowers of rams' horns shall sound a mighty
alarm to terrify the heart of the enemy, and therewith the javelins
shall fly out to bring down the slain. Then the sound of the horns
shall cease, but the Priests shall continue to blow a shrill staccato
blast on the trumpets to direct the battle until they have thrown
seven times against the enemy formation. And then they shall
sound a soft, a sustained, and a shrill sound on the trumpets of
Retreat.

It is according to this Rule that the Priests shall sound the
trumpets for the three divisions. With the first throw, the *Priests*
shall sound *on the trumpets* a mighty alarm to direct the *battle*
until they have thrown seven times. Then the Priests *shall sound*
for them on the trumpets *of Retreat a soft, a sustained, and a*
shrill sound, and they shall return to their positions in the formation.

Then the Priests shall blow the trumpets of Summons and the
two divisions of foot-soldiers shall advance from the gates and
shall stand between the formations. And the Priests shall then
blow the trumpets of Massacre, and the Levites and all the
blowers of rams' horns shall sound an alarm, a mighty blast, and
therewith   **IX**   they shall set about to bring down the slain with
their hands. All the people shall cease their clamour but the Priests
shall continue to blow the trumpets of Massacre to direct the

battle until the enemy is smitten and put to flight; and the Priests shall blow to direct the battle.

And when they are smitten before them, the Priests shall sound the trumpets of Summons and all the foot-soldiers shall rally to them from the midst of the front formations, and the six divisions, together with the fighting division, shall take up their stations. Altogether, they shall be seven formations: twenty-eight thousand fighting men and six thousand horsemen.

All these shall pursue the enemy to destroy him in an everlasting destruction in the battle of God. The Priests shall sound for them the trumpets of Pursuit, and they shall deploy against all the enemy in a pursuit to destruction; and the horsemen shall thrust them back on the flanks of the battle until they are utterly destroyed.

And as the slain men fall, the Priests shall trumpet from afar; they shall not approach the slain lest they be defiled with unclean blood. For they are holy, and they shall not profane the anointing of their priesthood with the blood of nations of vanity.

The Rule for changes in battle order to form the position of a square with towers, a concave line with towers, a convex line with towers, a shallow convex line obtained by the advance of the centre, or by the advance of both flanks to terrify the enemy

The shields of the towers shall be three cubits long and their spears eight cubits. The tower shall advance from the formation and shall have one hundred shields to each side; in this *manner*, the tower shall be surrounded on three sides by three hundred shields. And it shall also have two gates, *one to the right* and one to the left.

They shall write on all the shields of the towers: on the first, *Michael, on the second, Gabriel, on the third, Sariel*, and on the fourth, *Raphael. Michael* and *Gabriel shall stand on the right, and Sariel* and *Raphael on the left.*

X . . . Furthermore, Moses taught us, 'Thou art in the midst of us, a mighty God and terrible, causing all our enemies to flee before *us.*' He taught our generations in former times saying, *When you draw near to battle, the Priest shall rise and speak to the people saying, Hear, O Israel! You draw near to battle this day* *against your enemies. Do not fear! Do not let your hearts be afraid! Do not be terrified, and have no fear! For your God goes with you to fight for you against your enemies that He may deliver you'* (Deut. xx, 2–4).

Our officers shall speak to all those prepared for battle. They shall strengthen by the power of God the freely devoted of heart, and shall make all the fearful of heart withdraw; they shall fortify all the mighty men of war. They shall recount that which Thou *saidst* through Moses: *When you go to war in your land against the oppressor who oppresses you, you shall blow the trumpets, and you shall be remembered before your God and shall be saved from your enemies* (Num. x, 9).

O God of Israel, who is like Thee
    in heaven or on earth?
Who accomplishes deeds and mighty works like Thine?
Who is like Thy people Israel
    which Thou hast chosen for Thyself
    from all the peoples of the lands;
the people of the saints of the Covenant,
    instructed in the laws
    and learned in wisdom . . .
who have heard the voice of Majesty
    and have seen the Angels of Holiness,
whose ear has been unstopped,
    and who have heard profound things?

Thou, O God, hast created the expanse of the heavens
    and the host of heavenly lights,
the tasks of the spirits
    and the dominion of the Holy Ones,
the treasury of glory
    and the canopy of the clouds.
Thou art Creator of the earth
    and of the laws dividing it into desert and grassland;
of all that it brings forth
    and of all its fruits *according to their kinds;*
of the circle of the seas
    and of the gathering-place of the rivers

and of the divisions of the deeps;
of the beasts and birds
and of the shape of Adam
and of the *generations of* his *seed*;
of the confusion of tongues
and of the scattering of the peoples,
of the dwelling in clans
and of the inheritance of lands;
. . . of the sacred seasons
and of the cycles of the years
and of time everlasting.

XI Truly, the battle is Thine! Their bodies are crushed by the might of Thy hand and there is no man to bury them.

Thou didst deliver Goliath of Gath, the mighty warrior, into the hands of David Thy servant, because in place of the sword and in place of the spear he put his trust in Thy great Name; for Thine is the battle. Many times, by Thy great Name, did he triumph over the Philistines. Many times hast Thou also delivered us by the hand of our kings through Thy loving-kindness, and not in accordance with our works by which we have done evil, nor according to our rebellious deeds.

Truly the battle is Thine and the power from Thee! It is not ours. Our strength and the power of our hands accomplish no mighty deeds except by Thy power and by the might of Thy great valour. This Thou hast taught us from ancient times, saying, *A star shall come out of Jacob, and a sceptre shall rise out of Israel. He shall smite the temples of Moab and destroy all the children of Sheth. He shall rule out of Jacob and shall cause the survivors of the city to perish. The enemy shall be his possession and Israel shall accomplish mighty deeds* (Num. xxiv, 17–19).

By the hand of Thine anointed, who discerned Thy testimonies, Thou hast revealed to us the *times* of the battles of Thy hands that Thou mayest glorify Thyself in our enemies by levelling the hordes of Belial, the seven nations of vanity, by the hand of Thy poor whom Thou hast redeemed *by Thy might* and by the fullness of Thy marvellous power. Thou hast opened the door of hope to the melting heart: Thou wilt do to them as Thou didst to Pharaoh, and to the captains of his chariots in the Red Sea. Thou wilt kindle the downcast of spirit and they shall be a flaming torch in the straw to consume ungodliness and never to cease till iniquity is destroyed.

From ancient times Thou hast foretold *the hour* when the might of Thy hand would be raised against the Kittim, saying, *Assyria shall fall by the sword of no man, the sword of no mere man shall devour him* (Isa. xxxi, 8). For Thou wilt deliver into the hands of the poor the enemies from all the lands, to humble the mighty of the peoples by the hand of those bent to the dust, to bring upon the *head of Thine enemies* the reward of the wicked, and to justify Thy true judgement in the midst of all the sons of men, and to make for Thyself an everlasting Name among the people *whom Thou hast redeemed* . . .

For Thou wilt fight with them from heaven . . .   **XII** For the multitude of the Holy Ones *is with Thee* in heaven, and the host of the Angels is in Thy holy abode, praising Thy Name. And Thou hast established in *a community* for Thyself the elect of Thy holy people. *The list* of the names of all their host is with Thee in the abode of Thy holiness; *the reckoning of the saints* is in Thy glorious dwelling-place. Thou hast recorded for them, with the graving-tool of life, the favours of *Thy* blessings and the Covenant of Thy peace, that Thou mayest reign *over them* for ever and ever and throughout all the eternal ages. Thou wilt muster the *hosts of* Thine elect, in their Thousands and Myriads, with Thy Holy Ones *and with all* Thine Angels, that they may be mighty in battle, *and may smite* the rebels of the earth by Thy great judgements, and that *they may triumph* together with the elect of heaven.

For Thou art *terrible*, O God, in the glory of Thy kingdom, and the congregation of Thy Holy Ones is among us for everlasting succour. We will despise kings, we will mock and scorn the mighty; for our Lord is holy, and the King of Glory is with us together with the Holy Ones. Valiant *warriors* of the angelic host are among our numbered men, and the Hero of war is with our congregation; the host of His spirits is with our foot-soldiers and horsemen. *They are as* clouds, as clouds of dew covering the earth, as a shower of rain shedding judgement on all that grows on the earth.

Rise up, O Hero!
Lead off Thy captives, O Glorious One!
Gather up Thy spoils, O Author of mighty deeds!

Lay Thy hand on the neck of Thine enemies
   and Thy feet on the pile of the slain!
Smite the nations, Thine adversaries,
   and devour the flesh of the sinner with Thy sword!
Fill Thy land with glory
   and Thine inheritance with blessing!
Let there be a multitude of cattle in Thy fields,
   and in Thy palaces silver and gold and precious stones!

O Zion, rejoice greatly!
O Jerusalem, show thyself amidst jubilation!
Rejoice, all you cities of Judah;
keep your gates ever open
   that the hosts of the nations
   may be brought in!

Their kings shall serve you
   and all your oppressors shall bow down before you;
   they shall lick the dust *of your feet.*
Shout for joy, *O daughters of* my people!
Deck yourselves with glorious jewels
   and rule over *the kingdoms of the nations!*
Sovereignty shall be to the Lord
   and everlasting dominion to Israel . . .

XIII The High Priest shall come, and his brethren the Priests and the Levites, and all the elders of the army shall be with him; and standing, they shall bless the God of Israel and all His works of truth, and shall execrate Belial there and all the spirits of his company. Speaking, they shall say:

Blessed be the God of Israel for all His holy purpose and for His works of truth! Blessed be all those who *serve* Him in righteousness and who know Him by faith!

Cursed be Belial for his sinful purpose and may he be execrated for his wicked rule! Cursed be all the spirits of his company for their ungodly purpose and may they be execrated for all their service of uncleanness! Truly they are the company of Darkness, but the company of God is one of *eternal* Light.

Thou art the God of our fathers; we bless Thy Name for ever. We are the people of Thine *inheritance*; Thou didst make a Covenant with our fathers, and wilt establish it with their children throughout eternal ages. And in all Thy glorious testimonies there has been a reminder of Thy mercies among us to succour the remnant, the survivors of Thy Covenant, that they might *recount* Thy works of truth and the judgements of Thy marvellous mighty deeds.

Thou hast created us for Thyself, *O God*, that we may be an everlasting people. Thou hast decreed for us a destiny of Light according to Thy truth. And the Prince of Light Thou hast appointed from ancient times to come to our support; *all the sons of righteousness are in his hand*, and all the spirits of truth are under his dominion. But Belial, the Angel of Malevolence, Thou hast created for the Pit; his *rule* is in Darkness and his purpose is to bring about wickedness and iniquity. All the spirits of his company, the Angels of Destruction, walk according to the precepts of Darkness; towards them is their *inclination*.

But let us, the company of Thy truth, rejoice in Thy mighty hand and be glad for Thy salvation, and exult because of Thy *succour and* peace. O God of Israel, who can compare with Thee in might? Thy mighty hand is with the poor. Which angel or prince can compare with Thy *redeeming* succour? *For Thou hast appointed* the day of battle from ancient times . . . *to come to the aid* of truth and to destroy iniquity, to bring Darkness low and to magnify Light . . . to stand for ever, and to destroy all the sons of Darkness . . .

XIV . . . And when they have risen from the slain to return to the camp, they shall all sing the Psalm of Return. And in the morning, they shall wash their garments, and shall cleanse themselves of the blood of the bodies of the ungodly. And they shall return to the positions in which they stood in battle formation before the fall of the enemy slain, and there they shall all bless the God of Israel. Rejoicing together, they shall praise His Name, and speaking they shall say:

Blessed be the God of Israel
    who keeps mercy towards His Covenant,
and the appointed times of salvation
    with the people He has delivered!
*

He has called them that staggered
    to *marvellous mighty deeds,*
and has gathered in the assembly of the nations
    to destruction without any remnant.
He has lifted up in judgement the fearful of heart
     and has opened the mouth of the dumb
     that they might praise the mighty works *of God.*
He has taught war *to the hand* of the feeble
     and steadied the trembling knee;
    he has braced the back of the smitten.
Among the poor in spirit *there is power*
    over the hard of heart,
and by the perfect of way
    all the nations of wickedness have come to an end:
    not one of their mighty men stands,
but we are the remnant *of Thy people.*

Blessed be Thy Name, O God of mercies,
    who hast kept the Covenant with our fathers.
In all our generations Thou hast bestowed
    Thy wonderful favours on the remnant *of Thy people*
    under the dominion of Belial.
During all the mysteries of his Malevolence
    he has not made *us* stray from Thy Covenant;
Thou hast driven his spirits *of destruction*
    far from *us,*
Thou hast preserved the soul of Thy redeemed
    when the men of his dominion acted wickedly.
Thou hast raised the fallen by Thy strength,
    but hast cut down the great in height
    and hast brought down the lofty.
There is no rescue for all their mighty men
    and no refuge for their swift men;
Thou givest to their honoured men a reward of shame,
all their empty existence *hast Thou turned to nothing.*

But we, Thy holy people, will praise Thy Name
    because of the works of Thy truth.
We will exalt Thy splendour because of Thy mighty deeds

> *in all the* seasons and appointed times for ever,
>   at the coming of day and at nightfall
>   and at the departure of evening and morning.
>   For great is the design of Thy glory
>   and of Thy wonderful mysteries on high
>   that *Thou shouldst raise up* dust before Thee
>   and lay low the 'gods'.
>   Rise up, rise up, O God of gods,
>   raise Thyself in might, King of Kings!
>   May all the sons of Darkness *scatter before Thee*!
>   The light of Thy greatness *shall shine forth*
>   *on* 'gods' and men.
>   *It shall be like a fire* burning
>   in the dark places of perdition;
>   it shall burn the sinners in the perdition of hell,
>   in an eternal blaze
>   . . . in all the eternal seasons.

They shall recite there *all the* war hymns. Afterwards they shall return to *their* camps . . .   **XV** For this shall be a time of distress for Israel, *and of the summons* to war against all the nations. There shall be eternal deliverance for the company of God, but destruction for all the nations of wickedness.

All those *who are ready* for battle shall march out and shall pitch their camp before the king of the Kittim and before all the host of Belial gathered about him for the Day *of Revenge* by the Sword of God.

Then the High Priest shall rise, with the *Priests*, his brethren, and the Levites, and all the men of the army, and he shall recite aloud the Prayer in Time of War *written in the Book* of the Rule concerning this time, and also all their Hymns. He shall marshal all the formations there, as is *written in the Book of War*, and the priest appointed for the Day of Revenge by the voice of all his brethren shall go forward to strengthen the *hearts of the fighting men*. Speaking, he shall say:

Be strong and valiant; be warriors! Fear not! Do not be *confused and do not let your hearts be afraid!* Do not be fearful; fear them not! Do not fall back . . . for they are a congregation of wickedness and all their works are in Darkness; they tend towards Darkness.

They make for themselves a refuge *in falsehood* and their power shall vanish like smoke. All the multitudes of their community . . . shall not be found. Damned as they are, all the substance of their wickedness shall quickly fade, like a flower in *the summer-time.*

Be brave and strong for the battle of God! For this day is *the time of the battle of* God against all the host of Belial, *and of the judgement of* all flesh. The God of Israel lifts His hand in His marvellous *might* against all the spirits of wickedness. *The hosts of* the warrior 'gods' gird themselves for battle, *and the* formations of the Holy Ones *prepare themselves,* for the Day *of Revenge . . .* **XVI** . . . For the God of Israel has called out the sword against all the nations, and He will do mighty deeds by the saints of His people.

And they shall obey all this Rule on the day when they stand before the camps of the Kittim

The Priests shall afterwards sound for them the trumpets of the Reminder, and the gates of war shall open; the foot-soldiers shall advance and the columns shall station themselves between the formations. The Priests shall sound for them the signal, 'Battle Array', and at the sound of the trumpets the columns *shall deploy* until every man is in his place. The Priests shall then sound a second signal *for them to advance,* and when they are within throwing distance of the formation of the Kittim, each man shall seize his weapon of war. Then the six *Priests shall blow on* the trumpets of Massacre a shrill staccato blast to direct the battle, and the Levites and all the blowers of rams' horns shall sound *a battle alarm,* a mighty clamour; and with this clamour they shall begin to bring down the slain from among the Kittim. All the people shall cease their clamour, *but the Priests shall continue to* sound the trumpets of Massacre, and battle shall be fought against the Kittim . . . And when *Belial* girds himself to come to the aid of the sons of darkness, and when the slain among the foot-soldiers begin to fall by the mysteries of God, and when all the men appointed for battle are put to ordeal by them, the Priests shall sound the trumpets of Summons for another formation of the reserve to advance into battle; and they shall take up their stand between the formations. And for those engaged *in battle* they shall sound the 'Retreat'.

Then the High Priest shall draw near, and standing before the formation, he shall strengthen by the power of God their hearts *and hands* in His battle . . .

XVII He will pay their reward with burning *fire by the hand of* those tested in the crucible. He will sharpen His weapons and will not tire until all the wicked nations are destroyed. Remember the judgement *of Nadab and* Abihu, sons of Aaron, by whose judgement God showed Himself holy in the eyes *of Israel. But Eleazar* and Ithamar He confirmed in an everlasting *priestly* Covenant.

Be strong and fear not; *for they tend* towards chaos and confusion, and they lean on that which is not and *shall not be. To the God* of Israel belongs all that is and shall be; *He knows* all the happenings of eternity. This is the day appointed by Him for the defeat and overthrow of the Prince of the kingdom of wickedness, and He will send eternal succour to the company of His redeemed by the might of the princely Angel of the kingdom of Michael. With everlasting light He will enlighten with joy *the children* of Israel; peace and blessing shall be with the company of God. He will raise up the kingdom of Michael in the midst of the gods, and the realm of Israel in the midst of all flesh. Righteousness shall rejoice on high, and all the children of His truth shall jubilate in eternal knowledge. And you, the sons of His Covenant, be strong in the ordeal of God! His mysteries shall uphold you until He moves His hand for His trials to come to an end.

After these words, the Priests shall sound to marshal them into the divisions of the formation; and at the sound of the trumpets the columns shall deploy until *every man is* in his place. Then the Priests shall sound a second signal on the trumpets for them to advance, and when the *foot*-soldiers approach throwing distance of the formation of the Kittim, every man shall seize his weapon of war. The Priests shall blow the trumpets of Massacre, *and the Levites and all* the blowers of rams' horns shall sound a battle alarm, and the foot-soldiers shall stretch out their hands against the host of the Kittim; *and at the sound of the alarm* they shall begin to bring down the slain. All the people shall cease their clamour, but the Priests shall continue to blow *the trumpets of Massacre and battle shall be fought against the Kittim* . . .

*

XVIII *In the seventh lot* when the great hand of God is raised in an everlasting blow against Belial and all the hosts of his kingdom, and when Assyria is pursued *amidst the shouts of Angels* and the clamour of the Holy Ones, the sons of Japheth shall fall to rise no more. The Kittim shall be crushed without *remnant, and no man shall be saved from among them.*

At that time, on the day when the hand of the God of Israel is raised against all the multitude of Belial, the Priests shall blow *the six trumpets* of the Reminder and all the battle formations shall rally to them and shall divide against all the *camps of the* Kittim to destroy them utterly. *And as* the sun speeds to its setting on that day, the High Priest shall stand, together *with the Levites* who are with him and the *tribal* chiefs *and the elders* of the army, and they shall bless the God of Israel there. Speaking they shall say:

Blessed be Thy Name, O God *of gods,* for Thou hast worked great marvels *with Thy people*! Thou hast kept Thy Covenant with us from of old, and hast opened to us the gates of salvation many times. For the *sake of Thy Covenant Thou hast removed our misery, in accordance with* Thy *goodness* towards us. Thou hast acted for the sake of Thy Name, O God of righteousness . . . *Thou hast worked a marvellous* miracle *for us,* and from ancient times there never was anything like it. For Thou didst know the time appointed for us and it has appeared *before us* this day . . . *Thou hast shown* us *Thy merciful hand* in everlasting redemption by causing *the dominion of* the enemy to fall back for ever. Thou hast shown us Thy mighty hand in *a stroke of destruction in the war against all* our enemies.

And now the day speeds us to the pursuit of their multitude . . . Thou hast delivered up the hearts of the brave so that they stand no more. For Thine is the power, and the battle is in Thy hands!
. . . **XIX** For our Sovereign is holy and the King of Glory is with us; the *host of his spirits is with our foot-soldiers and horsemen. They are as clouds, as clouds of dew* covering the earth, and as a shower of rain shedding righteousness on *all that grows there.*

Rise up, O Hero!
Lead off Thy captives, O Glorious One!
Gather up Thy spoils, O Author of mighty deeds!
Lay Thy hand on the neck of Thine enemies

and Thy feet *on the pile of the slain!*
Smite the nations, Thine adversaries,
   and devour flesh with Thy sword!
Fill Thy land with glory
   and Thine inheritance with blessing!
Let there be a multitude of cattle in Thy fields,
   and in Thy palaces
   silver and gold and precious stones!

O Zion, rejoice greatly!
   Rejoice all you cities of Judah!
Keep your gates ever open
   that the hosts of the nations
   may be brought in!
Their kings shall serve you
   and all your oppressors shall bow down before you;
   they shall lick the dust of your feet.
Shout for joy, O daughters of my people!
Deck yourselves with glorious jewels
   and rule over the kingdom of the nations!
Sovereignty shall be to the Lord
   and everlasting dominion to Israel.

Then they shall gather in the camp that night to rest until the morning. And in the morning they shall go to the place where the formation stood before the warriors of the Kittim fell, as well as the multitudes of Assyria, and the hosts of all the *assembled* nations to discover whether the multitude of the stricken are dead with none to bury them, those who fell there under the Sword of God. And the High Priest shall draw near, *with his vicar, and the chief Priests* and the Levites with the Prince of the battle, and all the chiefs of the formations and their numbered men; *they shall return to the positions which they held before the* slain *began to fall* from among the Kittim, and there they shall praise the God the Most High . . .

The Temple Scroll

Discovered in 1956 in Cave 11, the Temple Scroll did not emerge from semi-clandestinity until the Six Day War in June 1967. It is the longest Qumran manuscript, measuring over twenty-eight feet. There are also other fragments pertaining to the same document from Cave 11 and from Cave 4. Originally it consisted of sixty-seven columns.

The major part of the scroll deals with the Temple (building and furniture) and cultic worship, especially sacrifices on Sabbaths and the many feasts of the year. Most of the legislation depends, directly or indirectly, on Exodus, Leviticus, and more particularly on Deuteronomy, but there are also occasional non-biblical regulations. The beginning of the manuscript is badly mutilated. Column I is missing. Columns III–XII are so fragmented that only a very hypothetical reconstruction, exclusively from biblical texts, is possible. I have decided not to translate them but indicate their probable contents in the summary that follows:

1. Covenant between God and Israel (II).
2. Building of the Temple, measurements of the Sanctuary, the Holy of Holies, the chambers and colonnades (III–VII).
3. Description of the mercy seat, the cherubim, the veil, the table, the golden lamp-stand, etc. (VII–XI).
4. Outline of the sacrifices and the altar (XI–XII).
5. Daily, weekly and monthly sacrifices and those offered on festivals (XIII–XXIX).
6. Buildings in the Temple courtyards: the stairhouse, the house of the laver, the house for sacred vessels, the slaughterhouse, etc. (XXX–XXXV).
7. The three courtyards of the Temple, one for the priests, one for Jewish men over twenty years of age, and one for women and children (XXXVI–XLV).
8. Purity regulations concerning the Temple and the city of the Sanctuary (XLVI–XLVIII).
9. Purity regulations concerning the cities of Israel (XLVIII–LI).
10. Judges and officers (LI).
11. Laws relating to idolatry and to sacrificial animals (LI–LIII).
12. Vows and oaths (LIII–LIV).

13. Laws against apostasy (LIV–LV).
14. Laws relating to priests and Levites and detailed statutes of the Jewish king (LVI–LIX).
15. Miscellaneous laws regarding priestly dues, idols, witnesses, the conduct of war, the rebellious son, crimes punishable by 'hanging', and incestuous relations (LX–LXVI).

The sequence of subjects generally follows the Bible, but an obvious effort has been made to systematise, harmonise and reinterpret the laws. Sections complementary to Scripture include the Temple legislation (III–XII, XXX–XLV), festivals (XVII–XXIX), purity material as rules relating to the Temple and the city (XLVI–XLVII), and the statutes of the king (LVI–LIX). The aim of the redactor is to present the message of the scroll not as an interpretation of the Bible, but as an immediate divine revelation. For this purpose, not only does he formulate the supplementary legislation as directly spoken by God, but also frequently substitutes 'I' for 'the Lord = YHWH' of Scripture.

Although the view has been advanced that the Temple Scroll is not a Qumran composition, the contrary thesis has a solid foundation. The relationship between this writing and the Damascus Document is particularly striking in the case of the prohibition of royal polygamy, of marriage between uncle and niece, and of marital relations within the city of the Sanctuary, to name the most significant instances. Note also that the death penalty of 'hanging' (probably crucifixion) reserved for traitors appears both in TS LXIV, and in the Nahum Commentary (cf. p. 285). Since the Damascus Document and the Nahum Commentary are more likely to depend on the Temple Scroll than vice versa, the latter may safely be dated to the second century BCE. But it may also have an antecedent history reaching back to the pre-Qumran age.

II *Behold, I will make a covenant.*

For it is something dreadful that I will do *to you. I myself will expel from before you* the Amorites, the Canaanites, the Hittites, *the Girgashites, the Perizzites, the Hivites and* the Jebusites. Take *care not to make a* covenant with the inhabitants of the country *which you are to* enter so that they may not prove a *snare for you.* You must destroy their *altars, smash their* pillars *and* cut down their *sacred trees and burn their* idols *with fire.* You must not desire silver and gold so *that you may not be ensnared by them;*

for that would be abominable to me. You must *not bring any abominable idol* into your house *and come* under the ban together with it. You shall *detest and abominate it,* for it is under the ban. You shall not worship *another* god, *for YHWH, whose name is Jealous,* is a jealous God. Take care not to make a *covenant with the inhabitants of the country so that, when they whore* after *their* gods *and* sacrifice to *them and invite you, you may not eat of their sacrifices and take their daughters for your sons, and their daughters may not whore after* their *gods* and cause *your sons to whore after them . . .*

XIII *This is what you shall offer on the altar: two yearling lambs* without blemish *every day as a perpetual holocaust. You shall offer the first in the morning; and you shall offer the other lamb in the evening; the corresponding grain-offering will be a* tenth of fine flour mixed with *a quarter of a hin of beaten oil; it shall be a perpetual holocaust of soothing odour, an offering by fire* to YHWH; and the corresponding drink-offering shall be a quarter *of a hin of* wine. *The priest who offers the holocaust shall receive the skin of* the burnt-*offering which he has offered. You shall offer the other lamb in the evening* with the same grain-*offering as in the* morning and with the corresponding drink-offering as an offering by fire, a soothing odour to YHWH . . .

On the *Sabbath* days you shall offer two *yearling rams without blemish and two* **XIV** *tenths of an ephah of fine flour, mixed with oil, for a grain-offering and the corresponding drink-offering. This is the holocaust of every Sabbath in addition to the perpetual holocaust and the corresponding drink-offering. On the first day of each month you shall offer a holocaust to YHWH: two young bulls, one ram, seven yearling rams without blemish and a grain-offering* of fine flour, *three tenths of an ephah* mixed *with half a hin of oil, and a drink-offering,* half a hin for *each young bull and a grain-offering of fine flour mixed with oil, two tenths of an ephah* with a third *of a hin, and wine for a drink-offering, one third of a hin for each ram; . . .* one tenth *of fine flour for* a grain-offering, *mixed with a quarter of a hin, and wine, a quarter of a hin* for each lamb . . . a soothing *odour* to YHWH on the first day of each month. This is the burnt-offering for each month for the months of the year . . . On the first day of the *first* month *the months of the year shall start; it shall be the first month of* the year *for you. You shall do no* work. *You shall offer a he-goat for a sin-offering.* It shall be offered by itself to expiate *for you. You shall offer a holocaust: a bullock,* a ram, *seven yearling* ram lambs *without blemish . . . additional to the burnt-offering for the new moon, and a grain-offering of three tenths of fine flour mixed with oil,* half a hin *for each bullock, and* wine for a drink-offering, *half a hin, a soothing odour to YHWH, and two* tenths of fine flour mixed *with oil, one third of a hin. You shall offer wine for a drink-offering,* one *third* of a hin for the ram, *an offering by fire, of soothing odour to YHWH; and one tenth of fine flour,* a grain-offering *mixed with a quarter of a hin of oil. You shall offer wine for a drink-offering, a quarter of a hin* for each *ram . . .* lambs and for the he-*goat . . .*   **XV** *. . .* For the ordination of the priests, one ram for each *day, and* baskets of bread for all the rams *of the ordination, one basket for* each *ram.* They shall divide all the rams and the baskets for the seven *days of the ordination for each* day; according to *their* divisions, *they shall offer to YHWH the right thigh* of the ram as a holocaust and *the fat covering the entrails and the* two kidneys and the fat on them *and on* the loins and the whole fat tail close to the backbone and the appendage of the liver and the corresponding grain-offering and drink-offering according to the *statute. They shall take one unleavened cake from the* basket and one cake of bread with oil and *one* wafer, *and they shall put it all on the fat* together with the offering of the right thigh. Those who sacrifice shall wave the rams and the baskets of bread as a wave-*offering* before YHWH. This is a holocaust, an offering by fire, of soothing odour before YHWH. *They shall burn everything on the altar over* the holocaust, to complete their ordination during the seven days of *ordination.*

If the High Priest is to *minister to YHWH, whoever* has been ordained to put on the vestments in place of his father, shall offer *a bull for* all the people and another for the priests. He shall offer the one for the priests first. The elders of the priests shall lay *their hands*   **XVI** on its *head* and after them the High Priest and all the *priests. They shall slaughter* the bull *before YHWH.* The elders of the priests shall take from the blood of the bull and *place it with their finger on the horns of the altar* and they shall pour *the blood* around the four corners of the *altar* ledge *. . . and they shall take from its blood and* place it *on his right ear lobe and on the* *thumb of his right hand and the big toe of his* right *foot. They shall sprinkle on him and his vestments some of the blood which was on the altar* . . . *he* shall be *holy* all his days. *He shall not go near any dead body.* He shall *not* render himself unclean *even for his father or mother, for he is* holy *to YHWH, his God* . . . *He shall offer on the* altar and burn *the fat of the first bull* . . . *all* the fat on the entrails and *the appendage of the liver and the two kidneys* and the fat on them and *the fat on* the loins, and the corresponding grain-offering and drink-*offering according to their statute,* he shall burn *them on the altar.* It shall be *a* burnt-offering, an offering by fire, of soothing odour *before YHWH. The flesh of the bull,* its skin and offal, they shall burn outside the *sanctuary city on a wood fire* in a place reserved for sin-offerings. There they shall burn *it with its head and legs* together with all its entrails. They shall burn all of it there except the fat. It is a sin-*offering.* He shall take the second bull, which is for the people, and by it he shall expiate *for all the people of* the assembly, by its blood and fat. As he did with the first bull, *so he shall do* with the bull of the assembly. He shall place with his finger some of its blood on the horns of the *altar, and the remainder of* its blood, he shall sprinkle on *the* four corners of the altar ledge, and *its fat and* the corresponding *grain-*offering and drink-offering, he shall burn on the altar. It is a sin-offering for the assembly   **XVII** . . . They shall rejoice because expiation has been made for them . . . This day *shall* be a holy gathering for them, *an eternal rule for all their generations* wherever they dwell . . .

Let them *prepare on the fourteenth* day of the first month *between dusk and dark the Passover of YHWH.* They shall sacrifice it before the evening offering and shall sacrifice . . . men from twenty years of age and over shall prepare it. They shall eat it at night in the holy courts. They shall rise early and each shall go to his tent . . .

On the fifteenth day of this month there shall be a holy gathering. You shall do no work of labour on it. It shall be a seven-day feast of unleavened bread for YHWH. You shall offer on each of these seven days a holocaust to YHWH: two young bulls, a ram, and seven ram lambs without blemish and a he-goat for a sin-offering and the corresponding grain-offering and drink-offering *according to the* statute for the young bulls, rams, lambs and the

he-goat. On the seventh day *there shall be an assembly* for
YHWH. You shall do no work on it.   **XVIII** . . . This shall be an
eternal rule for you *for your generations wherever you dwell.*
Then they shall offer the one ram, once, on the day of the waving
of the sheaf.

You shall count seven complete Sabbaths from the day of your
bringing the sheaf of *the wave-offering. You shall* count until the
morrow of the seventh Sabbath. You shall count *fifty* days. You
shall bring a new grain-offering to YHWH from your homes, *a
loaf of fine flour,* freshly baked with leaven. They are firstfruits to
YHWH, wheat bread, twelve *cakes, two* tenths of fine flour in
each cake . . .   **XIX** . . . *On this* day there shall be *a holy gathering, an eternal rule* for their generations. *They* shall *do* no work.
It is the feast of Weeks and the feast of Firstfruits, an eternal
memorial.

You *shall count* seven weeks from the day when you bring the
new grain-offering to YHWH, the bread of firstfruits. Seven full
Sabbaths *shall elapse* until you have counted fifty days to the
morrow of the seventh Sabbath. *You* shall *bring* new wine for a
drink-offering, four hins from all the tribes of Israel, one third of a
hin for each tribe.

They shall offer on this day with the wine twelve rams to
YHWH; all the chiefs of the clans of Israel.   **XX** . . . They shall
prepare them . . . and they shall burn their fat on the altar, *the
fat covering the entrails* and the fat that is on them, and *the
appendage of the liver with* the kidneys he shall remove and the fat
on *them,* and that which is on the loins and the fat tail close to the
backbone. They shall *burn all on the altar* together with the corresponding grain-offering and drink-offering, an offering by fire,
of soothing odour *before YHWH.* They shall offer every grain-
offering joined to a drink-offering according to *the statute.* They
shall take a handful from *every* grain-offering offered either with
frankincense or dry, this being its *memorial portion,* and burn it
on the altar. They shall eat the remainder in the *inner* courtyard.
The priests shall eat it unleavened. It shall not be eaten with
leaven. It shall be *eaten* on that day *before* sunset. They shall salt
all their offerings. You shall never allow the covenant of salt to fail.

They shall offer to YHWH an offering from the rams and the
lambs, the right thigh, the breast, *the cheeks, the stomach* and the

foreleg as far as the shoulder bone, and they shall wave them as a wave-offering.   **XXI**   *The priests'* portions *shall* be the thigh of the offering and the breast . . . *The priests* shall drink there first and the Levites *second* . . . After them the whole people, from the great to the small, shall begin to drink the new wine. They *shall not eat* any unripe grapes from the vines, for *on* this *day* they shall expiate for the *tirosh.* The children of Israel shall rejoice before YHWH, an eternal *rule* for their generations wherever they dwell. They shall rejoice on *this day for they have begun* to pour out an intoxicating drink-offering, the new wine, on the altar of YHWH, year by year.

You shall count from that day seven weeks, seven times seven days, forty-nine days; there shall be seven full Sabbaths; until the morrow of the seventh Sabbath you shall count fifty days. You shall then offer new oil from the homes of *the* tribes of the *children of* Israel, half a hin from a tribe, new beaten oil . . . **XXII** . . . *With* this oil they shall light the lamps . . . The Levites shall slaughter *the lambs and the rams and* the priests, the sons of Aaron, *shall* sprinkle their blood *on the altar all around . . . and* they shall burn their fat on the altar of the *holocaust . . . and the corresponding grain-offering* and drink-offering, they shall burn over the fats . . . *an offering by fire, of soothing odour to* YHWH . . . The cheeks and the stomach shall be the priests' portion according to the statute concerning them. They shall give to the Levites the shoulder. Afterwards they shall bring the offerings out to the children of Israel, and the children of Israel shall give the priests one ram, one lamb, and to the Levites, one ram, one lamb, and to each tribe, one ram, one lamb. They shall eat them on that day in the outer courtyard before YHWH, an eternal rule for their generations, year by year. Afterwards they shall eat from the olives and anoint themselves with the new oil, for on this day they shall expiate for *all the* oil of the land before YHWH once yearly. They shall rejoice   **XXIII** . . .

The High Priest shall offer the *holocaust of the Levites* first, and afterwards he shall send up in smoke the holocaust of the tribe of Judah, and *when he* is sending it up in smoke, they shall slaughter before him the he-goat first and he shall lift up its blood in a bowl to the altar and with his finger he shall put *some* of the blood to the four horns of the altar of the holocaust and to the four corners of the altar ledge, and shall toss the blood towards the base of the altar ledge all around. He shall burn its fat on the altar, the fat covering the entrails and that over the entrails. The appendage of the liver with the kidneys he shall remove as well as the fat over them and on the loins. He shall send up in smoke all of them on the altar together with the corresponding grain-offering and drink-offering, an offering by fire of soothing odour to YHWH. **XXIV** ... *Thus they must do to every* young bull, and to every ram and to *every lamb* and its limbs shall remain apart. The corresponding *grain-offering* and drink-offering shall be on it, an *eternal* rule for your generations before YHWH.

After this holocaust he shall offer the holocaust of the tribe of Judah separately. As he has done with the holocaust of the Levites, so shall he do with the holocaust of the children of Judah after the Levites. On the second day he shall first offer the holocaust of Benjamin and after it he shall offer the holocaust of the children of Joseph, Ephraim and Manasseh together. On the third day, he shall offer the holocaust of Reuben separately, and the holocaust of Simeon separately. On the fourth day he shall offer the holocaust of Issachar separately and the holocaust of Zebulun separately. On the fifth day he shall offer the holocaust of Gad separately and the holocaust of Asher separately . . . **XXV** . . .

In the *seventh month, on the first day of the month, you shall have* a sacred rest, a remembrance announced by a trumpet blast, a *holy gathering. You shall offer a holocaust, an offering by fire, of soothing odour* before YHWH. You shall *offer one young bull*, one ram, seven yearling *lambs without blemish and one he-goat for a sin-offering, and* the corresponding grain-offering and drink-offering according to the statute concerning them, *of soothing odour to YHWH, in addition to* the perpetual *holocaust and the* holocaust of the new moon. Afterwards *you shall offer* this *holocaust* at the third part of the day, an eternal rule for your generations, *wherever you dwell.* You shall rejoice on this day. On it you shall do no work. A sacred rest shall this day be for you.

The tenth of this month is the Day of Atonement. You shall mortify yourselves. For any person who does not mortify himself on this self-same day shall be cut off from his people. You shall offer on it a holocaust to YHWH: one young bull, one ram, seven ram lambs, one he-goat for a sin-offering, in addition to the sin-offering of the atonement and the corresponding grain-offering and drink-offering according to the statute concerning the young bull, the ram, the lambs and the he-goat. For the sin-offering of the atonement you shall offer two rams for holocaust. The High Priest shall offer one for himself and his father's house **XXVI** ... *The High Priest shall cast lots on the two goats, one* lot for YHWH and one for Azazel. He shall slaughter the goat *on* which *YHWH's lot has fallen and shall lift up* its blood in a golden bowl which is in *his* hand, *and do* with its blood *as he has done with the blood of* his young bull and shall expiate with it for all the people of the assembly. He shall send up in smoke its fat and the corresponding grain- and drink-offering on the altar of the holocaust. Its flesh, skin and dung they shall burn beside his young bull. It is a sin-offering for the whole assembly. He shall expiate with it for all the people of the assembly and it shall be forgiven to them. He shall wash his hands and feet of the blood of the sin-offering and shall come to the living goat and shall confess over its head the iniquities of the children of Israel together with all their guilt, all their sins. He shall put them on the head of the goat and despatch it to Azazel in the desert by the hand of the man who is waiting ready. The goat shall bear all the iniquities of the children of Israel.   **XXVII** ... *and he shall expiate* for all the children of Israel and it shall be forgiven to them ... Afterwards he shall offer the young bull, the ram, and *the lambs, according to* the statute relating to them, on the altar of the holocaust, and the holocaust will be accepted for the children of Israel, an eternal rule for their generations. Once a year this day shall be for them a memorial. They shall do no work on it, for it shall be *to* them a Sabbath of sacred rest. Whoever shall do work on it or shall not mortify himself on it, shall be cut off from the midst of his people. A Sabbath of sacred rest, a holy gathering shall this day be for you. You shall sanctify it as a memorial wherever you dwell and you shall do no work ...

XXVIII ... *On* the second *day:* twelve young bulls, *two rams,* fourteen *lambs* and one he-goat *for a sin-offering and the corresponding grain-offering and drink-offering* according to the statute concerning the young bulls, the rams, the lambs *and* the he-goat; it is an offering by fire, of soothing odour to YHWH.

On the third day eleven young bulls, two rams, fourteen lambs and one he-goat for a sin-offering and the corresponding grain-offering and drink-offering according to the statute concerning the young bulls, the rams, the lambs and the he-goat.

On the fourth day ten young bulls, two rams, fourteen yearling ram lambs and one he-goat for a sin-offering and the corresponding grain-offering and drink-offering for the young bulls, **XXIX** . . . *each on its* day according to the law of this statute, always from the children of Israel in addition to their freewill-offerings in regard to all that they offer, their drink-offerings and all their gifts that they shall bring to me in order to be acceptable. I shall accept them and they shall be my people and I shall be for them for ever. I will dwell with them for ever and ever and will sanctify my sanctuary by my glory. I will cause my glory to rest on it until the day of creation on which I shall create my sanctuary, establishing it for myself for all time according to the covenant which I have made with Jacob in Bethel.

XXX . . . In the house which you shall build . . . you *shall make* a staircase north of the Temple, a square house, twenty cubits from one corner to the other alongside its four corners. Its distance from the wall of the Temple shall be seven cubits on the north-west. You shall make the width of its wall four cubits . . . like the Temple and its inside from corner to corner twelve *cubits.* There shall be a square column in its middle, in the centre; its width four cubits on each side around which the stairs wind . . . **XXXI** In the upper chamber of *this house you shall make a* gate opening to the roof of the Temple and a way shall be made through this gate towards the entrance . . . of the Temple by which one can reach the upper chamber of the Temple. Overlay with gold all this stairhouse, its walls, its gates and its roof, from inside *and from* outside, its column and its stairs. *You* shall do everything as I tell you. You shall make a square house for the laver in the south-east, on all its sides, each twenty-one cubits; fifty cubits distant from the altar. The width of the wall shall be four cubits, and the height twenty cubits . . . Make gates for it on the east, on the north and on the west. The width of the gates shall be four cubits and the height seven **XXXII** . . . You shall make in the wall of this house, on the inside, recesses . . . They shall be overlaid with gold on which they shall place their clothes which they have worn on arrival . . .

You shall make a trench around the laver beside its house and the trench shall go *from the house of* the laver to a cavity. It shall descend *rapidly* to the ground where the water shall flow and disappear. It shall not be touched by any man for it is mingled with the blood of the holocaust.   **XXXIII** ... You shall make a house east of the house of the *laver* according to the measurement of *the house of the basin.* Its wall shall be at a distance of seven cubits from the wall of the house of the laver. Its whole building and rafters shall be like those of the house of the laver. It shall have two gates on the north and the south, one opposite the other, according to the measurement of the gates of the house of the laver. Inside all the walls of this house shall have apertures, their width and depth two cubits each and their height four with which the entrails and the feet are raised to the altar ...   **XXXIV** ... Afterwards they shall slaughter the young bulls and collect *the blood* in bowls and toss it around the altar base. They shall open the wheels and strip the skin of the young bulls from their flesh and cut them up into pieces, salt the pieces, wash the entrails and the legs, salt them and send them up in smoke on the fire which is on the altar, each young bull with its pieces beside it and the corresponding grain-offering of fine flour on it, the wine of the drink-offering beside it and some of it on it. The priests, the sons of Aaron, shall send everything up in smoke on the altar, an offering by fire, of soothing odour before YHWH. You shall make chains hanging from the rafters of the twelve columns   **XXXV** ... whoever is not a priest shall die, and ... he *who* is not clothed in the *holy vestments in which* he was ordained, they too shall be put to death and shall not *profane the* sanctuary of their God, thus incurring the iniquity of mortal guilt. You shall sanctify the environs of the altar, the Temple, the laver and the colonnade and they shall be most holy for ever and ever.

You shall make a place west of the Temple, a colonnade of pillars standing around for the sin-offerings and the guilt-offerings, divided from one another, the sin-offerings of the priests, the he-goats, and the sin-offerings of the people and their guilt-offerings. None of these shall be mingled one with another, for their places shall be divided from one another in order that the priests may not err concerning all the sin-offerings of the people, and all the rams of the guilt-offerings, thus incurring the sin of guilt . . .

XXXVI . . . The gate shall be forty *cubits* wide. Each side shall be *according to this measurement. The width* of *its* wall shall be seven cubits, *and* its *height forty*-five *cubits to the rafters* of *its* roof. The width of its chambers shall be twenty-six cubits from corner to corner. The gates of entrance and exit: the gate shall be fourteen cubits wide and twenty-eight cubits high from the threshold to the lintel. The height of the rafters above the lintel shall be fourteen cubits. The gate shall be roofed with a panelling of cedar wood overlaid with pure gold. Its doors shall be overlaid with fine gold.

From the corner of the gate to the second angle of the court-yard, there shall be one hundred and twenty cubits. Thus shall be the measurement of all these gates of the inner courtyard. The gates shall lead inside into the courtyard.   **XXXVII** You shall make inside the courtyard seats for the priests, and tables in front of the seats, in the inner colonnade by the outer wall of the court-yard, places made for the priests and their sacrifices, for the firstfruits and the tithes, for their peace-offering sacrifices which they shall sacrifice. The sacrifices of the peace-offerings of the children of Israel shall not be mingled with the sacrifices of the priests.

In the four corners of the courtyard you shall make for them a place for cooking-stoves where they shall seethe their sacrifices *and* sin-offerings.   **XXXVIII** . . . There they shall eat . . . the bird, the turtle-dove and the young pigeons . . .

You shall make a second courtyard around *the* inner *courtyard,* one hundred cubits wide, and four hundred and eighty cubits long on the east side, and thus shall be the width and length of all its sides: to the south, to the west and to the north. Its wall shall be four cubits wide and twenty-eight cubits high. Chambers shall be made in the wall outside and between each chamber there shall be three-*and-a-half cubits*   **XXXIX** . . . No woman shall come there, nor a child until the day that he has fulfilled the rule *and has paid for* himself *a ransom* to YHWH, half a shekel, an eternal rule, a memorial wherever they dwell. The shekel consists of twenty *gerahs.*

. . . Afterwards they shall enter from the age of twenty . . . The

names of the gates of this courtyard shall be according to the names *of* the children of Israel: Simeon, Levi and Judah in the east; Reuben, Joseph and Benjamin in the south; Issachar, Zebulun and Gad in the west; Dan, Naphtali and Asher in the north. Between each gate the measurement shall be: from the north-eastern corner to the gate of Simeon, ninety-nine cubits, and the gate twenty-eight cubits. From this gate of Simeon to the gate of Levi, ninety-nine cubits, and the gate, twenty-eight cubits . . .   **XL** . . . You shall make a third courtyard . . . in length about one thousand six *hundred* cubits from one corner to the next. Each side shall be according to this measurement: on the east, the south, the west and the north. The wall shall be seven cubits wide and forty-nine cubits high. Chambers shall be made between its gates along the foundation as far up as its 'crowns'.* There shall be three gates in the east, three in the south, three in the west and three in the north. The gates shall be fifty cubits wide and their height seventy cubits. Between one gate and another there shall be three hundred and sixty cubits. From the corner to the gate of Simeon, three hundred and sixty cubits. From the gate of Simeon to the gate of Levi, likewise. From the gate of Levi to the gate of Judah, likewise three *hundred and* sixty cubits . . .
XLI . . . From the gate of Issachar *to the gate of Zebulun,* *three* hundred *and sixty* cubits. From the gate of Zebulun to the gate of Gad, three hundred and sixty cubits. From the gate *of* Gad to the northern corner, three hundred and sixty cubits. From this corner to the gate of Dan: three hundred and sixty cubits. Thus from the gate of Dan to the gate of Naphtali, three hundred and sixty cubits. From the gate of Naphtali to the gate of Asher, three hundred and sixty cubits. From the gate of Asher to the eastern corner, three hundred and sixty cubits. The gates shall jut outwards from the wall of the courtyard seven cubits, and extend inwards from the wall to the courtyard thirty-six cubits. The entrance of the gate shall be fourteen cubits wide and twenty-eight cubits high up to the lintel. The rafters at the doorways shall be of cedar wood and overlaid with gold. The doors shall be overlaid with pure gold. Between each gate inwards you shall make storehouses,   **XLII** *rooms and colonnades.*

The room shall be ten cubits wide, twenty cubits long, and

* = crenellations: Yadin.

fourteen cubits high . . . The wall shall be two cubits wide. On the outside there shall be storehouses. *The storehouse shall be ten cubits wide and* twenty cubits *long.* The wall shall be two cubits wide *and fourteen cubits high* up to the lintel. Its entrance shall be three cubits wide. *You shall make in this way* all the storehouses and the *corresponding* rooms. The colonnade . . . shall be ten cubits wide. Between each gate *you shall make eighteen* storehouses and the corresponding eighteen rooms . . .

You shall make a staircase next to the walls of the gates towards the colonnade. Winding stairs shall go up to the second and third colonnades and to the roof. You shall build storehouses and corresponding rooms and colonnades as on the ground floor. The second and the third levels shall follow the measurement of the lower one. On the roof of the third you shall make pillars roofed with rafters from one pillar to the next providing a place for tabernacles. The pillars shall be eight cubits high and the tabernacles shall be made on their roof each year at the feast of the Tabernacles for the elders of the congregation, for the princes, the heads of the fathers' houses of the children of Israel, the captains of the thousands, the captains of the hundreds, who will ascend and dwell there until the sacrificing of the holocaust on the festival which is the feast of the Tabernacles, each year . . . **XLIII** . . . on the days of the firstfruits of the corn, of the *wine (tirosh) and the oil, and at the festival of the offering of* wood. On these days the tithe shall be eaten. They shall not put aside anything from it from one year to another. For they shall eat it in this manner. From the feast of the Firstfruits of the corn of wheat they shall eat the corn until the next year, until the feast of the Firstfruits, and they shall drink the wine from the day of the festival of Wine until the next year, until the day of the festival of the Wine, and they shall eat the oil from its festival, until the next year, until the festival, the day of offering the new oil on the altar. Whatever is left to last beyond their festivals shall be sanctified by being burnt with fire. It shall no longer be eaten for it is holy. Those who live within a distance of three days' walk from the sanctuary shall bring whatever they can bring. If they cannot carry it, they shall sell it for money and buy with it corn, wine, oil, cattle and sheep, and shall eat them on the days of the festivals. On working days they shall not eat from this in their weariness for it is holy. On the holy days it shall be eaten, but it shall not be eaten on working days.   **XLIV** . . .

You shall allot *the rooms and the corresponding chambers. From the gate of Simeon* to the gate of Judah shall be for the priests . . . All that is to the right and to the left of the gate of Levi, you shall allot to Aaron, your brother, one hundred and eight rooms and corresponding chambers and two tabernacles which are on the roof. You shall allot to the sons of Judah the area from the gate of Judah to the corner: fifty-four rooms and corresponding chambers and the tabernacle that is over them. You shall allot to the sons of Simeon the area from the gate of Simeon to the second corner: their rooms, the corresponding chambers and tabernacles. You shall allot to the sons of Reuben the area from the corner which is beside the sons of Judah to the gate of Reuben: fifty-two rooms and the corresponding chambers and tabernacles. The area from the gate of Reuben to the gate of Joseph you shall allot to the sons of Joseph, to Ephraim and Manasseh. The area from the gate of Joseph to the gate of Benjamin you shall allot to the sons of Kohath from the Levites. The area from the gate of Benjamin to the western corner you shall allot to the sons of Benjamin. The area from this corner to the gate of Issachar you shall allot to the sons of Issachar . . .   **XLV** . . . The second* *priestly course* shall enter on the left . . . and the first† shall leave on the right. They shall not mingle with one another nor their vessels. *Each* priestly course shall come to its place and they shall stay there. One shall arrive and the other leave on the eighth day. They shall clean the rooms, one after the other, when the first priestly course leaves. There shall be no mingling there.

No man who has had a nocturnal emission shall enter the sanctuary at all until three days have elapsed. He shall wash his garments and bathe on the first day and on the third day he shall wash his garments and bathe, and after sunset he shall enter the sanctuary. They shall not enter my sanctuary in their impure uncleanness and render it unclean. No man who has had sexual intercourse with his wife shall enter anywhere into the city of the sanctuary where I cause my name to abide, for three days. No blind man shall enter it in all his days and shall not profane the

* = incoming.   † = outgoing.

city where I abide, for I, YHWH, abide amongst the children of Israel for ever and ever.

Whoever is to purify himself of his flux shall count seven days for his purification. He shall wash his garments on the seventh day and bathe his whole body in running water. Afterwards he shall enter the city of the sanctuary. No one unclean through contact with a corpse shall enter there until he has purified himself. No leper nor any man smitten in his body shall enter there until he has purified himself . . .

XLVI . . . You shall make a terrace round about, outside the outer courtyard, fourteen cubits wide like the entrances of all the gates. You shall make twelve steps leading to it by which the children of Israel shall ascend there to enter my sanctuary.

You shall make a one-hundred-cubits-wide ditch around the sanctuary which shall divide the holy sanctuary from the city so that no one can rush into my sanctuary and defile it. They shall sanctify my sanctuary and hold it in awe because I abide among them.

You shall make for them latrines outside the city where they shall go out, north-west of the city. These shall be roofed houses with holes in them into which the filth shall go down. It shall be far enough not to be visible from the city, at three thousand cubits . . .

XLVII . . . Their cities *shall be* pure . . . for ever. The city which I will sanctify, causing my name and *my* sanctuary to abide *in it,* shall be holy and pure of all impurity with which they can become impure. Whatever is in it shall be pure. Whatever enters it shall be pure: wine, oil, all food and all moistened food shall be clean. No skin of clean animals slaughtered in their cities shall be brought there to the city of the sanctuary. But in their cities they may use them for any work they need. But they shall not bring them to the city of my sanctuary, for the purity of the skin corresponds to that of the flesh. You shall not profane the city where I cause my name and my sanctuary to abide. For it is in the skins of animals slaughtered in the sanctuary that they shall bring their wine and oil and all their food to the city of my sanctuary. They shall not pollute my sanctuary with the skins of animals slaughtered in their country which are tainted.* You cannot render any city among your cities as pure as my city, for the purity of the skin of the animal corresponds to the purity of its flesh. If you slaughter it in my sanctuary, it shall be pure for my sanctuary, but if you slaughter it in your cities, it shall be pure only for your cities. Whatever is pure for the sanctuary, shall be brought in skins fit for the sanctuary, and you shall not profane my sanctuary and my city where I abide with tainted skins.

XLVIII ... You may eat *the following* flying *insects*: every kind of great locust, every kind of long-headed locust, every kind of green locust, and every kind of desert locust. These are among the flying insects which you may eat: those which walk on four legs and have legs jointed above their feet to leap with them on the ground and wings to fly with. You shall not eat the carcass of any bird or beast but may sell it to a foreigner. You shall not eat any abominable thing, for you are a holy people to YHWH, your God.

You are the sons of YHWH, your God. You shall not gash yourselves or shave your forelocks in mourning for the dead, nor shall you tattoo yourselves, for you are a holy people to YHWH, your God. You shall not profane your land.

You shall not do as the nations do; they bury their dead everywhere, they bury them even in their houses. Rather you shall set apart areas in the midst of your land where you shall bury your dead. Between four cities you shall designate an area for burial. In every city you shall set aside areas for those stricken with leprosy, with plague and with scab, who shall not enter your cities and profane them, and also for those who suffer from a flux; and for menstruating women, and women after childbirth, so that they may not cause defilement in their midst by their impure uncleanness ... XLIX ... If a man dies in your cities, the house in which the dead man has died shall be unclean for seven days. Whatever is in the house and whoever enters the house shall be unclean for seven days. Any food on which water has been poured shall be unclean, anything moistened shall be unclean. Earthenware vessels shall be unclean and whatever they contain shall be unclean for every clean man. The open vessels shall be unclean for every Israelite with whatever is moistened in them.

On the day when the body is removed from there, they shall

* = unfit for the Temple.

cleanse the house of all pollution of oil, wine and water moisture. They shall rub the house's floor, walls and doors and shall wash with water the bolts, doorposts, thresholds and lintels. On the day when the body is removed from there, they shall purify the house and all its utensils, hand-mills and mortars, all utensils of wood, iron and bronze and all utensils capable of purification. Clothes, sacks and skins shall be washed. As for the people, whoever has been in the house or has entered the house shall bathe in water and shall wash his clothes on the first day. On the third day they shall sprinkle purifying water on them and shall bathe. They shall wash their garments and all the utensils in the house.

On the seventh day they shall sprinkle them a second time. They shall bathe, wash their clothes and utensils and shall be clean by the evening of the impurity contracted from the dead so as to be fit to touch their pure things . . .   **L** . . . Whoever touches the bone of a dead person in the fields, or one slain by the sword, or a dead body or the blood of a dead person, or a tomb, he shall purify himself according to the rule of this statute. But if he does not purify himself according to the statute of this law, he is unclean, his uncleanness being still in him. Whoever touches him must wash his clothes, bathe and he shall be clean by the evening.

If a woman is with child and it dies in her womb, as long as it is dead in her, she shall be unclean like a tomb. Any house that she enters shall be unclean with all its utensils for seven days. Whoever touches it shall be unclean till the evening. If anyone enters the house with her, he shall be unclean for seven days. He shall wash his clothes and bathe in water on the first day. On the third day he shall sprinkle and wash his clothes and bathe. On the seventh day he shall sprinkle a second time and wash his clothes and bathe. At sunset he shall be clean.

As for all the utensils, clothes, skins and all the materials made of goat's hair, you shall deal with them according to the statute of this law. All earthenware vessels shall be broken for they are unclean and can no more be purified ever.

All creatures that teem on the ground you shall proclaim unclean: the weasel, the mouse, every kind of lizard, the wall gecko, the sand gecko, the great lizard and the chameleon . . .

LI . . . You shall *not* render yourselves unclean by them. *Whoever* *touches them* dead shall be unclean *until the* evening. He shall wash his clothes and bathe *in water and at* sunset he shall be clean. Whoever carries any of their bones, their carcass, skin, flesh or claw shall wash his clothes and bathe in water. After sunset he shall be clean. You shall forewarn the children of Israel about all the impurities.

They shall not render themselves unclean by those of which I tell you on this mountain and they shall not be unclean.

For I, YHWH, abide among the children of Israel. You shall sanctify them and they shall be holy. They shall not render themselves abominable by anything that I have separated for them as unclean and they shall be holy.

You shall establish judges and officers in all your towns and they shall judge the people with just judgement. They shall not be partial in their judgement. They shall not accept bribes, nor shall they twist judgement, for the bribe twists judgement, overturns the works of justice, blinds the eyes of the wise, produces great guilt, and profanes the house by the iniquity of sin. Justice and justice alone shall you pursue that you may live and come to inherit the land that I give you to inherit for all days. The man who accepts bribes and twists just judgement shall be put to death. You shall not be afraid to execute him.

You shall not do in your land as the nations do. Everywhere they sacrifice, plant sacred trees, erect sacred pillars and set up carved stones to bow down before them . . . **LII** . . . You shall not plant *any tree as a sacred tree beside my altar to be made by you.* You shall not erect a sacred pillar *that is hateful to me.* You shall not make anywhere in your land a carved stone to bow down before it. You shall not sacrifice to me any cattle or sheep with a grave blemish, for they are abominable to me. You shall not sacrifice to me any cattle or sheep or goat that is pregnant, for this would be an abomination to me. You shall not slaughter a cow or a ewe and its young on the same day, neither shall you kill a mother with her young.

Of all the firstlings born to your cattle or sheep, you shall sanctify for me the male animals. You shall not use the firstling of your cattle for work, nor shall you shear the firstling of your small cattle. You shall eat it before me every year in the place that I shall choose. Should it be blemished, being lame or blind or afflicted with any grave blemish, you shall not sacrifice it to me. It is within your towns that you shall eat it. The unclean and the clean among you together may eat it like a gazelle or a deer. It is the blood alone that you shall not eat. You shall spill it on the ground like water and cover it with dust. You shall not muzzle an ox while it is threshing. You shall not plough with an ox and an ass harnessed together. You shall not slaughter clean cattle or sheep or goat in any of your towns, within a distance of three days' journey from my sanctuary. It is rather in my sanctuary that you shall slaughter it, making of it a holocaust or peace-offering. You shall eat and rejoice before me in the place on which I choose to set my name. Every clean animal with a blemish, you shall eat it within your towns, away from my sanctuary at a distance of thirty stadia. You shall not slaughter it close to my sanctuary for its flesh is tainted. You shall not eat in my city, which I sanctify by placing my name in it, the flesh of cattle, sheep or goat which has not entered my sanctuary. They shall sacrifice it there, toss its blood to the base of the altar of holocaust and shall burn its fat.   **LIII** *When I extend your frontiers as I have told you, and if the place where I have chosen to set my name is too distant,* and you say, 'I will eat meat', because you long for it, *whatever you desire,* you may eat, *and you may slaughter* any of your small cattle or cattle which I give you according to my blessing. You may eat it within your towns, the clean and the unclean together, like gazelle or deer meat. But you shall firmly abstain from eating the blood. You shall spill it on the ground like water and cover it with dust. For the blood is the life and you shall not eat the life with the flesh so that it may be well with you and with your sons after you for ever. You shall do that which is correct and good before me, for I am YHWH, your God.

But all your devoted gifts and votive donations you shall bring when you come to the place where I cause my name to abide, and you shall sacrifice them there before me as you have devoted and vowed them with your mouth. When you make a vow, you shall not tarry in fulfilling it, for surely I will require it of you and you shall become guilty of a sin. You shall keep the word uttered by your lips, for your mouth has vowed freely to perform your vow.

When a man makes a vow to me or swears an oath to take upon

himself a binding obligation, he must not break his word. Whatever has been uttered by his mouth, he shall do it.

When a woman makes a vow to me, or takes upon herself a
binding obligation by means of an oath in her father's house, in
her youth, if her father hears of her vow or the binding obligation
which she has taken upon herself and remains silent, all her vows
shall stand, and her binding obligation which she has taken upon
herself shall stand. If, however, her father definitely forbids her
on the day that he hears of it, none of her vows or binding obligations which she has taken upon herself shall stand, and I will
absolve her because her father has forbidden her **LIV** *when he
heard of them. But if he annuls them after* the day *that he has*
heard *of them, he shall bear* her guilt: *her father has annulled
them. Any vow* or binding oath made by a woman *to mortify herself,* her husband may confirm *it* or annul it on the day that he
hears of it, and I will absolve her.

But any vow of a widow or a divorced woman, whatever she has
taken upon herself shall stand in conformity with all that her
mouth has uttered.

Everything that I command you today, see to it that it is kept.
You shall not add to it, nor detract from it.

If a prophet or a dreamer appears among you and presents you
with a sign or a portent, even if the sign or the portent comes true,
when he says, 'Let us go and worship other gods whom you have
not known!', do not listen to the words of that prophet or that
dreamer, for I am testing you to discover whether you love
YHWH, the God of your fathers, with all your heart and soul. It is
YHWH, your God, that you must follow and serve, and it is Him
that you must fear and His voice that you must obey, and you
must hold fast to Him. That prophet or dreamer shall be put to
death for he has preached rebellion against YHWH, your God,
who brought you out of the land of Egypt and redeemed you from
the house of bondage, to lead you astray from the path that I have
commanded you to follow. You shall rid yourself of this evil.

If your brother, the son of your father or the son of your
mother, or your son, or your daughter, or the wife of your bosom,
or your friend who is like your own self, seeks to entice you
secretly, saying, 'Let us go and worship other gods whom you have
not known', neither you, **LV** *nor* your fathers, some of the gods

of the peoples that are round about you, whether near you or far off from you, from the one end of the earth to *the other, you shall not yield to him or listen to him, nor shall your eye pity* him, nor shall you spare *him, nor shall you conceal him; but you shall kill him; your hand shall be first against him to put him to death, and afterwards the hand of all the people. You shall stone him to death with stones because he sought to* draw you away *from me who brought you out of the land of Egypt, out of the house of bondage. And all Israel shall hear, and fear, and never again do such an evil thing* among you. If in one *of your cities in which I* give you to *dwell* you hear this said: 'Men, sons of *Belial* have arisen in your midst and have led astray all the inhabitants of their city saying, "Let us go and worship gods whom you have not known!",' you shall inquire, search and investigate carefully. If the matter is proven true that such an abomination has been done in Israel, you shall surely put all the inhabitants of that city to the sword. You shall place it and all who are in it under the ban, and you shall put the beasts to the sword. You shall assemble all the booty in the city square and shall burn it with fire, the city and all the booty, as a whole-offering to YHWH, your God. It shall be a ruin for ever and shall never be rebuilt. Nothing from that which has been placed under the ban shall cleave to your hand so that I may turn from my hot anger and show you compassion. I will be compassionate to you and multiply you as I told your fathers, provided that you obey my voice, keeping all my commandments that I command you today, to do that which is correct and good before YHWH, your God.

If among you, in one of your towns that I give you, there is found a man or a woman who does that which is wrong in my eyes by transgressing my covenant, and goes and worships other gods, and bows down before them, or before the sun or the moon, or all the host of heaven, if you are told about it, and you hear about this matter, you shall search and investigate it carefully. If the matter is proven true that such an abomination has been done in Israel, you shall lead out that man or that woman and stone him to death with stones.

LVI . . . *You shall go to the Levitical priests* or to the *judges then in office;* you shall seek their guidance and *they* shall *pronounce on* the matter for which *you have sought their guidance,* *and they shall proclaim* their judgement to you. You shall act in conformity with the law that they proclaim to you and the saying that they declare to you from the book of the Law. They shall issue to you a proclamation in truth from the place where I choose to cause my name to abide. Be careful to do all that they teach you and act in conformity with the decision that they communicate to you. Do not stray from the law which they proclaim to you to the right or to the left. The man who does not listen but acts arrogantly without obeying the priest who is posted there to minister before me, or the judge, that man shall die. You shall rid Israel of evil. All the people shall hear of it and shall be awe-stricken, and none shall ever again be arrogant in Israel.

When you enter the land which I give you, take possession of it, dwell in it and say, 'I will appoint a king over me as do all the nations around me!', you may surely appoint over you the king whom I will choose. It is from among your brothers that you shall appoint a king over you. You shall not appoint over you a foreigner who is not your brother. He, the king, shall definitely not acquire many horses, neither shall he lead the people back to Egypt for war to acquire many horses and much silver and gold, for I told you, 'You shall never again go back that way'. He shall not acquire many wives that they may not turn his heart away from me. He shall not acquire very much silver and gold.

When he sits on the throne of his kingdom, they shall write for him this law from the book which is before the priests. **LVII** This is the law *that they shall write for him . . . They shall count,* on the day that they appoint him king, the sons of Israel from the age of twenty to sixty years according to their standard units. He shall install at their head captains of thousands, captains of hundreds, captains of fifties and captains of tens in all their cities. He shall select from among them one thousand by tribe to be with him: twelve thousand warriors who shall not leave him alone to be captured by the nations. All the selected men whom he has selected shall be men of truth, God-fearers, haters of unjust gain and mighty warriors. They shall be with him always, day and night. They shall guard him from anything sinful, and from any foreign nation in order not to be captured by them. The twelve princes of his people shall be with him, and twelve from among the priests, and from among the Levites twelve. They shall sit together with him to proclaim judgement and the law so that his heart shall not be lifted above them, and he shall do nothing without them concerning any affair.

He shall not marry as wife any daughter of the nations, but shall take a wife for himself from his father's house, from his father's family. He shall not take another wife in addition to her, for she alone shall be with him all the time of her life. But if she dies, he may marry another from his father's house, from his family. He shall not twist judgement; he shall take no bribe to twist a just judgement and shall not covet a field or a vineyard, any riches or house, or anything desirable in Israel. He shall not rob

LVIII . . . When the king hears of any nation or people intent on plundering whatever belongs to Israel, he shall send for the captains of thousands and the captains of hundreds posted in the cities of Israel. They shall send with the captain one tenth of the people to go with the king to war against their enemies, and they shall go with him. But if a large force enters the land of Israel, they shall send with him one fifth of the warriors. If a king with chariots and horses and a large force comes, they shall send with him one third of the warriors, and the two remaining divisions shall guard their city and their boundaries so that no marauders invade their land. If the war presses the king hard, they shall send to him half of the people, the men of the army, but the other half of the people shall not be severed from their cities.

If they triumph over their enemies, smash them, put them to the sword and carry away their booty, they shall give the king his tithe of this, the priests one thousandth and the Levites one hundredth from everything. They shall halve the rest between the combatants and their brothers whom they have left in their cities.

If the king goes to war against his enemies, one fifth of the people shall go with him, the warriors, all the mighty men of valour. They shall avoid everything unclean, everything shameful, every iniquity and guilt. He shall not go until he has presented himself before the High Priest who shall inquire on his behalf for a decision by the Urim and Tummim.* It is at his word that he shall go and at his word that he shall come, he and all the children of Israel who are with him. He shall not go following his heart's counsel until the High Priest has inquired for a decision by the

* The High Priest's instruments of divination.

Urim and Tummim. He shall then succeed in all his ways on which he has set out ... **LIX** ... and they shall disperse them in many lands and they shall become a *horror*, a byword, a mockery. With a heavy yoke and in extreme want, they shall there serve gods made by human hands, of wood and stone, silver and gold. During this time their cities shall become a devastation, a laughing-stock and a wasteland, and their enemies shall devastate them. They shall sigh in the lands of their enemies and scream because of the heavy yoke. They shall cry out but I will not listen; they shall scream but I will not answer them because of their evil doings. I will hide my face from them and they shall become food, plunder and prey. None shall save them because of their wickedness, because they have broken my covenant and their soul has loathed my law until they have incurred every guilt. Afterwards they will return to me with all their heart and all their soul, in conformity with all the words of this law, and I will save them from the hand of their enemies and redeem them from the hand of those who hate them, and I will bring them to the land of their fathers. I will redeem them, and increase them and exult over them. I will be their God and they shall be my people.

The king whose heart and eyes have gone astray from my commandments shall never have one to sit on the throne of his fathers, for I will cut off his posterity for ever so that it shall no more rule over Israel. But if he walk after my rules and keep my commandments and do that which is correct and good before me, no heir to the throne of the kingdom of Israel shall be cut off from among his sons for ever. I will be with him and will save him from the hand of those who hate him and from the hand of those who seek his life. I will place all his enemies before him and he shall rule over them according to his pleasure and they shall not rule over him. I will set him on an upward, not on a downward, course, to be the head and not the tail, that the days of his kingdom may be lengthened greatly for him and his sons after him.

LX ... To the Levites shall belong the tithe of the corn, the wine and the oil that they have sanctified to me first; the shoulder from those who slaughter a sacrifice and a proportion of the booty, the plunder and the catch of birds, wild animals and fish, one hundredth; the tithe from the young pigeons and from the honey one fiftieth. To the priests shall belong one hundredth of the young pigeons, for I have chosen them from all your tribes to attend on me and minister before me and bless my name, he and his sons always. If a Levite come from any town anywhere in Israel where he sojourns to the place where I will choose to cause my name to abide, if he come with an eager soul, he may minister like his brethren the Levites who attend on me there. He shall have the same share of food with them, besides the inheritance from his father's family.

When you enter the land which I give you, do not learn to practise the abominations of those nations. There shall be found among you none who makes his son or daughter pass through fire, nor an augur or a soothsayer, a diviner or a sorcerer, one who casts spells or a medium, or wizards or necromancers. For they are an abomination before me, all who practise such things, and it is because of these abominations that I drive them out before you. You shall be perfect towards YHWH, your God . . . **LXI** . . . and *who utters a word* in *my name which I have* not commanded *him to* utter, or who *speaks in the name of other* gods, that prophet shall be put to death. If you say in your heart, 'How shall we know the word which YHWH has not uttered?', when the word uttered by the prophet in the name of YHWH is not fulfilled and does not come true, that is not a word that I have uttered. The prophet has spoken arrogantly; do not fear him.

A single witness may not come forward against a man in the matter of any iniquity or sin which he has committed. It is on the evidence of two witnesses or three witnesses that a case can be established. If a malicious witness comes forward against a man to testify against him in a case of a crime, both disputants shall stand before me and before the priests and the Levites and before the judges then in office, and the judges shall inquire, and if the witness is a false witness who has testified falsely against his brother, you shall do to him as he proposed to do to his brother. You shall rid yourselves of evil. The rest shall hear of it and shall be awe-stricken and never again shall such a thing be done in your midst. You shall have no mercy on him: life for life, eye for eye, tooth for tooth, hand for hand, foot for foot.

When you go to war against your enemies, and you see horses and chariots and an army greater than yours, be not afraid of them, for I am with you who brought you out of the land of Egypt . . . **LXII** . . . *If any man has betrothed a woman but has not yet married her, he shall return* home. Otherwise he may die in the war and another man may take her. *The officers shall continue* to address the army and say, 'If any man is afraid and has lost heart, he shall go and return. Otherwise he may render his kinsmen as faint-hearted as himself.'

When the judges have finished addressing the army, they shall appoint army captains at the head of the people.

When you approach a city to fight it, first offer it peace. If it seeks peace and opens its gates to you, then all the people found in it shall become your forced labourers and shall serve you. If it does not make peace with you, but is ready to fight a war against you, you shall besiege it and I will deliver it into your hands. You shall put all its males to the sword, but the women, the children, the beasts and all that is in the city, all its booty, you may take as spoil for yourselves. You may enjoy the use of the booty of your enemies which I give you. Thus shall you treat the very distant cities, those which are not among the cities of these nations. But in the cities of the peoples which I give you as an inheritance, you shall not leave alive any creature. Indeed you shall utterly exterminate the Hittites, the Amorites, the Canaanites, the Hivites, the Jebusites, the Girgashites and the Perizzites as I have commanded you, that they may not teach you to practise all the abominations that they have performed to their gods.

LXIII . . . In a case of murder *the elders of* that city *shall bring down* the heifer to a ravine with an ever-flowing stream which has never been sown or cultivated, and there they shall break its neck.

The priests, the sons of Levi, shall come forward, for I have chosen them to minister before me and bless my name, and every dispute and every assault shall be decided by their word. All the elders of the city nearest to the body of the murdered man shall wash their hands over the head of the heifer whose neck has been broken in the ravine. They shall declare, 'Our hands did not shed this blood, nor did our eyes see it happen. Accept expiation for Thy people Israel whom Thou hast redeemed, O YHWH, and do not permit the guilt of innocent blood to rest among Thy people, Israel. Let this blood be expiated for them.' You shall rid Israel of the guilt of innocent blood, and you shall do that which is correct and good before YHWH, your God. When you go to war against your enemies, and I deliver them into your hands, and you capture some of them, if you see among the captives a pretty woman and desire her, you may take her to be your wife. You shall bring her to your house, you shall shave her head, and cut her nails. You shall discard the clothes of her captivity and she shall dwell in your house, and bewail her father and mother for a full month. Afterwards you may go to her, consummate the marriage with her and she will be your wife. But she shall not touch whatever is pure for you for seven years, neither shall she eat of the sacrifice of peace-offering until seven years have elapsed. Afterwards she may eat.　　**LXIV** ... If a man has a disobedient and rebellious son who refuses to listen to his father and mother, nor listens to them when they chastise him, his father and mother shall take hold of him and bring him to the elders of his city, to the gate of his place. They shall say to the elders of his town, 'This son of ours is disobedient and rebellious; he does not listen to us; he is a glutton and a drunkard.' All the men of his city shall stone him with stones and he shall die, and you shall rid yourselves of evil. All the children of Israel shall hear of it and be awe-stricken. If a man slanders his people and delivers his people to a foreign nation and does evil to his people, you shall hang him on a tree and he shall die. On the testimony of two witnesses and on the testimony of three witnesses he shall be put to death and they shall hang him on the tree. If a man is guilty of a capital crime and flees abroad to the nations, and curses his people, the children of Israel, you shall hang him also on the tree, and he shall die. But his body shall not stay overnight on the tree. Indeed you shall bury him on the same day. For he who is hanged on the tree is accursed of God and men. You shall not pollute the ground which I give you to inherit. If you see your kinsman's ox or sheep or donkey straying, do not neglect them; you shall indeed return them to your kinsman. If your kinsman does not live near you, and you do not know who he is, you shall bring the animal to your house and it shall be with you until he claims it.　　**LXV** ... When a bird's nest happens to lie before you by the roadside, on any tree or on the ground, with fledglings or eggs, and the hen is sitting on the fledglings or the eggs, you shall not take the hen with the young. You shall surely let the hen

escape and take only the young so that it may be well with you and
your days shall be prolonged. When you build a new house, you
shall construct a parapet on the roof so that you do not bring
blood-guilt on your house if anyone should fall from it.

When a man takes a wife, has sexual intercourse with her and
takes a dislike to her, and brings a baseless charge against her,
ruining her reputation, and says, 'I have taken this woman, approached her, and did not find the proof of virginity in her', the
father or the mother of the girl shall take the girl's proof of virginity and bring it to the elders at the gate. The girl's father shall say
to the elders, 'I gave my daughter to be this man's wife; he has
taken a dislike to her and has brought a baseless charge against
her saying, "I have not found the proof of virginity in your daughter." Here is the proof of my daughter's virginity.' They shall
spread out the garment before the elders of that city. The elders of
that city shall take that man and chastise him. They shall fine him
one hundred pieces of silver which they shall give to the father of
the girl, because the husband has tried to ruin the reputation of an
Israelite virgin . . .   **LXVI** . . . *When a virgin betrothed to a man
is found by another man in the city and he lies with her, they shall
bring both of them to the gate* of that city and stone them with
stones and they shall be put to death: the girl because she has not
shouted for help, although she was in the city, and the man
because he has dishonoured his neighbour's wife. You shall rid
yourselves of evil. If the man has found the woman in the fields in
a distant place hidden from the city, and raped her, only he who
has lain with her shall be put to death. To the girl they shall do
nothing since she has committed no crime worthy of death. For
this affair is like that of a man who attacks his neighbour and
murders him. For it was in the fields that he found her and the
betrothed girl shouted for help, but none came to her rescue.

When a man seduces a virgin who is not betrothed, but is suitable to him according to the rule, and lies with her, and he is
found out, he who has lain with her shall give the girl's father fifty
pieces of silver and she shall be his wife. Because he has dishonoured her, he may not divorce her all his days. A man shall not
take his father's wife and shall not lift his father's skirt. A man
shall not take the wife of his brother and shall not lift the skirt of
his brother, the son of his father or the son of his mother, for this

is unclean. A man shall not take his sister, the daughter of his father or the daughter of his mother, for this is abominable. A man shall not take his father's sister or his mother's sister, for this is immoral. A man shall not take the daughter of his brother or the daughter of his sister for this is abominable . . .

Miqsat Ma'ase Ha-Torah

SOME OBSERVANCES OF THE LAW

When the contents of the six Cave 4 manuscripts of this work are assembled into a single account, they amount to 120 lines mostly of a fragmentary nature. The document begins with a sectarian calendar (omitted here), continues with a series of special rules, and ends with an exhortation. Miqsat Ma'ase Ha-Torah has been called an epistle, but since it lacks the introductory and concluding formulae of a letter, it is more likely to be a kind of legal tractate. It is addressed to a single leading personality who is compared to King David. The *dramatis personae* consist of a 'we' party, a 'you' party, and a 'they' party. The group responsible for MMT (as it is known), who refer to themselves as 'we', seek to detach the leader of the 'you' party from the erroneous views propounded by the 'they' party. The official editors claim that the document was written by the Teacher of Righteousness and sent to the Wicked Priest; that the views of the 'we' party are akin to those of the Sadducees; and that the 'they' party are the Pharisees. However, these are no more than hypotheses. In particular, the identification of the author with the Teacher of Righteousness is less likely than that of the leader of the 'you' group with the man who was to become the Wicked Priest, probably Jonathan Maccabaeus.

This extract includes some of the Special Rules and the most complete section of *The Exhortation*.

Among the chief topics of controversy are questions of ritual purity, including the law on slaughter, the 'red heifer' ritual, the exclusion of the blind and the deaf, the law relating to lepers, the fourth-year fruit and tithe of cattle, the ban on dogs in Jerusalem, and the law regulating contact with dead bodies, together with some rules on marriage and intermarriage. MMT is particularly important as a source of ancient legal debate. It is unique among the Dead Sea Scrolls and foreshadows the halakhic process developed and practised by later rabbis.

Special Rules Concerning Purity

And concerning the purity of the heifer of the sin-offering, he who slaughters it and he who burns it and he who collects its ashes and he who sprinkles the water of purification – all these are to be pure at sunset so that the pure shall sprinkle the impure.

And furthermore concerning the skins *and bones of unclean animals, they shall not make from their bones* and from their *skins* handles of *vessels* . . .

And furthermore concerning the skin of the carcass of a clean *animal,* he who carries their carcass shall not touch the *sacred* purity.

And concerning pregnant animals we consider *that one should not sacrifice* the mother and the unborn young on the same day.

And concerning eating, we consider that the unborn young may be eaten . . . provided it has been slaughtered.

And concerning the Ammonite and the Moabite and the bastard *and the man whose testicles* have been crushed *and one* whose penis *has been cut off* who enter the congregation, . . . *and* they take *wives so as to be* one bone with them . . .

And furthermore we consider *that they should not . . . have intercourse* with them . . . *and they should* not unite with them so as to make them *into one bone* . . .

And furthermore concerning the blind who do not see how to beware of all minglings . . . and do not see the minglings which entail guilt-offering. And furthermore concerning the deaf who have not heard the decrees and judgements and purity rules and have not heard the judgements of Israel – for he who has not seen and has not heard them does not know how to practise them; yet they come to the pure food of the Sanctuary . . .

And dogs are not to be brought to the sacred camp for they may eat some of the bones from the Sanctuary to which meat is still attached. For Jerusalem is the sacred camp and is the place which He has chosen from all the tribes of Israel, for Jerusalem is the head of the camps of Israel.

And furthermore *concerning the* planting of fruit trees planted in the land of Israel, they are like firstfruits destined for the priests. And the tithe of the cattle and sheep is for the priests.

And furthermore concerning the lepers, we *say that they shall not* come into contact with the sacred pure food for they shall be separated . . .

Furthermore it is written that from the time the leper has

shaved and washed, he shall stay outside . . . *for seven* days. And now while their impurity is with them . . . *they shall not come into contact* with the sacred pure food of the house.

And concerning *the impurities* of a man, we say that every bone to which flesh is or *is not* attached is to be treated according to the law of the dead or slain . . .

And concerning fornication practised by the people, they should be *sons of* holiness, as it is written, *Israel is holy* (Jer. ii, 3).

And concerning *his clean* animal, *it is written that it shall not be mated with a different kind.*

And concerning his clothes, it is written that they shall not be of mixed material.

And he shall not sow his field and vineyard *with two kinds.* For they are holy and the sons of Aaron are most *holy.* And you know that some of the priests and *the people mingle and they* unite and defile the *holy* seed and also their *seed* with whores . . .

And furthermore it is written *in the Book of Moses that You shall not bring an abominable thing into your house* (cf. Deut. vii, 26) *for* an abominable thing is detestable.

From 'The Exhortation'

And it shall come to pass when all these things befall you in the end of days, the blessing and the curse, then you will call them to mind and return to Him with all your heart and all your soul (Deut. xxx, 1–2) at the end of days . . . *and the blessings came* in the days of Solomon the son of David. And the curses came from in the days of Jeroboam the son of Nebat until Jerusalem and Zedekiah king of Judah were exiled that He will *bring* them to . . . And we recognise that some of the blessings and curses which are written in the *Book of* Moses have come. And this is at the end of days when they will come back to Israel for *ever . . .*

Remember the kings of Israel and understand their works that each of them who feared *the* Torah was saved from troubles, and to those who were seekers of the Law, their iniquities were pardoned.

Remember David, that he was a man of piety, and that he was also saved from many troubles and pardoned.

We have also written to you concerning some of the observances of the Law (*miqsat ma'ase ha-Torah*), which we think are
beneficial to you and your people. For *we have noticed* that prudence and knowledge of the Law are with you.

Understand all these matters and ask Him to straighten your
counsel and put you far away from thoughts of evil and the counsel of Belial. Consequently, you will rejoice at the end of time
when you discover that some of our sayings are true. And it will be
reckoned for you as righteousness when you perform what is right
and good before Him, for your own good and for that of Israel.

Purities

This passage comes from the first of ten Cave 4 manuscripts dealing with purity matters. It deals with uncleanness caused by bodily fluxes and issues of blood and with the means of its removal.

Let him not begin to cast his lot. He shall lie on a bed of sorrow and sit in a seat of sighs. He shall dwell in isolation with all the unclean, and away from food purity at a distance of twelve cubits in the wing assigned to him on the north-west of every dwelling-house according to this measure. Every man from among the unclean . . . he shall bathe in water *on the seventh day* and wash his clothes, and afterwards he may eat. For this is what he said, *He shall cry, Unclean, unclean* (Lev. xiii, 45), as long as *the* plague *affects him.*

A woman with a seven-day issue of blood shall not touch a man with a flux, nor any vessel touched by a man who has a flux, nor anything he has lain or sat on. But if she has touched them, she shall wash her garments and bathe, and afterwards she may eat. Above all, she shall not mingle with the pure *during* her seven days so that she may not pollute the *camps* of the Holy of Israel. Neither shall she touch any woman with a long-term issue of blood. And the person, either male or female, who counts the seven days (cf. Lev. xv, 13) shall not touch the menstruant during her uncleanness. Only when she has purified herself *from* her uncleanness may she be touched, for the blood of the menstruant is reckoned as a flux for anyone who touches it. And if he has touched *bodily flux or* semen, he *shall* be unclean. *And he who has* touched a man from among all these unclean persons during the seven days of *his* cleansing he shall not eat. If he has become unclean because of a corpse, *he shall bathe in water*, wash his garments and afterwards he may *eat.*

HYMNS AND POEMS

• •

The Thanksgiving Hymns

The poems contained in the Hymns Scroll are similar to the biblical Psalms. They are mostly hymns of thanksgiving, individual prayers as opposed to those intended for communal worship, expressing a rich variety of spiritual and doctrinal detail. But the two fundamental themes running through the whole collection are those of salvation and knowledge. The sectary thanks God continually for having been saved from the 'lot' of the wicked, and for his gift of insight into the divine mysteries. He, a 'creature of clay', has been singled out by his Maker to receive favours of which he feels himself unworthy and he alludes again and again to his frailty and total dependence on God. Whereas some of the Hymns give expression to thoughts and sentiments common to all the members of the sect, others, particularly nos. 1, 2, and 7–11, appear to refer to the experiences of a teacher abandoned by his friends and persecuted by his enemies. Several scholars tend to ascribe the authorship of these to the Teacher of Righteousness, and even consider that he may be responsible for all the Hymns. But although this hypothesis is not impossible, no sure conclusion can yet be reached. Nor are we in a position to date any particular composition. The most we can say is that the collection as such probably attained its final shape during the last pre-Christian century.

Philo's account of the banquet celebrated by the contemplative Essenes, or Therapeutae, on the Feast of Pentecost may indicate the use to which the Hymns were put. He reports that when the President of the meeting had ended his commentary on the Scriptures, he rose and chanted a hymn, either one of his own making or an old one, and after him each of his brethren did likewise (*The Contemplative Life*). Similarly, it is probable that the psalms of this Scroll were recited by the Guardian and newly initiated members at the Feast of the Renewal of the Covenant. Hymn 4 expressly refers to the oath of the Covenant, and Hymn 5 appears to be a poetic commentary on the liturgy marking the entry into the Community. Indeed, the relative poverty of principal themes may be due to the fact that all this poetry was intended for a special occasion and its inspirational scope was thereby limited.

Hymn 1

. . . As Thou hast said by the hand of Moses,
   Thou forgivest transgression, iniquity, and sin,
   and pardonest rebellion and unfaithfulness.

For the bases of the mountains shall melt
   and fire shall consume the deep places of Hell,
but Thou wilt deliver
   all those that are corrected by Thy judgements,
that they may serve Thee faithfully
   and that their seed may be before Thee for ever.
   Thou wilt keep Thine oath
   and wilt pardon their transgression;
   Thou wilt cast away all their sins.

Thou wilt cause them to inherit all the glory of Adam
   and abundance of days.

Hymn 2

I give Thee thanks
   because of the spirits which Thou hast given to me!
I *will bring forth* a reply of the tongue
   to recount Thy righteous deeds,
and the forbearance . . .
   and the works of Thy mighty right hand,
   and *the pardon* of the sins of the forefathers.
I will bow down and implore Thy mercy
   on my sins and wicked deeds,
   and on the perversity of *my heart,*
for I have wallowed in uncleanness,
   and have *turned aside* from the counsel *of Thy truth*
and I have not laboured . . .
   For Thine, Thine is righteousness,

and an everlasting blessing be upon Thy Name!
According to Thy righteousness,
  let *Thy servant* be redeemed
  and the wicked be brought to an end.

For I have understood that *it is Thou*
  who dost establish the path of whomsoever Thou choosest;
Thou dost hedge him in with *true* discernment
  that he may not sin against Thee,
and that his humility *may bear fruit*
  through Thy chastisement.
Thou dost purify his heart in *Thy trials.*
Preserve Thy servant, *O God*, lest he sin against Thee,
  or stagger aside from any word of Thy will.
Strengthen the *loins of Thy servant*
  that he may resist the spirits *of falsehood,*
that he may walk in all that Thou lovest,
  and despise all that Thou loathest,
  that he may do that which is good in Thine eyes.
Destroy their *dominion* in my bowels,
  for *within* Thy servant is a spirit of *flesh.*

Hymn 3

. . . All these things *Thou didst establish in Thy wisdom.*
Thou didst appoint all Thy works
  before ever creating them:
the host of Thy spirits
  and the Congregation *of Thy Holy Ones,*
the heavens and all their hosts
  and the earth and all it brings forth.
In the seas and deeps . . .
  . . . an everlasting task;
for Thou hast established them from before eternity.

. . . and they shall recount Thy glory
  throughout all Thy dominion
For Thou hast shown them that
  which they had not *seen*

by removing all ancient things
    and creating new ones,
by breaking asunder things anciently established,
    and raising up the things of eternity.
For *Thou art from the beginning*
    and shalt endure for ages without end.
And Thou hast *appointed* all these things
    in the mysteries of Thy wisdom
    to make known Thy glory *to all.*

But what is the spirit of flesh
    that it should understand all this,
and that it should comprehend
    the great *design of Thy wisdom*?
What is he that is born of woman
    in the midst of all Thy terrible *works*?
He is but an edifice of dust,
    and a thing kneaded with water,
whose beginning *is sinful iniquity,*
    and shameful nakedness,
    and a fount of uncleanness,
and over whom a spirit of straying rules.
If he is wicked he shall become *a sign for* ever,
    and a wonder to every generation,
    and an object of horror to all flesh.

By Thy goodness alone is man righteous,
    and with Thy many mercies *Thou strengthenest him.*
Thou wilt adorn him with Thy splendour
    and wilt *cause him to reign amid* many delights
    with everlasting peace and length of days.
For Thou hast spoken,
    and Thou wilt not take back Thy word.

And I, Thy servant,
    I know by the spirit which Thou hast given to me
    that Thy words are truth,
and that all Thy works are righteousness,
    and that Thou wilt not take back Thy word . . .

Hymn 4

Blessed art Thou, O Lord
   who hast given understanding
   to the heart of *Thy* servant
that he may understand all these things
. . . and resist *the works* of wickedness
   and bless justly all those who choose Thy will,
and that he may love all that Thou lovest
   and loathe all that Thou *hatest.*
Thou shalt instruct Thy servant
   . . . spirits of man
for Thou hast cast their lot according to the spirits
   between good and evil
   to accomplish their task.
And I know through the understanding
   which comes from Thee,
that in Thy goodwill towards man
   Thou hast increased *his inheritance* in Thy Holy Spirit
   and thus Thou hast drawn me near to understanding of Thee.
And the closer I approach,
   the more am I filled with zeal
   against all the workers of iniquity
   and the men of deceit.

For none of those who approach Thee
   rebels against Thy command,
nor do any of those who know Thee
   alter Thy words;
for Thou art righteous,
   and all Thine elect are truth.
Thou wilt blot out all injustice and wickedness for ever,
   and Thy righteousness shall be revealed
   before the eyes of all Thy creatures.

I know through Thy great goodness;
and with an oath I have undertaken
   never to sin against Thee,

nor to do anything evil in Thine eyes.
And thus do I bring into community
    all the men of my Council.

I will cause each man to draw near
    in accordance with his understanding,
and according to the greatness of his inheritance,
    so will I love him.
I will not honour an evil man,
    nor consider *the bribes of shame*;
I will *not* barter Thy truth for riches,
    nor one of Thy precepts for bribes.
But *I will* love *each man*
    according to his *speech*
and according as Thou removest him far from Thee,
    so will I hate him;
and none of those who have turned *from* Thy Covenant
    will I bring into the Council *of Thy truth.*

Hymn 5

I thank Thee, O Lord,
    as befits the greatness of Thy power
    and the multitude of Thy marvels for ever and ever.
Thou art a merciful God and rich in *favours,*
    pardoning those who repent of their sin
    and visiting the iniquity of the wicked.
Thou delightest in the free-will offering *of the righteous*
    but iniquity Thou hatest always.
Thou hast favoured me, Thy servant,
    with a spirit of knowledge,
that I may choose truth *and goodness*
    and loathe all the ways of iniquity.
And I have loved Thee freely
    and with all my heart;
contemplating the mysteries of Thy wisdom
    I have sought Thee.
For this is from Thy hand
    and *nothing is done* without *Thy will* . . .

I have loved Thee freely
   and with all my heart and soul
I have purified . . .
   that I might not turn aside from any of Thy commands.
I have clung to the Congregation . . .
   that I might not be separated from any of Thy laws.

I know through the understanding which comes from Thee
   that righteousness is not in a hand of flesh,
   that man *is not master of* his way
   and that it is not in mortals to direct their step.
I know that the inclination of every spirit
   is in Thy hand;
Thou didst establish *all* its *ways* before ever creating it,
   and how can any man change Thy words?
Thou alone didst *create* the just
   and establish him from the womb
   for the time of goodwill,
that he might hearken to Thy Covenant
   and walk in all Thy ways,
and that *Thou mightest show Thyself great* to him
   in the multitude of Thy mercies,
and enlarge his straitened soul to eternal salvation,
   to perpetual and unfailing peace.
Thou wilt raise up his glory
   from among flesh.

But the wicked Thou didst create
   for *the time* of Thy *wrath,*
Thou didst vow them from the womb
   to the Day of Massacre,
   for they walk in the way which is not good.
They have despised *Thy Covenant*
   and their souls have loathed Thy *truth;*
they have taken no delight in all Thy commandments
   and have chosen that which Thou hatest.

For according to the mysteries of Thy *wisdom,*
   Thou hast ordained them for great chastisements
   before the eyes of all Thy creatures,

that *for all* eternity
    they may serve as a sign *and a wonder*,
and that *all men* may know Thy glory
    and Thy tremendous power.

But what is flesh
    that it should understand *these things*?
    And how should *a creature of* dust direct his steps?
It is Thou who didst shape the spirit
    and establish its work *from the beginning*;
    the way of all the living proceeds from Thee.
I know that no riches equal Thy truth,
    and *have therefore desired*
    to enter the Council of Thy holiness.
I know that Thou hast chosen them before all others
    and that they shall serve Thee for ever.
Thou wilt *take no bribe for the deeds of iniquity*,
    nor ransom for the works of wickedness;
for Thou art a God of truth
    and *wilt destroy* all iniquity *for ever*,
and no *wickedness* shall exist before Thee.

. . . Because I know all these things
    my tongue shall utter a reply.
Bowing down and *confessing all* my transgressions,
    I will seek *Thy* spirit *of knowledge*;
cleaving to Thy spirit of *holiness*,
    I will hold fast to the truth of Thy Covenant,
that *I may serve* Thee in truth and wholeness of heart,
    and that I may love *Thy Name*.

Blessed art Thou, O Lord,
    Maker *of all things and mighty in* deeds:
    all things are Thy work!
Behold, Thou art pleased to favour *Thy servant*,
    and hast graced me with Thy spirit of mercy
    and *with the radiance* of Thy glory.
Thine, Thine is righteousness,
    for it is Thou who hast done all *these things*!

I know that Thou hast marked the spirit of the just,
  and therefore I have chosen to keep my hands clean
  in accordance with *Thy* will:
the soul of Thy servant *has loathed*
  every work of iniquity.
And I know that man is not righteous
  except through Thee,
and therefore I implore Thee
  by the spirit which Thou hast given *me*
  to perfect Thy *favours* to Thy servant *for ever*,
purifying me by Thy Holy Spirit,
  and drawing me near to Thee by Thy grace
  according to the abundance of Thy mercies
. . . *Grant me* the place *of Thy loving-kindness*
  which *Thou hast* chosen for them that love Thee
  and keep *Thy commandments*,
that they may stand in Thy presence *for* ever.
. . . Let no scourge *come* near him
  lest he stagger aside from the laws of Thy Covenant.
. . . I *know, O Lord,*
  that Thou art merciful and compassionate,
  long-suffering and *rich* in grace and truth,
  pardoning transgression *and sin.*
Thou repentest of *evil against them that love Thee*
  and keep *Thy* commandments,
that return to Thee with faith
  and wholeness of heart
. . . to serve Thee
  and to do that which is good in Thine eyes.
Reject not the face of Thy servant

Hymn 6

. . . Thou art long-suffering in Thy judgements
  and righteous in all Thy deeds.

By Thy wisdom *all things exist from* eternity,
  and before creating them Thou knewest their works
  for ever and ever.

Nothing is done *without Thee*
    and nothing is known unless Thou desire it.

Thou hast created all the spirits
    and hast established a statute and law
    for all their works.
Thou hast spread the heavens for Thy glory
    and hast *appointed* all *their hosts*
    according to Thy will;
the mighty winds according to their laws
    before they became angels *of holiness*
    . . . and eternal spirits in their dominions;
the heavenly lights to their mysteries,
    the stars to their paths,
the clouds to their tasks,
    the thunderbolts and lightnings to their duty,
and the perfect treasuries of snow and hail
    to their purposes,
. . . to their mysteries.

Thou hast created the earth by Thy power
    and the seas and deeps *by Thy might.*
Thou hast fashioned *all* their *inhabitants*
    according to Thy wisdom,
    and hast appointed all that is in them
    according to Thy will.

And to the spirit of man
    which Thou hast formed in the world,
Thou hast given dominion over the works of Thy hands
    for everlasting days and unending generations.
. . . in their ages
Thou hast allotted to them tasks
    during all their generations,
and judgement in their appointed seasons
    according to the rule *of the two spirits.*
For Thou hast established their ways
    for ever and ever,
and hast ordained from eternity

their visitation for reward and chastisements;
Thou hast allotted it to all their seed
   for eternal generations and everlasting years . . .
In the wisdom of Thy knowledge
   Thou didst establish their destiny before ever they were.
All things *exist* according to *Thy will*
   and without Thee nothing is done.

These things I know
   by the wisdom which comes from Thee,
for Thou hast unstopped my ears
   to marvellous mysteries.

And yet I, a shape of clay
   kneaded in water,
a ground of shame
   and a source of pollution,
a melting-pot of wickedness
   and an edifice of sin,
a straying and perverted spirit
   of no understanding,
   fearful of righteous judgements,
what can I say that is not foreknown,
   and what can I utter that is not foretold?
All things are graven before Thee
   on a written Reminder
   for everlasting ages,
and for the numbered cycles
   of the eternal years
   in all their seasons;
they are not hidden or absent from Thee.

What shall a man say
   concerning his sin?
And how shall he plead
   concerning his iniquities?
And how shall he reply
   to righteous judgement?
For Thine, O God of knowledge,

like the sound of the roaring of many waters
    so have *all* the deceivers thundered against me;
    all their thoughts were devilish *schemings.*

They have cast towards the Pit the life of the man
    whose mouth Thou hast confirmed,
and into whose heart
    Thou hast put teaching and understanding,
that he might open a fountain of knowledge
    to all men of insight.
They have exchanged them for lips of uncircumcision,
    and for the foreign tongue
of a people without understanding,
    that they might come to ruin in their straying.

Hymn 7

I thank Thee, O Lord,
    for Thou hast placed my soul
    in the bundle of the living,
and hast hedged me about
    against all the snares of the Pit.

Violent men have sought after my life
    because I have clung to Thy Covenant.
For they, an assembly of deceit,
    and a horde of Belial,
know not that my stand
    is maintained by Thee,
and that in Thy mercy Thou wilt save my soul
    since my steps proceed from Thee.

From Thee it is
    that they assail my life,
that Thou mayest be glorified
    by the judgement of the wicked,
and manifest Thy might through me
    in the presence of the sons of men;
for it is by Thy mercy that I stand.

And I said, Mighty men
    have pitched their camps against me,
and have encompassed me
    with all their weapons of war.
They have let fly arrows
    against which there is no cure,
and the flame of their javelins
    is like a consuming fire among trees.
The clamour of their shouting
    is like the bellowing of many waters,
like a storm of destruction
    devouring a multitude of men;
as their waves rear up,
    Naught and Vanity spout upward to the stars.
But although my heart melted like water,
    my soul held fast to Thy Covenant,
and the net which they spread for me
    has taken their own foot;
they have themselves fallen
    into the snares which they laid for my life.
But my foot remains upon level ground;
    apart from their assembly I will bless Thy Name.

Hymn 8

I thank Thee, O Lord,
    for Thou hast *fastened* Thine eye upon me.
Thou hast saved me from the zeal
    of lying interpreters,
and from the congregation of those
    who seek smooth things.
Thou hast redeemed the soul of the poor one
    whom they planned to destroy
    by spilling his blood because he served Thee.

Because *they knew not*
    that my steps were directed by Thee,
they made me an object of shame and derision
    in the mouth of all the seekers of falsehood.

'He shall not purify himself with water contained in a vessel' (The Damascus Document, page 111). Large limestone goblet for ritual use, produced on a lathe, from Qumran, 1st century CE

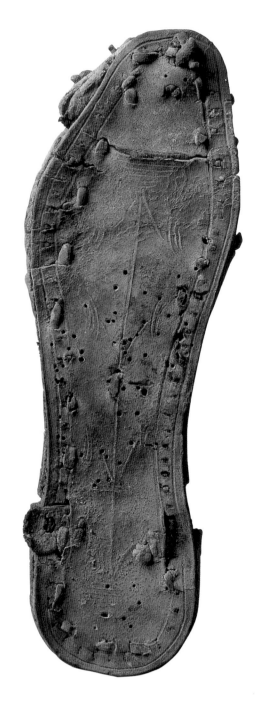

'No man shall walk in the field to do business on the Sabbath'
(The Damascus Document, page 111). Sandal from Qumran,
1st century BCE–1st century CE

But Thou, O my God, hast succoured
  the soul of the poor and the needy
    against one stronger than he;
Thou hast redeemed my soul
  from the hand of the mighty.
Thou hast not permitted their insults to dismay me
  so that I forsook Thy service
    for fear of the wickedness of the *ungodly*,
or bartered my steadfast heart for folly . . .

Hymn 9

. . . They caused *me* to be
  like a ship on the deeps of the *sea*,
and like a fortified city
  before *the aggressor*,
and like a woman in travail
  with her first-born child,
upon whose belly pangs have come
  and grievous pains,
filling with anguish her child-bearing crucible.

For the children have come to the throes of Death,
  and she labours in her pains who bears a man.
For amid the throes of Death
  she shall bring forth a man-child,
and amid the pains of Hell
  there shall spring from her child-bearing crucible
    a Marvellous Mighty Counsellor;
and a man shall be delivered from out of the throes.

When he is conceived
  all wombs shall quicken,
and the time of their delivery
  shall be in grievous pains;
they shall be appalled
  who are with child.
And when he is brought forth
  every pang shall come upon the child-bearing crucible.

And they, the conceivers of Vanity,
    shall be prey to terrible anguish;
the wombs of the Pit
    shall be prey to all the works of horror.
The foundations of the wall shall rock
    like a ship upon the face of the waters;
the heavens shall roar
    with a noise of roaring,
and those who dwell in the dust,
    as well as those who sail the seas,
    shall be appalled by the roaring of the waters.

All their wise men
    shall be like sailors on the deeps,
for all their wisdom shall be swallowed up
    in the midst of the howling seas.
As the Abysses boil
    above the fountains of the waters,
the towering waves and billows shall rage
    with the voice of their roaring;
and as they rage,
    Hell and Abaddon shall open
and all the flying arrows of the Pit
    shall send out their voice to the Abyss.

And the gates *of Hell* shall open
    on all the works of Vanity;
and the doors of the Pit shall close
    on the conceivers of wickedness;
and the everlasting bars shall be bolted
    on all the spirits of Naught.

Hymn 10

I thank Thee, O Lord,
    for Thou hast redeemed my soul from the Pit,
and from the hell of Abaddon
    Thou hast raised me up to everlasting height.

I walk on limitless level ground,
and I know there is hope for him
    whom Thou hast shaped from dust
    for the everlasting Council.
Thou hast cleansed a perverse spirit of great sin
    that it may stand with the host of the Holy Ones,
and that it may enter into community
    with the congregation of the Sons of Heaven.
Thou hast allotted to man an everlasting destiny
    amidst the spirits of knowledge,
that he may praise Thy Name in a common rejoicing
    and recount Thy marvels before all Thy works.

And yet I, a creature of clay,
    what am I?
Kneaded with water,
    what is my worth and my might?
For I have stood in the realm of wickedness
    and my lot was with the damned;
the soul of the poor one was carried away
    in the midst of great tribulation.
Miseries of torment dogged my steps
while all the snares of the Pit were opened
    and the lures of wickedness were set up
    and the nets of the damned were spread on the waters;
while all the arrows of the Pit
    flew out without cease,
    and, striking, left no hope;
while the rope beat down in judgement
    and a destiny of wrath fell upon the abandoned
    and a venting of fury upon the cunning.
It was a time of the wrath of all Belial
    and the bonds of death tightened without any escape.

The torrents of Belial shall reach
    to all sides of the world.
In all their channels
    a consuming fire shall destroy
    every tree, green and barren, on their banks;

unto the end of their courses
 it shall scourge with flames of fire,
and shall consume the foundations of the earth
 and the expanse of dry land.
The bases of the mountains shall blaze
 and the roots of the rocks shall turn
 to torrents of pitch;
it shall devour as far as the great Abyss.

The torrents of Belial shall break into Abaddon,
 and the deeps of the Abyss shall groan
 amid the roar of heaving mud.
The land shall cry out because of the calamity
 fallen upon the world,
 and all its deeps shall howl.
And all those upon it shall rave
 and shall perish amid the great misfortune.
For God shall sound His mighty voice,
 and His holy abode shall thunder
 with the truth of His glory.
The heavenly hosts shall cry out
 and the world's foundations
 shall stagger and sway.
The war of the heavenly warriors shall scourge the earth;
 and it shall not end before the appointed destruction
 which shall be for ever and without compare.

Hymn 11

I thank Thee, O Lord,
 for Thou art as a fortified wall to me,
 and as an iron bar against all destroyers

. . . Thou hast set my feet upon rock . . .
 that I may walk in the way of eternity
and in the paths which Thou hast chosen . . .

Hymn 12

I thank Thee, O Lord,
   for Thou hast illumined my face by Thy Covenant . . .

I seek Thee,
   and sure as the dawn
   Thou appearest as *perfect Light* to me.
Teachers of lies *have smoothed* Thy people *with words,*
   and *false prophets* have led them astray;
they perish without understanding
   for their works are in folly.
For I am despised by them
   and they have no esteem for me
   that Thou mayest manifest Thy might through me.
They have banished me from my land like a bird from its nest;
all my friends and brethren are driven far from me
   and hold me for a broken vessel.

And they, teachers of lies and seers of falsehood,
   have schemed against me a devilish scheme,
to exchange the Law engraved on my heart by Thee
   for the smooth things which they speak to Thy people.
And they withhold from the thirsty the drink of Knowledge,
   and assuage their thirst with vinegar,
that they may gaze on their straying,
   on their folly concerning their feast-days,
   on their fall into their snares.

But Thou, O God,
   dost despise all Belial's designs;
it is Thy purpose that shall be done
   and the design of Thy heart
   that shall be established for ever.
As for them, they dissemble,
   they plan devilish schemes.
They seek Thee with a double heart
   and are not confirmed in Thy truth.

A root bearing poisoned and bitter fruit
    is in their designs;
they walk in stubbornness of heart
    and seek Thee among idols,
and they set before themselves
    the stumbling-block of their sin.
They come to inquire of Thee
    from the mouth of lying prophets deceived by error
who speak *with strange* lips to Thy people,
    and an alien tongue,
that they may cunningly turn
    all their works to folly.

For *they hearken* not *to* Thy *voice*,
    nor do they give ear to Thy word;
of the vision of knowledge they say, 'It is unsure',
    and of the way of Thy heart, 'It is not the way'.
But Thou, O God, wilt reply to them,
chastising them in Thy might
    because of their idols
    and because of the multitude of their sins,
that they who have turned aside from Thy Covenant
    may be caught in their own designs.
Thou wilt destroy in Judgement
    all men of lies,
    and there shall be no more seers of error;
for in Thy works is no folly,
    no guile in the design of Thy heart.
But those who please Thee
    shall stand before Thee for ever;
those who walk in the way of Thy heart
    shall be established for evermore.

Clinging to Thee, I will stand.
I will rise against those who despise me
    and my hand shall be turned
    against those who deride me;
for they have no esteem for me
    that *Thou mayest* manifest Thy might through me.

Thou hast revealed Thyself to me in Thy power
    as perfect Light,
    and Thou hast not covered my face with shame.
All those who are gathered in Thy Covenant
    inquire of me,
and they hearken to me who walk in the way of Thy heart,
    who array themselves for Thee
    in the Council of the holy.

Thou wilt cause their law to endure for ever
    and truth to go forward unhindered,
and Thou wilt not allow them to be led astray
    by the hand of the damned
    when they plot against them.
Thou wilt put the fear of them into Thy people
    and wilt make of them a hammer
    to all the peoples of the lands,
that at the Judgement they may cut off
    all those who transgress Thy word.

Through me Thou hast illumined
    the face of the Congregation
    and hast shown Thine infinite power.
For Thou hast given me knowledge
    through Thy marvellous mysteries,
and hast shown Thyself mighty within me
    in the midst of Thy marvellous Council.
Thou hast done wonders before the Congregation
    for the sake of Thy glory,
that they may make known Thy mighty deeds to all the living.

But what is flesh to be worthy of this?
What is a creature of clay
    for such great marvels to be done,
whereas he is in iniquity from the womb
    and in guilty unfaithfulness until his old age?
Righteousness, I know, is not of man,
    nor is perfection of way of the son of man:
to the Most High God belong all righteous deeds.

The way of man is not established
    except by the spirit which God created for him
    to make perfect a way for the children of men,
that all His creatures may know
    the might of His power,
and the abundance of His mercies
    towards all the sons of His grace.

As for me, shaking and trembling seize me
    and all my bones are broken;
my heart dissolves like wax before fire
    and my knees are like water
    pouring down a steep place.
For I remember my sins
    and the unfaithfulness of my fathers.
When the wicked rose against Thy Covenant
    and the damned against Thy word,
I said in my sinfulness,
    'I am forsaken by Thy Covenant.'
But calling to mind the might of Thy hand
    and the greatness of Thy compassion,
I rose and stood,
    and my spirit was established
    in face of the scourge.

I lean on Thy grace
    and on the multitude of Thy mercies,
for Thou wilt pardon iniquity,
    and through Thy righteousness
    Thou wilt purify man of his sin.
Not for his sake wilt Thou do it,
    but for the sake of Thy glory.
For Thou hast created the just and the wicked . . .

Hymn 13

I thank Thee, O Lord,
   for Thou hast not abandoned me
   whilst I sojourned among a people *burdened with sin.*

Thou hast not judged me
   according to my guilt,
   nor hast Thou abandoned me
   because of the designs of my inclination;
but Thou hast saved my life from the Pit.
Thou hast brought *Thy servant deliverance*
   in the midst of lions destined for the guilty,
and of lionesses which crush the bones of the mighty
   and drink the blood of the brave.

Thou hast caused me to dwell with the many fishers
   who spread a net upon the face of the waters,
   and with the hunters of the children of iniquity;
Thou hast established me there for justice.
Thou hast confirmed the counsel of truth in my heart
   and the waters of the Covenant for those who seek it.
Thou hast closed up the mouth of the young lions
   whose teeth are like a sword,
   and whose great teeth are like a pointed spear,
   like the venom of dragons.
All their design is for robbery
   and they have lain in wait;
but they have not opened their mouth against me.

For Thou, O God, hast sheltered me
   from the children of men,
and hast hidden Thy Law *within me*
   against the time when Thou shouldst reveal
   Thy salvation to me.
For Thou hast not forsaken me
   in my soul's distress,

and Thou hast heard my cry
    in the bitterness of my soul;
and when I groaned,
    Thou didst consider my sorrowful complaint.
Thou hast preserved the soul of the poor one
    in the den of lions
    which sharpened their tongue like a sword.
Thou hast closed up their teeth, O God,
    lest they rend the soul of the poor and needy.
Thou hast made their tongue go back
    like a sword to its scabbard
    lest the soul of Thy servant *be blotted out.*

Thou hast dealt wondrously with the poor one
    to manifest Thy might within me
    in the presence of the sons of men.
Thou hast placed him in the melting-pot,
    like gold in the fire,
and like silver refined
    in the melting-pot of the smelters,
    to be purified seven times.
The wicked and fierce have stormed against me
    with their afflictions;
    they have pounded my soul all day.
But Thou, O my God,
    hast changed the tempest to a breeze;
Thou hast delivered the soul of the poor one
    like *a bird from the net*
    and like prey from the mouth of lions.

Hymn 14

Blessed art Thou, O Lord,
    for Thou hast not abandoned the fatherless
    or despised the poor.
For Thy might *is boundless*
    and Thy glory beyond measure
    and wonderful Heroes minister to Thee;
yet *hast Thou done marvels* among the humble

. . . Thou hast unstopped my ears
    to the correction of those who reprove with justice
. . . *Thou hast saved me* from the congregation of *vanity*
    and from the assembly of violence;
Thou hast brought me into the Council of . . .
    and hast purified me of sin.
And I know there is hope
    for those who turn from transgression
    and for those who abandon sin
. . . and to walk without wickedness
    in the way of Thy heart.
I am consoled for the roaring of the peoples,
    and for the tumult of kingdoms when they assemble;
for in a little while, I know,
      Thou wilt raise up survivors among Thy people
      and a remnant within Thine inheritance.
Thou wilt purify and cleanse them of their sin
    for all their deeds are in Thy truth.
Thou wilt judge them in Thy great loving-kindness
    and in the multitude of Thy mercies
    and in the abundance of Thy pardon,
    teaching them according to Thy word;
and Thou wilt establish them in Thy Council
    according to the uprightness of Thy truth.

Thou wilt do these things for Thy glory
    and for Thine own sake,
to *magnify* the Law and *the truth*
    and to enlighten the members of Thy Council
    in the midst of the sons of men,
that they may recount Thy marvels
    for everlasting generations
    and *meditate* unceasingly upon Thy mighty deeds.
All the nations shall acknowledge Thy truth,
    and all the people Thy glory.

For Thou wilt bring Thy glorious *salvation*
    to all the men of Thy Council,
    to those who share a common lot

with the Angels of the Face.
And among them shall be no mediator to *invoke Thee*,
    and no messenger *to make* reply;
for . . .
They shall reply according to Thy glorious word
    and shall be Thy princes in the company *of the Angels.*

They shall send out a bud *for ever*
    like a flower *of the fields,*
and shall cause a shoot to grow
    into the boughs of an everlasting Plant.
It shall cover the whole *earth* with its shadow
    and its crown shall reach to the *clouds*;
its roots shall go down to the Abyss
    and all the rivers of Eden shall water its branches.
. . . A source of light
    shall become an eternal ever-flowing fountain,
and in its bright flames
    all the *sons of iniquity* shall be consumed;
it shall be a fire to devour all sinful men
    in utter destruction.

They who bore the yoke of my testimony
    have been led astray *by teachers of lies,*
    and have rebelled against the service of righteousness.
Whereas Thou, O my God, didst command them
    to mend their ways
by walking in the way of *holiness,*
    where no man goes who is uncircumcised
    or unclean or violent,
they have staggered aside from the way of Thy heart
    and languish in *great* wretchedness.
A counsel of Belial is in their heart
    and in accordance with their wicked design
    they wallow in sin.

I am as a sailor in a ship
    amid furious seas;
their waves and all their billows

roar against me.
There is no calm in the whirlwind
    that I may restore my soul,
no path that I may straighten my way
    on the face of the waters.
The deeps resound to my groaning
    and *my soul has journeyed* to the gates of death.

But I shall be as one who enters a fortified city,
    as one who seeks refuge behind a high wall
    until deliverance comes;
    I will *lean on* Thy truth, O my God.
For Thou wilt set the foundation on rock
    and the framework by the measuring-cord of justice;
and the tried stones *Thou wilt lay*
    by the plumb-line *of truth*,
to *build* a mighty *wall* which shall not sway;
    and no man entering there shall stagger.

For no enemy shall ever invade *it*
    since its doors shall be doors of protection
    through which no man shall pass;
and its bars shall be firm
    and no man shall break them.
No rabble shall enter in with their weapons of war
    until all the *arrows* of the war of wickedness
    have come to an end.

And then at the time of Judgement
    the Sword of God shall hasten,
and all the sons of His truth shall awake
    to *overthrow* wickedness;
all the sons of iniquity shall be no more.
The Hero shall bend his bow;
the fortress shall open on to endless space
and the everlasting gates shall send out weapons of war.
They shall be mighty
    from end to end *of the earth*
and there shall be no escape

for the guilty of heart *in their battle*;
they shall be utterly trampled down
    without any *remnant.*
There shall be no hope
    in the greatness *of their might,*
      no refuge for the mighty warriors;
for *the battle shall be* to the Most High God . . .
Hoist a banner,
    O you who lie in the dust!
O bodies gnawed by worms,
    raise up an ensign for *the destruction of wickedness*!
The sinful shall be destroyed
    in the battles against the ungodly.

The scourging flood when it advances
    shall not invade the stronghold . . .
As for me, I am dumb . . .
my arm is torn from its shoulder
    and my foot has sunk into the mire.
My eyes are closed by the spectacle of evil,
    and my ears by the crying of blood.
My heart is dismayed by the mischievous design,
    for Belial is manifest in their evil inclination.
All the foundations of my edifice totter
    and my bones are pulled out of joint;
my bowels heave like a ship in a violent tempest
    and my heart is utterly distressed.
A whirlwind engulfs me
    because of the mischief of their sin.

Hymn 15

I thank Thee, O Lord,
    for Thou hast upheld me by Thy strength.
Thou hast shed Thy Holy Spirit upon me
    that I may not stumble.

Thou hast strengthened me
    before the battles of wickedness,

'With this oil they shall light the lamps' (The Temple Scroll, page 149).
Herodian pottery lamp with a palm-fibre wick, from Qumran,
1st century BCE–1st century CE

'David son of Jesse was wise and brilliant like the light of the sun; he was a scribe, intelligent and perfect in all his ways before God and men' (An Account of David's Poems, page 235). Pottery inkwell from Qumran, late 1st century BCE–early 1st century CE

and during all their disasters
    Thou hast not permitted that fear
    should cause me to desert Thy Covenant.
Thou hast made me like a strong tower, a high wall,
    and hast established my edifice upon rock;
eternal foundations
    serve for my ground,
and all my ramparts are a tried wall
    which shall not sway.

Thou hast placed me, O my God,
    among the branches of the Council of Holiness;
Thou hast *established my mouth* in Thy Covenant,
    and my tongue is like that of Thy disciples;
    whereas the spirit of disaster is without a mouth
    and all the sons of iniquity without a reply;
    for the lying lips shall be dumb.
For Thou wilt condemn in Judgement
    all those who assail me,
distinguishing through me
    between the just and the wicked.
For Thou knowest the whole intent of a creature,
    Thou discernest every reply,
and Thou hast established my heart
    on Thy teaching and truth,
directing my steps into the paths of righteousness
    that I may walk before Thee
    in the land *of the living,*
into paths of glory and *infinite* peace
    which shall *never* end.
For Thou knowest the inclination of Thy servant,
that I have not relied *upon the works of my hands*
    to raise up *my heart,*
nor have I sought refuge
    in my own strength.
I have no fleshly refuge,
and Thy servant has no righteous deeds
    to deliver him from the *Pit of no* forgiveness.
But I lean on the *abundance of Thy mercies*

and hope *for the greatness* of Thy grace,
that Thou wilt bring *salvation* to flower
    and the branch to growth,
providing refuge in Thy strength
    and raising up my heart.

For in Thy righteousness
    Thou hast appointed me for Thy Covenant,
and I have clung to Thy truth
    and *gone forward in Thy ways.*

Thou hast made me a father to the sons of grace,
    and as a foster-father to men of marvel;
they have opened their mouths like little babes . . .
    like a child playing in the lap of its nurse.
Thou hast lifted my horn above those who insult me,
    and those who attack me
    sway like the boughs of a tree;
my enemies are like chaff before the wind,
    and my dominion is over the sons *of iniquity,*
For Thou hast succoured my soul, O my God,
    and hast lifted my horn on high.
And I shall shine in a seven-fold light
    in *the Council appointed by* Thee for Thy glory;
for Thou art an everlasting heavenly light to me
    and wilt establish my feet
    upon level ground for ever.

Hymn 16

I *thank Thee, O Lord,*
    for Thou hast enlightened me through Thy truth.
In Thy marvellous mysteries,
and in Thy loving-kindness to a man *of vanity,*
and in the greatness of Thy mercy to a perverse heart
    Thou hast granted me knowledge.

Who is like Thee among the gods, O Lord,
    and who is according to Thy truth?

Who, when he is judged,
    shall be righteous before Thee?
For no spirit can reply to Thy rebuke
    nor can any withstand Thy wrath.

Yet Thou bringest all the sons of Thy truth
    in forgiveness before Thee,
to cleanse them of their faults
    through Thy great goodness,
and to establish them before Thee
    through the multitude of Thy mercies
    for ever and ever.

For Thou art an eternal God;
    all Thy ways are determined for ever *and ever*
    and there is none other beside Thee.
And what is a man of Naught and Vanity
    that he should understand Thy marvellous mighty deeds?

Hymn 17

I thank Thee, O God,
    for Thou hast not cast my lot
    in the congregation of Vanity,
    nor hast Thou placed my decree
    in the council of the cunning.
Thou hast called me to Thy grace
    and to *Thy* forgiveness Thou hast brought me,
and, by the multitude of Thy mercies,
    to all judgements of *righteousness.*
As for me, I am an unclean *man,*
    and from the womb of her who conceived me
I am an unclean man,
    and from the womb of her who has conceived me
I am in sinful guilt,
    and from the breast of my mother in injustice,
    and in the bosom *of my nurse* in great impurity.
And from my youth I am in blood,
    and until *my old age in the iniquity of the flesh.*

But Thou, O my God,
Thou hast established my feet in the way of Thy heart,
 and hast opened my ears to *Thy wonderful* tidings,
 and my heart to understand Thy truth . . .

Hymn 18

I *thank Thee, O Lord,*
 for Thou hast placed me beside a fountain of streams
 in an arid land,
and close to a spring of waters
 in a dry land,
and beside a watered garden
 in a wilderness.

For Thou didst set a plantation
 of cypress, pine, and cedar for Thy glory,
trees of life beside a mysterious fountain
 hidden among the trees by the water,
and they put out a shoot
 of the everlasting Plant.
But before they did so, they took root
 and sent out their roots to the watercourse
that its stem might be open to the living waters
 and be one with the everlasting spring.

And all *the beasts* of the forest
 fed on its leafy boughs;
its stem was trodden by all who passed on the way
 and its branches by all the birds.
And all the *trees* by the water rose above it
 for they grew in their plantation;
but they sent out no root to the watercourse.

And the bud of the shoot of holiness
 of the Plant of truth
 was hidden and was not esteemed;
and being unperceived,
 its mystery was sealed.

Thou didst hedge in its fruit, *O God*,
    with the mystery of mighty Heroes
    and of spirits of holiness
    and of the whirling flame of fire.
No *man shall approach* the well-spring of life
or drink the waters of holiness
    with the everlasting trees,
    or bear fruit with *the Plant* of heaven,
who seeing has not discerned,
    and considering has not believed
    in the fountain of life,
who has turned *his hand against* the everlasting *bud*.

And I was despised by tumultuous rivers
    for they cast up their slime upon me.

But Thou, O my God, hast put into my mouth
    as it were rain for all *those who thirst*
    and a fount of living waters which shall not fail.
When they are opened they shall not run dry;
they shall be a torrent *overflowing its banks*
    and like the *bottomless* seas.
They shall suddenly gush forth
    which were hidden in secret,
and shall be like the waters of the Flood
    to every tree, both the green and the barren;
    to every beast and bird *they shall be an abyss*.
The trees shall sink like lead in the mighty waters,
    fire *shall burn among them*
and they shall be dried up;
but the fruitful Plant
    by the everlasting *spring*
shall be an Eden of glory
    bearing fruits *of life*.

By my hand Thou hast opened for them
    a well-spring and ditches,
that all their channels may be laid out
    according to a certain measuring-cord,

and the planting of their trees
   according to the plumb-line of the sun,
that *their boughs may become*
   a beautiful Branch of glory.
When I lift my hand to dig its ditches
   its roots shall run deep into hardest rock
   and its stem . . . in the earth;
   in the season of heat it shall keep its strength.
But if I take away my hand
   it shall be like a thistle *in the wilderness*;
its stem shall be like nettles in a salty land,
   and thistles and thorns shall grow from its ditches,
   and brambles and briars.—
Its border *trees* shall be like the wild grapevine
   whose foliage withers before the heat,
   and its stem shall not be open to *the spring*.

Behold, I am carried away with the sick;
   I am acquainted with scourges.
I am forsaken in *my sorrow* . . .
   and without any strength.
For my sore breaks out in bitter pains
   and in incurable sickness impossible to stay;
my heart laments within me
   as in those who go down to Hell.
My spirit is imprisoned with the dead
   for *my life* has reached the Pit;
my soul languishes *within me*
   day and night without rest.

My wound breaks out like burning fire
   shut up in *my bones,*
whose flames devour me for days on end,
   diminishing my strength for times on end
   and destroying my flesh for seasons on end.
The pains fly out *towards me*
   and my soul within me languishes even to death.
My strength has gone from my body
   and my heart runs out like water;

my flesh is dissolved like wax
    and the strength of my loins is turned to fear.

My arm is torn from its socket
    and I can lift my hand *no more*;
My *foot* is held by fetters
    and my knees slide like water;
    I can no longer walk.
I cannot step forward lightly,
    for my legs and arms are bound by shackles
    which cause me to stumble.
The tongue has gone back which Thou didst make
    marvellously mighty within my mouth;
    it can no longer give voice.
I have no word for my disciples
    to revive the spirit of those who stumble
    and to speak words of support to the weary.
My circumcised lips are dumb . . .

. . . *For* the throes of death *encompass me*
    and Hell is upon my bed;
my couch utters a lamentation
    and my pallet the sound of a complaint.
My eyes are like fire in the furnace
    and my tears like rivers of water;
my eyes grow dim with waiting,
    for my salvation is far from me
    and my life is apart from me.

But behold,
    from desolation to ruin,
    and from the pain to the sore,
    and from the travail to the throes,
my soul meditates on Thy marvellous works.
In Thy mercies Thou hast not cast me aside;
season by season, my soul shall delight
    in the abundance of mercy.
I will reply to him who slanders me
    and I will rebuke my oppressor;

I will declare his sentence unjust
    and declare Thy judgement righteous.

For I know by Thy truth,
    and I choose Thy judgement upon me:
I delight in my scourges
    for I hope for Thy loving-kindness.
Thou hast put a supplication
    in the mouth of Thy servant
and Thou hast not threatened my life
    nor rejected my peace.
Thou hast not failed my expectation,
    but hast upheld my spirit in face of the scourge.

For it is Thou who hast founded my spirit
    and Thou knowest my intent;
    in my distress Thou hast comforted me.
I delight in forgiveness,
    and am consoled for the former transgression;
for I know there is hope in Thy grace
    and expectation in Thy great power.
For no man can be just in Thy judgement
    or *righteous in* Thy trial.
Though one man be more just than another,
    one person *more* wise *than another,*
one mortal more glorious
    than another creature *of clay,*
    yet is there no power to compare with Thy might.
There is no *bound* to Thy glory,
    and to Thy wisdom, no measure . . .

. . . and my oppressor shall *not* prevail against me.
I will be a stumbling-block to *those who swallow me up,*
    and a snare to all those who battle against me;
I will be for my enemies a cause of shame,
    and a cause of disgrace
    to those who murmur against me.
For Thou, O my God . . .
    Thou wilt plead my cause;

for it is according to the mystery of Thy wisdom
    that Thou hast rebuked me.

Thou wilt conceal the truth until *its* time,
    and righteousness until its appointed moment.
Thy rebuke shall become my joy and gladness,
    and my scourges shall turn to *eternal* healing
    and everlasting *peace.*
The scorn of my enemies shall become a crown of glory,
    and my stumbling shall change to everlasting might.

For in Thy . . .
    and my light shall shine forth in Thy glory.
For as a light from out of the darkness,
    so wilt Thou enlighten me.
Thou wilt bring healing to my wound,
    and marvellous might in place of my stumbling,
    and everlasting space to my straitened soul.
For Thou art my refuge, my high mountain,
    my stout rock and my fortress;
in Thee will I shelter
    from all the *designs of ungodliness*
for Thou wilt succour me with eternal deliverance.

For Thou hast known me from the time of my father,
    and hast chosen me from the womb.
From the belly of my mother
    Thou hast dealt kindly with me,
and from the breast of her who conceived me
    have Thy mercies been with me.
Thy grace was with me in the lap of her who reared me,
    and from my youth Thou hast illumined me
    with the wisdom of Thy judgement.

Thou hast upheld me with certain truth;
    Thou hast delighted me with Thy Holy Spirit
    and *hast opened my heart* till this day.
Thy just rebuke accompanies my *faults*
    and Thy safeguarding peace delivers my soul.

The abundance of Thy forgiveness is with my steps
   and infinite mercy accompanies Thy judgement of me.
Until I am old Thou wilt care for me;
   for my father knew me not
   and my mother abandoned me to Thee.
For Thou art a father
   to all *the sons* of Thy truth,
and as a woman who tenderly loves her babe,
   so dost Thou rejoice in them;
and as a foster-father bearing a child in his lap
   so carest Thou for all Thy creatures.

Hymn 19

I thank Thee, O Lord

. . . and nothing exists except by Thy will;
none can consider *Thy deep secrets*
   or contemplate Thy *mysteries*.
What then is man that is earth,
   that is shaped *from clay* and returns to the dust,
that Thou shouldst give him to understand such marvels
   and make known to him the counsel of *Thy truth*?

Clay and dust that I am,
   what can I devise unless Thou wish it,
   and what contrive unless Thou desire it?
What strength shall I have
   unless Thou keep me upright,
and how shall I understand
   unless by the spirit which Thou hast shaped for me?
What can I say unless Thou open my mouth
   and how can I answer unless Thou enlighten me?
Behold, Thou art Prince of gods
   and King of majesties,
Lord of all spirits,
   and Ruler of all creatures;
nothing is done without Thee,
   and nothing is known without Thy will.

Beside Thee there is nothing,
    and nothing can compare with Thee in strength;
in the presence of Thy glory there is nothing,
    and Thy might is without price.

Who among Thy great and marvellous creatures
    can stand in the presence of Thy glory?
    How then can he who returns to his dust?
For Thy glory's sake alone hast Thou made all these things.

Hymn 20

Blessed art Thou, O Lord,
    God of mercy *and abundant* grace,
for Thou hast made known *Thy wisdom to me*
    that I should recount Thy marvellous deeds,
    keeping silence neither by day nor *by night!*

For I have trusted in Thy grace.
In Thy great goodness,
    and in *the multitude of Thy mercies*

. . . For I have leaned on Thy truth

. . . *And unless* Thou rebuke,
    there is no stumbling;
unless Thou foreknow it,
    there is no scourge;
    nothing is done without Thy *will.*

I will cling to Thy ways
    according to my knowledge *of Thy* truth;
contemplating Thy glory
    I will recount Thy wonderful works,
and understanding *Thy goodness*
    I will lean on the multitude of Thy mercies
    and hope for Thy forgiveness.

For Thou Thyself hast shaped *my spirit*
    and established me *according to Thy will;*

and Thou hast not placed my support in gain,
   nor does my *heart delight in riches*;
   Thou hast given me no fleshly refuge.
The might of warriors *rests* on abundant delights,
   and on plenty of corn and wine and oil;
   they pride themselves in possessions and wealth.
But the righteous is like a green *tree*
   beside streams of water,
   bringing forth leaves and multiplying its branches;
for *Thou hast chosen them*
   from among the children of men
   that they may all grow fat from the land.

Thou wilt give to the children of Thy truth
   unending joy and everlasting *gladness*,
and according to the measure of their knowledge,
   so shall they be honoured one more than another.

And likewise for the son of man . . .
   Thou wilt increase his portion
   in the knowledge of Thy truth,
and according to the measure of his knowledge,
   so shall he be honoured . . .
For the soul of Thy servant has loathed *riches* and gain,
   and he has not *desired* exquisite delights.
My heart rejoices in Thy Covenant
   and Thy truth delights my soul.
I shall flower *like the lily*
   and my heart shall be open to the everlasting fountain;
   my support shall be in the might from on high.

. . . My heart is stricken with terror,
   and my loins with trembling;
my groaning goes down to the Abyss,
   and is shut up in the chambers of Hell.
I am greatly afraid when I hear of Thy judgement
   of the mighty Heroes,
and of Thy trial of the host
   of Thy Holy Ones . . .

Hymn 21

I thank Thee, my God,
   for Thou hast dealt wondrously to dust,
   and mightily towards a creature of clay!
I thank Thee, I thank Thee!

What am I, that Thou shouldst *teach* me
   the counsel of Thy truth,
and give me understanding
   of Thy marvellous works;
that Thou shouldst lay hymns of thanksgiving
   within my mouth
   and *praise* upon my tongue,
and that of my circumcised lips
   Thou shouldst make a seat of rejoicing?
I will sing Thy mercies,
   and on Thy might I will meditate all day long.
I will bless Thy Name evermore.
I will declare Thy glory in the midst of the sons of men
   and my soul shall delight in Thy great goodness.

I know that Thy word is truth,
   and that righteousness is in Thy hand;
that all knowledge is in Thy purpose,
   and that all power is in Thy might,
   and that every glory is Thine.
In Thy wrath are all chastisements,
   but in Thy goodness is much forgiveness
   and Thy mercy is towards the sons of Thy goodwill.
For Thou hast made known to them
   the counsel of Thy truth,
and hast taught them Thy marvellous mysteries.

For the sake of Thy glory
   Thou hast purified man of sin
that he may be made holy for Thee,
   with no abominable uncleanness

and no guilty wickedness;
that he may be one *with* the children of Thy truth
    and partake of the lot of Thy Holy Ones;
that bodies gnawed by worms may be raised from the dust
    to the counsel *of Thy truth,*
and that the perverse spirit may be lifted
    to the understanding *which comes from Thee;*
that he may stand before Thee
    with the everlasting host
    and with *Thy* spirits *of holiness,*
to be renewed together with all the living
    and to rejoice together with them that know.

Hymn 22

I thank Thee, my God!
I praise Thee, my Rock!

. . . For Thou hast made known to me the counsel of Thy truth
    and hast taught me Thy marvellous mysteries;

and hast revealed Thy *wonders* to me.
I have beheld Thy marvels *towards the children* of grace,
    and I know *that* righteousness is Thine,
that in Thy mercies there is *hope for me,*
    but without Thy grace *destruction* without end.
But a fountain of bitter mourning opens for me,
    and my tears fall down.
Distress is not hidden from my eyes
    when I think of the evil inclinations of man,
of his return *to dust,*
    I understand and observe sin and the sorrow of guilt.
They enter my heart and reach into my bones . . .

I will groan with the zither of lamentation
    in all grief-stricken mourning and bitter complaint
until iniquity and *wickedness* are consumed
    and the disease-bringing scourge is no more.
Then will I play on the zither of deliverance

and the harp of joy,
on the tabors of prayer and the pipe of praise
   without end.

Who among all Thy creatures
   is able to recount *Thy wonders*?
May Thy Name be praised
   by the mouth of all men!
May they bless Thee for ever
   in accordance with *their understanding*,
and proclaim Thee with the voice of praise
   in the company of *the Sons of Heaven*!
There shall be neither groaning nor complaint
   and wickedness *shall be destroyed for ever*;
Thy truth shall be revealed in eternal glory
   and everlasting peace.
Blessed art *Thou, O my Lord*,
who hast given to *Thy servant*
   the knowledge of wisdom
that he may comprehend Thy wonders,
   and recount Thy . . .
   in Thy abundant grace!
Blessed art Thou,
   O God of mercy and compassion,
for the might of Thy *power*
   and the greatness of Thy truth,
and for the multitude of Thy favours
   in all Thy works!
Rejoice the soul of Thy servant with Thy truth
   and cleanse me by Thy righteousness.
Even as I have hoped in Thy goodness,
   and waited for Thy grace,
so hast Thou freed me from my calamities
   in accordance with Thy forgiveness;
and in my distress Thou hast comforted me
   for I have leaned on Thy mercy.

Blessed art Thou, O Lord,
   for it is Thou who hast done these things!

Thou hast set *hymns of praise*
  within the mouth of Thy servant,
and hast established for me a response of the tongue . . .

Hymn 23

. . . I will praise Thy Name among them that fear Thee.
Bowing down in prayer I will beg Thy favours
  from season to season always:
when light emerges from *its dwelling-place*,
and when the day reaches its appointed end
    in accordance with the laws
    of the Great Light of heaven;
when evening falls and light departs
    at the beginning of the dominion of darkness,
at the hour appointed for night,
and at its end when morning returns
    and the shadows retire to their dwelling-place
    before the approach of light;
always;
    at the genesis of every period
    and at the beginning of every age
    and at the end of every season,
according to the statute and signs
    appointed to every dominion
    by the certain law from the mouth of God,
by the precept which is and shall be
    for ever and ever without end.
Without it nothing is nor shall be,
    for the God of knowledge established it
    and there is no other beside Him.

I, the Master, know Thee O my God,
    by the spirit which Thou hast given to me,
and by Thy Holy Spirit I have faithfully hearkened
    to Thy marvellous counsel.
In the mystery of Thy wisdom
    Thou hast opened knowledge to me,
and in Thy mercies
    Thou hast unlocked for me the fountain of Thy might.

. . . Before Thee no man is just . . .
that he may understand all Thy mysteries
   or give answer *to Thy rebuke.*
But the children of Thy grace
   shall delight in Thy correction
   and watch for Thy goodness,
for in Thy mercies *Thou wilt show Thyself to them*
   and they shall know Thee;
at the time of Thy glory
   they shall rejoice.
Thou hast caused them to draw near
   in accordance *with their knowledge,*
and hast admitted them
   in accordance with their understanding,
and in their divisions they shall serve Thee
   throughout their dominion
without ever turning aside from Thee
   or transgressing Thy word.

Behold, *I was taken* from dust
   and fashioned *out of clay*
as a source of uncleanness,
   and a shameful nakedness,
a heap of dust,
   and a kneading *with water,*

. . . and a house of darkness,
   a creature of clay returning to dust,
returning *at the appointed time*
   to dwell in the dust whence it was taken.

How then shall dust reply to its Maker,
   and how understand His *works?*
How shall it stand before Him who reproves it?

. . . *and the Spring of* Eternity,
the Well of Glory
   and the Fountain of Knowledge.
Not even *the wonderful* Heroes *can* declare all Thy glory

or stand in face of Thy wrath,
and there is none among them
    that can answer Thy rebuke;
for Thou art just and none can oppose Thee.
How then can man who returns to his dust?
I hold my peace;
    what more shall I say than this?
I have spoken in accordance with my knowledge,
    out of the righteousness given to a creature of clay.
And how shall I speak unless Thou open my mouth;
    how understand unless Thou teach me?
How shall I seek Thee unless Thou uncover my heart,
    and how follow the way that is straight
unless *Thou guide me?*
How shall my foot stay on *the path*
unless Thou give it strength? . . .

Hymn 24

. . . *How* shall I look,
    unless Thou open my eyes?

Or hear,
    unless Thou unstop my ears?
My heart is astounded,
for to the uncircumcised ear
    a word has been disclosed,
and a heart *of stone*
    has understood the right precepts.

I know it is for Thyself
    that Thou hast done these things, O God;
for what is flesh
    that Thou shouldst act marvellously *towards it?*
It is Thy purpose to do mightily
    and to establish all things for Thy glory.
Thou hast created the host of knowledge
    to declare Thy mighty deeds to flesh,
    and the right precepts to him that is born *of woman.*

Thou hast *caused the perverse heart to enter*
   into a Covenant with Thee,
and hast uncovered the heart of dust
that it may be preserved from evil
   and saved from the snares of judgement
   in accordance with Thy mercies.

And I, a creature *of clay*
   kneaded with water,
a heap of dust
   and a heart of stone,
for what am I reckoned to be worthy of this?
For into an ear of dust *Thou hast put a new word*
   and hast engraved on a heart of *stone* things everlasting.
Thou hast caused *the straying spirit* to return
   that it may enter into a Covenant with Thee,
and stand *before Thee for ever*
   in the everlasting abode,
illumined with perfect Light for ever,
   with *no more* darkness,
for unending *seasons of joy*
and *unnumbered* ages of peace . . .

A Fragment

Thou didst open *his fountain*
   that he might rebuke the creature of clay for his way,
and him who is born of woman
   for the guilt of his deeds;
that he might open *the fount of* Thy truth
   to a creature whom Thou upholdest by Thy might;
that he might be, according to Thy truth,
   a messenger *in the season* of Thy goodness;
that to the humble he might bring
   glad tidings of Thy great mercy,
proclaiming salvation
   from out of the fountain *of holiness*
   to the contrite of spirit,
and everlasting joy to those who mourn.

A Fragment

. . . Chant, O beloved, sing to the King *of glory*.
 Rejoice, in the congregation of God.
Exult in the tents of salvation.
 Give thanks in the dwelling
 of holiness,
 extol together with the eternal host.
Magnify our God and glorify our King.
Sanctify His name with powerful lips
 and a victorious tongue.
Lift up alone your voice in all ages,
 Let a joyous meditation be heard.
Burst out in eternal rejoicings
 and prostrate incessantly in the common assembly.
Bless the wonderful Maker of exalted things,
 Him who proclaims the power of His hand,
sealing mysteries and revealing secrets,
 lifting up those who stumble and fall,
restoring the progress of those who hope for knowledge
 and humbling the meetings of the everlastingly haughty;
sealing the mysteries of *splendour*
 and establishing *the* wonders of glory.

Apocryphal Psalms

The incomplete Psalms Scroll from Cave 11 contains seven non-canonical poems interspersed among the canonical Psalms. One of these figures as Psalm 151 in the Greek Psalter, and four further compositions have been preserved in Syriac translation. Three previously unknown poems and an extract from the Hebrew version of Sirach li also feature in the Scroll.

In Psalms 151A and B or Syriac Psalm i, the stories of the election of David, the shepherd boy, as ruler of Israel, and his victory over Goliath, are poetically retold. Psalm 154 or Syriac Psalm ii is a sapiential hymn, and Psalm 155 or Syriac Psalm iii is an amalgam of an individual complaint and thanksgiving. Part of it is an alphabet acrostic, i.e. the lines begin with consecutive letters of the Hebrew alphabet. *Plea for Deliverance* is an individual thanksgiving hymn, the beginning of which is lost. The *Zion Psalm*, of which lines 1–3 and 8–15 are also in a fragmentary Psalms scroll from Cave 4, is another alphabetic acrostic hymn praising Jerusalem. Finally, the *Psalm of the Creation* is a further sapiential hymn.

A midrashic account of the poetic activities of David credits him with 4,050 compositions, subdivided into psalms, songs for the daily holocaust, songs for the Sabbath sacrifice, songs for festivals and songs for exorcism. The mention of fifty-two Sabbaths and the 364 days indicates that the author envisaged the solar year of the Qumran calendar.

The figure of 4,050 should be viewed against the equally prolific literary achievement claimed for Solomon in 1 Kings v, 12 (3,000 proverbs and 1,005 songs according to the Hebrew text; 3,000 proverbs and 5,000 songs according to the Septuagint). As for Josephus, he attributes to Solomon 1,005 *books* of poems and 3,000 *books* of parables (*Antiquities* VIII).

Only this catalogue, written in prose, is definitely sectarian. The psalms themselves probably belong to the second century BCE at the latest, but they may even date to the third century BCE.

Psalm 151A

Hallelujah. Of David, son of Jesse.

1 I was smaller than my brothers, and younger than the sons of
   my father.
   He made me shepherd of His flock, and a ruler over His kids.
2 My hands have made a pipe and my fingers a lyre.
   I have rendered glory to the Lord; I have said so in my soul.
3 The mountains do not testify to Him, and the hills do not tell
   of Him.
   The trees praise my words and the flocks my deeds.
4 For who can tell and speak of and recount the works of the
   Lord?
   God has seen all, He has heard all, and He listens to all.
5 He sent His prophet to anoint me, Samuel to magnify me.
   My brothers went out to meet him, beautiful of figure, beautiful of appearance.
6 They were tall of stature with beautiful hair, yet the Lord did
   not choose them.
7 He sent and took me from behind the flock, and anointed me
   with holy oil.
   As a prince of His people, and a ruler among the sons of His
   Covenant.

Psalm 151B

*The first display of David's power after God's prophet had
anointed him.*

1 Then I saw the Philistine taunting *from the enemy lines . . .*

Psalm 154

1 *Glorify God with a great voice. Proclaim His majesty in the
   congregation of the many.*
2 *Glorify His name amid the multitude of the upright and
   recount His greatness with the faithful.*

3 *Join* your souls to the good and to the perfect to glorify the Most High.

4 Assemble together to make known His salvation.
And be not slow in making known His strength, and His majesty to all the simple.

5 For wisdom is given to make known the glory of the Lord.

6 And to recount the greatness of His deeds she is made known to man,

7 to declare His strength to the simple, and to give insight into His greatness to those without understanding,

8 they who are far from her gates, who have strayed from her entrances.

9 For the Most High is the Lord of Jacob, and His majesty is over all His works.

10 And a man who glorifies the Most High is accepted by Him as one bringing an offering,

11 as one offering he-goats and calves, as one causing the altar to grow fat on a multitude of burnt-offerings, as an agreeable incense by the hand of the righteous.

12 From the doors of the righteous her voice is heard, and from the congregation of the devout her song.

13 When they eat their fill, she is mentioned, and when they drink in community together.

14 Their meditation is on the Law of the Most High, and their words are for making known His strength.

15 How far from the wicked is her word, and her knowledge from the insolent.

16 Behold the eyes of the Lord have compassion on the good,

17 and His mercy is great over those who glorify Him; from an evil time He saves *their* souls.

18 *Bless* the Lord who redeems the humble from the hand of strangers
and delivers the perfect from the hand of the wicked;

19 *who lifts up a horn out of* Jacob, *and a judge out of Israel.*

20 *He desires His tabernacle in Zion, and chooses Jerusalem for ever.*

Psalm 155

1 O Lord, I have called to Thee, hear me.

2 I have spread out my hands towards Thy holy dwelling-place.

3 Turn Thine ear and grant me my request,

4 and do not withhold my plea from me.

5 Construct my soul and do not cast it away,

6 and do not leave it alone before the wicked.

7 May the true judge turn away from me the rewards of evil.

8 Lord, do not judge me according to my sins, for no living man is righteous before Thee.

9 Lord, cause me to understand Thy Law and teach me Thy judgements.

10 And the multitude shall hear of Thy deeds, and peoples shall honour Thy glory.

11 Remember me and forget me not, and bring me not to unbearable hardships.

12 Put away from me the sin of my youth, and may my sins not be remembered against me.

13 Lord, cleanse me from the evil plague, and let it not return to me.

14 Dry up its roots within me, and permit not its leaves to flourish in me.

15 Lord, Thou art glory; therefore my plea is fulfilled before Thee.

16 To whom shall I cry so that he will grant it to me? What more can the *power* of the sons of men do?

17 From before Thee, O Lord, comes my trust.
I cried to the Lord and He answered me; He healed the brokenness of my heart.

18 I was sleepy *and I* slept; I dreamt and also *I awoke.*

19 *Lord, Thou didst support me when my heart was stricken, and I called upon the Lord my saviour.*

20 Now I will see their shame; I have relied on Thee, and I will not be ashamed. Render glory for ever and ever.

21 Redeem Israel, Thy pious one, O Lord, and the house of Jacob, Thine elect.

Prayer for Deliverance

For no worm thanks Thee, nor a maggot recounts Thy loving-kindness.

Only the living thank Thee, all they whose feet totter, thank Thee, when Thou makest known to them Thy loving-kindness, and causest them to understand Thy righteousness.

For the soul of all the living is in Thy hand; Thou hast given breath to all flesh.

O Lord, do towards us according to Thy goodness, according to the greatness of Thy mercies, and according to the greatness of Thy righteous deeds.

The Lord listens to the voice of all who love His name and does not permit His loving-kindness to depart from them.

Blessed be the Lord, doer of righteous deeds, who crowns His pious ones with loving-kindness and mercies.

My soul shouts to praise Thy name, to praise with jubilation Thy mercies,

to announce Thy faithfulness; there is no limit to Thy praises.

I belonged to death because of my sins, and my iniquities had sold me to Sheol.

But Thou didst save me, O Lord, according to the greatness of Thy mercies, according to the greatness of Thy righteous deeds.

I, too, have loved Thy name, and have taken refuge in Thy shadow.

When I remember Thy power, my heart is strengthened and I rely on Thy mercies.

Forgive my sins, O Lord, and purify me of my iniquity.

Grant me a spirit of faithfulness and knowledge; let me not be dishonoured in ruin.

Let not Belial dominate me, nor an unclean spirit; let pain and the evil inclination not possess my bones.

For Thou, O Lord, art my praise, and I hope in Thee every day.

My brethren rejoice with me and the house of my father is astounded by Thy graciousness.

. . . for ever I will rejoice in Thee.

Apostrophe to Zion

I will remember you, O Zion, for a blessing;
with all my might I love you;
your memory is to be blessed for ever.
Your hope is great, O Zion;
Peace and your awaited salvation will come.
Generation after generation shall dwell in you,
and generations of the pious shall be your ornament.
They who desire the day of your salvation
shall rejoice in the greatness of your glory.
They shall be suckled on the fullness of your glory,
and in your beautiful streets they shall make tinkling sounds.
You shall remember the pious deeds of your prophets,
and shall glorify yourself in the deeds of your pious ones.
Cleanse violence from your midst;
lying and iniquity, may they be cut off from you.
Your sons shall rejoice within you,
and your cherished ones shall be joined to you.
How much they have hoped in your salvation,
and how much your perfect ones have mourned for you.
Your hope, O Zion, shall not perish,
and your expectation will not be forgotten.
Is there a just man who has perished?
Is there a man who has escaped his iniquity?
Man is tried according to his way,
each is repaid according to his deeds.
Your oppressors shall be cut off from around you, O Zion,
and all who hate you shall be dispersed.
Your praise is pleasing, O Zion;
it rises up in all the world.
Many times I will remember you for a blessing;
I will bless you with all my heart.
You shall attain to eternal righteousness,
and shall receive blessings from the noble.
Take the vision which speaks of you,
and the dreams of the prophets requested for you.
Be exalted and increase, O Zion;

Praise the Most High, your Redeemer!
May my soul rejoice in your glory!

Hymn to the Creator

The Lord is great and holy, the Most Holy for generation after generation.

Majesty goes before Him, and after Him abundance of many waters.

Loving-kindness and truth are about His face; truth and judgement and righteousness are the pedestal of His throne.

He divides light from obscurity; he establishes the dawn by the knowledge of His heart.

When all His angels saw it, they sang, for He showed them that which they had not known.

He crowns the mountains with fruit, with good food for all the living.

Blessed be the master of the earth with His power, who establishes the world by His wisdom.

By his understanding He stretched out the heaven, and brought forth *wind* from His *stores.*

He made *lightnings for the rain,* and raised mist from the end *of the earth.*

An Account of David's Poems

David son of Jesse was wise and brilliant like the light of the sun; he was a scribe, intelligent and perfect in all his ways before God and men.

YHWH gave him an intelligent and brilliant spirit, and he wrote 3,600 psalms and 364 songs to sing before the altar for the daily perpetual sacrifice, for all the days of the year; and 52 songs for the Sabbath offerings; and 30 songs for the New Moons, for Feast-days and for the Day of Atonement.

In all, the songs which he uttered were 446, and 4 songs to make music on behalf of those stricken by evil spirits.

In all, they were 4,050.

All these he uttered through prophecy which was given him from before the Most High.

Lamentations

Several fragments of a poem inspired by the biblical Book of Lamentations have been preserved in Cave 4. Only the second offers a text long enough for intelligible translation.

> *. . . How* solitary *lies* the city,

> *. . .* the princess of all the peoples is desolate
>   like a forsaken woman;
> and all her daughters are forsaken
>   *like* a forsaken woman,
> like a woman hurt and forsaken
>   by her *husband.*
> All her palaces and *her* walls are
>   like a barren woman;
> and like a sheltered woman,
>   are all *her* paths;

> *. . .* and all her daughters are like women
>   mourning for *their husbands;*
>   *. . .* like women
>   deprived of their only children.
> Weep, weep, *Jerusalem*

> *. . . her tears flow* upon her cheeks
>   because of her sons *. . .*

Songs for the Holocaust
of the Sabbath

Fragments of a document concerned with heavenly worship were first published by J. Strugnell under the title 'The Angelic Liturgy', *Congress Volume Oxford, Supplements to Vetus Testamentum*, VII (Leiden, 1960), 318–45. The full material, including eight manuscripts from Cave 4, small fragments from Cave 11 and a large fragment from Masada (1039–200), was subsequently edited by Carol Newsom (*Songs of the Sabbath Sacrifice: A Critical Edition*, Harvard Semitic Studies 27, Atlanta, 1985). The songs contain angelic praises of God assigned to the first thirteen sabbaths, i.e. the first quarter of the solar year. They imply the simultaneity of heavenly and earthly worship. Although often obscure, the poems depict the celestial sanctuary, the throne-chariot, and the various groups participating in the angelic liturgy; they also include the words of the benedictions sung by the seven archangels.

The main source of inspiration is the Book of Ezekiel, especially chapters i and x in connection with the throne-chariot and xl–xlviii for the heavenly sanctuary. The *Merkabah*, or divine throne-chariot, was a central subject in ancient and medieval Jewish esotericism and mysticism. Hence this early post-biblical manifestation of the speculation is of considerable historical importance for the study of the so-called *Merkabah* mysticism and of the *Hekhaloth* ('heavenly palaces') literature.

The presence of this Qumran document in the fortress of Masada is best explained by assuming either that a number of Essenes joined the revolutionaries and took with them some of their manuscripts, or that the rebels occupied the Qumran area after its evacuation by the Community and later transferred some Essene manuscripts to their final place of resistance.

Here are some selections from the Songs:

Songs for the Holocaust of the Sabbath

I

For the Master. Song of the holocaust of the seventh Sabbath on the sixteenth of the month.

Praise the most high God, O you high among all the gods of knowledge.

Let the holy ones of the 'gods' sanctify the King of glory, who sanctifies by His holiness all His Holy ones.

O Princes of the praises of all the 'gods', praise the God of majestic praises,

For in the splendour of praises is the glory of His kingship.

In it are contained the praises of all the 'gods' together with the splendour of all *His* kingship.

Exalt His exaltation on high, O 'gods', above the gods on high, and His glorious divinity above all the highest heights.

For He *is the God of gods*, of all the Princes on high, and the King of kings of all the eternal councils.

By a discerning goodwill expressed by the words of His mouth *all the gods on high* come into being, at the opening of His lips, all the eternal spirits, by His discerning goodwill, all His creatures in their undertakings.

Exult, O you who exult *in His knowledge, with* an exultation among the wonderful 'gods';

utter His glory with the tongue of all who utter knowledge;

may His wonderful exultation be in the mouth of all who utter *His knowledge.*

For He is the God of all who exult in everlasting knowledge, and

the Judge through His might of all the spirits of understanding.

Celebrate O all celebrating gods, the King of majesty, for all the gods of knowledge celebrate His glory,

and all the spirits of righteousness celebrate His truth, and seek acceptance of their knowledge by the judgements of His mouth,

and of their celebrations when His mighty hand executes judgements of reward.

Sing to the God of power with an offering of the princely spirit, a song of divine joy, and a jubilation among all the holy, a wonderful song for eternal rejoicing.

With these all the *foundations of the holy* of holies shall praise, the pillars bearing the highest abode, and all the corners of its structure.

Sing to the God *who is* awesome in strength . . .

II

The figures of the 'gods' shall praise Him, *the most holy* spirits . . . of glory; the floor of the marvellous innermost chambers, the spirits of the eternal gods, all . . . *figures of the innermost* chamber of the King, the spiritual works of the marvellous firmament are purified with salt, spirits of knowledge, truth *and* righteousness in the holy of holies, forms of the living 'gods', forms of the illuminating spirits. All their *works of art* are marvellously linked, many-coloured *spirits*, artistic figures of the 'gods', engraved all around their glorious bricks, glorious figures on bricks of splendour and majesty. All their works of art are living 'gods', and their artistic figures are holy angels. From beneath the marvellous innermost *chambers* comes a sound of quiet silence . . .

III

The *cherubim* prostrate themselves before Him and bless. As they rise, a whispered divine voice *is heard*, and there is a roar of praise. When they drop their wings, there is a *whispered* divine voice. The cherubim bless the image of the throne-chariot above the firmament, *and* they praise *the majesty* of the luminous firmament beneath His seat of glory. When the wheels advance, angels of holiness come and go. From between His glorious wheels, there is as it were a fiery vision of most holy spirits. About them, the appearance of rivulets of fire in the likeness of gleaming brass, and a work of . . . radiance in many-coloured glory, marvellous pigments, clearly mingled. The spirits of the living 'gods' move perpetually with the glory of the marvellous chariots. The whispered voice of blessing accompanies the roar of their advance, and they praise the Holy One on their way of return. When they ascend, they ascend marvellously and when they settle, they stand still. The sound of joyful praise is silenced and there is a whispered blessing of the 'gods' in all the camps of God.

IV

The 'gods' praise Him *when they take* up their station, and all the *spirits of* the clear firmament rejoice in His glory. A sound of blessing is heard from all His divisions speaking of the firmaments of His glory, and His gates praise with a resounding voice. When the gods of knowledge enter by the doors of glory, and when the holy angels depart towards their realm, the entrance doors and the gates of exit proclaim the glory of the King, blessing and praising all the spirits of God when they depart and enter by the gates. None among them skips over a precept, nor do they . . . against the saying of the King . . . They run not away from the path, nor slip away from His domain. They are neither too high for His commission nor too lowly. For He shall be compassionate in the realm of His furious, destroying *anger*; He will not judge in the provinces of His glorious wrath. The fear of the King of 'gods' is awe-inspiring to *all* the 'gods' . . .

V

. . . At their marvellous stations are spirits, many-coloured like the work of a weaver, splendid engraved figures. In the midst of a glorious appearance of scarlet, colours of the most holy spiritual light, they hold to their holy station before *the* King, spirits of *pure* colours in the midst of an appearance of whiteness. The likeness of the glorious spirit is like a work of art of sparkling fine gold. All their pattern is clearly mingled like the work of art of a weaver. These are the Princes of those marvellously clothed for service, the Princes of the kingdom, the kingdom of the holy ones of the King of holiness in all the heights of the sanctuaries of His glorious kingdom.

HOROSCOPES, LITURGIES, BLESSINGS AND CURSES

· ·

'Horoscopes' or Astrological Physiognomies

Three documents from Cave 4, one in Hebrew and two in Aramaic, all dating probably to the end of the first century BCE, contain fragments of 'horoscopes' or, more precisely, astrological physiognomies claiming a correspondence between the features and destiny of a person and the configuration of the stars at the time of his birth.

The Hebrew text, published by J. M. Allegro, is written in a childish cipher. The text runs from left to right instead of the normal right to left and uses, in addition to the current 'square' Hebrew alphabet, letters borrowed from the archaic Hebrew (or Phoenician) and Greek scripts. The spiritual qualities of three individuals described in the work are reflected in their share of Light and Darkness. The first man is very wicked: eight parts of Darkness to a single part of Light. The second man is largely good: six parts of Light against three parts of Darkness. The last is almost perfect: eight portions of Light and only one of Darkness.

As far as physical characteristics are concerned, shortness, fatness and irregularity of features are associated with wickedness, their opposites reflect virtue.

Whether the sectaries forecast the future by means of astrology, or merely used horoscope-like compositions as literary devices, is impossible to decide at present, though I am inclined towards the latter alternative. That such texts are found among the Scrolls should not, however, surprise anyone. For if many Jews frowned on astrology, others, such as the Hellenistic Jewish writer Eupolemus, credited its invention to Abraham!

I

His thighs are long and lean, and his toes are thin and long. He is of the second Column. His spirit consists of six parts in the House of Light and three in the Pit of Darkness. And this is his birthday on which he is to be born: in the foot of the Bull. He will be meek. And his animal is the bull.

II

His head . . . *and his cheeks are* fat. His teeth are of uneven length. His fingers are thick, and his thighs are thick and very hairy, each one. His toes are thick and short. His spirit consists of eight parts in the House of Darkness and one from the House of Light.

III

His eyes are black and glowing . . . His voice is gentle. His teeth are fine and well aligned. He is neither tall, nor short . . . And his fingers are thin and long. And his thighs are smooth . . . *And his toes* are well aligned. His spirit consists of eight parts *in the House of Light, of* the second Column, and one *in the House of Darkness. And this is* his birthday on which he is to be born.

The Words of the Heavenly Lights

Surviving in three fragmentary manuscripts from Cave 4, 'The Words of the Heavenly Lights' are collective prayers for the days of the week which are full of biblical reminiscences. In the best-preserved of them the Sabbath and the fourth day are expressly mentioned in the surviving text.

I

I . . . Amen! Amen!

II . . . We pray Thee, O Lord, do in accordance with Thyself, in accordance with the greatness of Thy might, Thou who didst pardon our fathers when they rebelled against Thy saying. Thou wert angry with them so as to wish to destroy them, but because of Thy love for them and for the sake of Thy Covenant – for Moses had atoned for their sin – and in order that Thy great might and the abundance of Thy mercy might be known to everlasting generations, Thou didst take pity on them. So let Thine anger and wrath against all *their* sin turn away from Thy people Israel. Remember Thy marvels which Thou didst for the poor of the nations. For we were called by Thy Name . . . to *cause* us *to repent* with all our heart and soul and to plant Thy Law in our heart *that we might never depart from it, straying neither* to right nor to left. For Thou wilt heal us of foolishness and of blindness and confusion *of heart* . . . *Behold* we were sold because of our iniquities but despite our offences Thou didst call us . . . Thou wilt save us from sinning against Thee . . . and to make us understand the testimonies . . .

III . . . Behold, all the nations are as nothing beside Thee, they are counted as void and naught before Thee. We have called on Thy Name alone. Thou hast created us for Thy glory and made us Thy children in the sight of all the nations. For Thou hast named Israel 'My son, my first-born', and hast chastised us as a man chastises his son. Thou hast brought us up throughout the years of our generations *by means of* evil diseases, famine, thirst, pestilence, and the sword . . . of Thy Covenant. Because Thou hast chosen us *from all* the earth *to be Thy people*, therefore hast Thou poured out Thine anger *and jealousy* upon us in all the fury of Thy wrath. Thou hast caused *the scourge* of Thy *plagues* to cleave to us of which Moses wrote, and Thy servants the Prophets, that Thou wouldst send evil against us in the last days . . .

IV . . . Thy dwelling-place . . . a resting-place in Jerusalem, *the city which* Thou hast *chosen* from all the earth that Thy *Name* might remain there for ever. For Thou hast loved Israel above all the peoples. Thou hast chosen the tribe of Judah and hast established Thy Covenant with David that he might be as a princely shepherd over Thy people and sit before Thee on the throne of Israel for ever. All the nations have seen Thy glory, Thou who hast sanctified Thyself in the midst of Thy people Israel. They brought their offering to Thy great Name, silver and gold and precious stones together with all the treasures of their lands, that they might glorify Thy people, and Zion Thy holy city, and the House of Thy majesty. And there was neither adversary nor misfortune, but peace and blessing . . . and they ate and were satisfied and grew fat . . .

V . . . *They forsook* the fount of living waters . . . and served a strange god in their land. Also, their land was ravaged by their enemies; for Thy fury and the heat of Thy wrath overflowed, in the fire of Thy jealousy, making of it a desert where no man could go and return. Yet notwithstanding all this, Thou didst not reject the seed of Jacob, neither didst Thou cast away Israel to destruction, breaking Thy Covenant with them. For Thou alone art a living God and there is none beside Thee. Thou didst remember Thy Covenant, Thou who didst rescue us in the presence of all the nations, and didst not forsake us amid the nations. Thou wert gracious towards Thy people Israel in all the lands to which Thou didst banish them, that they might remember to return to Thee and to hearken to Thy voice *according to* all Thou hadst commanded by the hand of Moses Thy servant.

For Thou hast shed Thy Holy Spirit upon us, bringing upon us Thy blessings, that we might seek Thee in our distress *and whisper* prayers in the ordeal of Thy chastisement. We have entered into distress, have been stricken and tried by the fury of the oppressor. For we also have tired God with our iniquity, we have wearied the Rock with *our* sins. *But* in order that we may profit, Thou hast not wearied us who leadest *us* in the way in *which we must walk. But* we have not heeded . . .

VI . . . *Thou hast taken away* all our transgressions and hast purified us of our sin for Thine own sake. Thine, Thine is righteousness, O Lord, for it is Thou who hast done all this! Now, on the day when our heart is humbled, we expiate our iniquity and the iniquity of our fathers, together with our unfaithfulness and rebellion. We have not rejected Thy trials and scourges; our soul has not despised them to the point of breaking Thy Covenant despite all the distress of our soul. For Thou, who hast sent our enemies against us, strengthenest our heart that we may recount Thy mighty deeds to everlasting generations. We pray Thee, O Lord, since Thou workest marvels from everlasting to everlasting, to let Thine anger and wrath retreat from us. Look on *our affliction* and trouble and distress, and deliver Thy people Israel *from all* the lands, near and far, *to which Thou hast banished them* . . .

VII . . . who deliverest us from all distress. Amen! *Amen!*

II

II . . . Remember, pray, that we are Thy people and that Thou hast carried us marvellously *on the wings of* eagles and hast brought us towards Thee. And like an eagle which rouses its nestlings and hovers over *its young*, spreads out its wings, takes one and carries it on *its pinions*, so we dwell apart and are not reckoned among the nations and . . . Thou art in our midst in the pillar of fire and the cloud *of* Thy holiness walking before us, and as it were Thy glory in our midst.

Blessings and Curses

The first four fragments are from a collection of blessings originally attached to the Scroll containing the Community Rule and the Messianic Rule. They have been skilfully pieced together by J. T. Milik, who dates them to around 100 BCE. They are followed by blessings and curses from Cave 4.

The Blessings were to be recited by the Master or Guardian, and were, as it seems, intended for the messianic age, and perhaps for the ceremony of the institution of the new Community. It is, however, possible that they were actually used during the course of some liturgy anticipating and symbolising the coming of the messianic era.

Also included are a Blessing and two Curses from scrolls found in Cave 4. The Curses of Melkiresha' reveals Satan's specific name (My King is Wickedness), the counterpart of Melkizedek (My King is Justice), chief of the Army of Light (see p. 303).

The Blessing of the Faithful

Words of blessing. The Master shall bless them that fear *God and do* His will, that keep His commandments, and hold fast to His holy *Covenant*, and walk perfectly *in all the ways of* His *truth*, whom He has chosen for an eternal Covenant which shall endure for ever.

> May the *Lord bless you from the Abode of His holiness*; may He open for you from heaven an eternal fountain which *shall not fail*! . . .
>
> May He *favour* you with every *heavenly* blessing; *may He teach you* the knowledge of the Holy Ones!
>
> *May He unlock for you the* everlasting *fountain; may He not withhold the waters of life from* them that thirst!

The Blessing of the High Priest

> May the Lord lift His countenance towards you; *may He delight in the* sweet odour *of your sacrifices*!

May He choose *all* them that sit in your priestly *college* . . .

May He *lift* His countenance towards all your congregation!

May He place upon your head *a diadem* . . . in *everlasting* glory;
   may He sanctify your seed in glory without end!

May He grant you everlasting *peace* . . .

May He fight *at the head of* your Thousands *until the generation
   of falsehood is ended* . . .

. . . May He lay the foundation of your peace for ever!

The Blessing of the Priests

Words of blessing. The *Master shall bless* the sons of Zadok the
Priests, whom God has chosen to confirm His Covenant for *ever,
and to inquire* into all His precepts in the midst of His people, and
to instruct them as He commanded; who have established *His
Covenant* on truth and watched over all His laws with righteousness and walked according to the way of His choice.

May the Lord bless you from His holy *Abode*, may He set you as a
   splendid jewel in the midst of the congregation of the saints!

May He *renew* for you the Covenant of the *everlasting* priesthood;
   may He sanctify you *for the House* of Holiness!

May He *judge all* the leaders by your works, and all *the princes* of
   the peoples by the words from out of your lips!

May He give you as your portion the firstfruits of *all delectable
   things*, may He bless by your hand the counsel of all flesh!

. . . May everlasting blessings be the crown upon your head!

. . . *For* He has chosen you *to* . . . and to number the saints and to
   bless your people . . . the men of the Council of God by your
   hand, and not by the hand of a prince . . .

. . . May you be as an Angel of the Presence in the Abode of Holiness to the glory of the God of *hosts* . . .

May you attend upon the service in the Temple of the Kingdom
   and decree destiny in company with the Angels of the Presence,
   in common council *with the Holy Ones* for everlasting ages and
   time without end; for *all* His judgements are *truth*!

May He make you holy among His people, and an *eternal* light *to
   illumine* the world with knowledge and to enlighten the face of
   the Congregation *with wisdom*!

May He consecrate you to the Holy of Holies! For *you are made* holy for Him and you shall glorify His Name and His holiness.

The Blessing of the Prince of the Congregation

The Master shall bless the Prince of the Congregation . . . and shall renew for him the Covenant of the Community that he may establish the kingdom of His people for ever, *that he may judge the poor with righteousness and* dispense justice with equity to the oppressed Schøyen of the land, and that he may walk perfectly before Him in all the ways *of truth,* and that he may establish His holy Covenant at the time of the affliction of those who seek God.

May the Lord raise you up to everlasting heights, and as a fortified tower upon a high wall!
May you smite the peoples with the might of your hand and ravage the earth with your sceptre; may you bring death to the ungodly with the breath of your lips!
May He shed upon you the spirit of counsel and everlasting might, the spirit of knowledge and of the fear of God; may righteousness be the girdle *of your loins* and may your reins be girdled *with faithfulness*!
May He make your horns of iron and your hooves of bronze; may you toss like a young bull *and trample the peoples* like the mire of the streets!
For God has established you as the sceptre. The rulers . . . *and all the kings of the* nations shall serve you. He shall strengthen you with His holy Name and you shall be as a *lion; and you shall not lie down until you have devoured the* prey . . .

A Blessing

The seat of Thy splendour and the footstool of Thy glory in the heights of Thy standing and Thy holy stepping-place. And Thy glorious chariots, their cherubim and their wheels and all *their* companies; foundations of fire and flames of brightness and shinings of majesty and streams of fire and wonderful luminaries;

majesty and splendour and glorious height, holy foundation and source *of* majesty and height of glory, *marvel of* thanksgivings and reservoir of might, splendour of praises and great in wonderful things and healings and miraculous deeds, foundation of wisdom and pattern of knowledge and source of understanding, source of prudence and holy counsel and true foundation, treasure-house of intelligence, building of righteousness and place of uprightness, *great* in loving-kindness and in good answers and true loving-kindness and everlasting mercies and mysteries of *marvels* in *their revelations* and holy weeks in their appointed time and squads of months . . .

Curses of Belial

. . . *The* council of the Community shall all say together, Amen, amen. Afterwards *they* shall damn Belial and all his guilty lot. They shall answer and say, Cursed be Belial in his hostile design, and damned in his guilty dominion. Cursed be all the spirits of his *lot* in their wicked design, and damned in their thoughts of unclean impurity. For they are the lot of darkness and their visitation is for eternal destruction. Amen, amen.

Cursed be the Wicked *One in all* . . . of his dominions, and may all the sons of Belial be damned in all the works of their service until their annihilation *for ever. Amen, amen.*

And *they shall continue to say: Be cursed, Angel* of Perdition and Spirit *of* Destruction, in all the thoughts of your *guilty* inclination *and all your abominable plots* and *your* wicked design, *and* may you be damned . . . Amen, amen.

Curses of Melkiresha'

May God set him apart for evil from the midst of the Sons of *Light because he has turned away from following Him.*

And they shall continue saying: Be cursed, Melkiresha', in all the thoughts *of your guilty inclination. May* God *deliver you up* for torture at the hands of the vengeful Avengers. May God not heed *when* you call on Him. *May He raise His angry face* towards you. May there be no greeting of 'Peace' for you in the mouth of all those who hold fast to the Fathers. *May you be cursed* with no remnant, and damned without escape.

Cursed be those who practise *their wicked designs* and establish in their heart your evil devices, plotting against the Covenant of God . . .

APOCALYPTIC WORKS

• •

The Triumph of Righteousness or Mysteries

Originally entitled *The Book of Mysteries* by J. T. Milik, these fragments expound the familiar theme of the struggle between good and evil, but their nature is difficult to determine. Perhaps they derive from a sermon, or from an apocalyptical writing.

I

They know not the mystery to come, nor do they understand the things of the past. They know not that which shall befall them, nor do they save their soul from the mystery to come.

And this shall be the sign for you that these things shall come to pass.

When the breed of iniquity is shut up, wickedness shall then be banished by righteousness as darkness is banished by the light. As smoke clears and is no more, so shall wickedness perish for ever and righteousness be revealed like a sun governing the world. All who cleave to the mysteries of sin shall be no more; knowledge shall fill the world and folly shall exist no longer.

This word shall surely come to pass; this prophecy is true. And by this may it be known to you that it shall not be taken back.

Do not all the peoples loathe iniquity? And yet it is spread by them all. Does not the fame of truth issue from the mouth of all the nations? Yet is there a lip or tongue which holds to it? Which nation likes to be oppressed by another stronger than itself, or likes its wealth to be wickedly seized? And yet which nation has not oppressed another, and where is there a people which has not seized *another's* wealth? . . .

II

... *The* sorcerers, experts in sin, have uttered the parable and proclaimed the riddle in advance. And then you will know ... your foolishness for the seal of the vision is sealed away from you. And you have not considered the mysteries of eternity and have not comprehended understanding.

A Messianic Apocalypse

Commonly referred to as the 'Resurrection fragment', this writing consists of eleven fragments, and possibly six further tiny pieces. This fragment is the largest and contains the remains of three columns of which the second, translated here, is the best preserved. The script is dated to the beginning of the first century B C E. Whether the designation 'apocalypse' is fully justified is a moot point: the writing comes across as a composition in verse akin to the poetry of the late biblical period. The surviving fragments do not appear to include anything patently sectarian. The term 'Messiah', probably in the singular, is used without the addition of Aaron or Israel, and the noun *'hasidim'*, absent from the big scrolls and little attested elsewhere, figures twice here. The divine name 'Lord' represents, not the Tetragram, but *Adonai* (four times). The poem incorporates Psalm cxlvi, 6–7 and Isaiah lxi, 1 and, as in the Gospels, healing and resurrection are linked to the idea of the Kingdom of God.

. . . *The* heavens and the earth will listen to His Messiah, and none therein will stray from the commandments of the holy ones.

Seekers of the Lord, strengthen yourselves in His service!

All you hopeful in your heart, will you not find the Lord in this?

For the Lord will consider the pious *hasidim* and call the righteous by name.

Over the poor His spirit will hover and will renew the faithful with His power.

And He will glorify the pious on the throne of the eternal Kingdom.

He who liberates the captives, restores sight to the blind, straightens the *bent* (Ps. cxlvi, 7–8).

And *for* ever I will cleave *to the* hopeful and in His mercy . . .

And the *fruit* . . . will not be delayed for anyone

And the Lord will accomplish glorious things which have never been . . .

. . . For He will heal the wounded, and revive the dead and bring good news to the poor (Isa. lxi, 1) . . .

WISDOM LITERATURE

• •

The Seductress

A long and relatively well-preserved Wisdom poem from Cave 4 depicts, by means of the metaphor of the harlot, the dangers and attraction of false doctrine. Palaeographically, the text is dated to the first century BCE, but the work may be much older, possibly antedating the Qumran sect.

> . . . She is ever prompt to oil her words,
>   and she flatters with irony,
>   deriding with iniquitous *lips.*
> Her heart is set up as a snare,
>   and her affections as a fowler's nets.
> Her eyes are defiled with iniquity,
>   her hands have seized hold of the Pit.
> Her legs go down to work wickedness,
>   and to walk in wrong-doings.
> Her . . . are foundations of darkness,
>   and a multitude of sins is in her skirts.
> Her . . . are darkness of night,
>   and her garments . . .
> Her clothes are shades of twilight,
>   and her ornaments plagues of corruption.
> Her couches are beds of corruption,
>   and her . . . depths of the Pit.
> Her inns are couches of darkness,
>   and her dominions in the midst of the night.
> She pitches her dwelling on the foundations of darkness,
>   she abides in the tents of silence.

Amid everlasting fire is her inheritance,
    not among those who shine brightly.
She is the beginning of all the ways of iniquity.
Woe and disaster to all who possess her!
    And desolation to all who hold her!
For her ways are ways of death,
    and her paths are roads of sin,
    and her tracks are pathways to iniquity,
    and her by-ways are rebellious wrong-doings.
Her gates are gates of death,
and from the entrance of the house
    she sets out towards the underworld.
None of those who enter there will ever return,
    and all who possess her will descend to the Pit.
She lies in wait in secret places . . .

In the city's squares she veils herself,
    and she stands at the gates of towns.
She will never rest from *whoring*,
    her eyes glance hither and thither.
She lifts her eyelids naughtily
    to stare at a virtuous man and join him,
    and an important man to trip him up,
    at upright men to pervert their way,
    and the righteous elect to keep them from the
       commandment,
    at the firmly established to bring them down wantonly,
    and those who walk in uprightness to alter the statute;
to cause the humble to rebel against God,
    and turn their steps away from the ways of justice,
    to bring insolence to their heart,
    so that they march no more in the paths of uprightness;
    to lead men astray to the ways of the Pit,
    and seduce with flatteries every son of man.

Exhortation to Seek Wisdom

Large fragments of a Wisdom poem in which a teacher encourages his 'people', his 'sons', the 'Simple', to search for Wisdom have been preserved in Cave 4. The script is believed to be late Hasmonaean, i.e. from the first half of the first century B C E. As is often the case in Wisdom literature, events of the patriarchal and Mosaic past are used for didactic purposes.

And you, sons of men, woe to you!
For man sprouts from his ground like grass,
 and his grace blossoms like a flower.
His glory blows away and his grass dries up,
 and the wind carries away its flower . . .
so that it is found no more . . .
They shall seek him but shall not find him,
 and there is no hope for him;
 and his days are like a shadow over the *earth*.
Now pray hearken to me, my people;
 heed me, O you Simple;
 become wise through the might of God.
Remember His miracles which He did in Egypt,
 and His marvels in the land of Ham.
Let your heart shake because of His fear,
 and do His will . . .

. . . Happy is the man to whom Wisdom has been given thus,
. . . nor let the wicked boast, saying:
It has not been given me . . .
 For God gave it to Israel,
 and with a good measure He measures it;
 and He will redeem all His people,
 and He will put to death those who hate His Wisdom.

Seek her and find her, grasp her and possess her!
With her is length of days and fatness of bone,
 the joy of the heart . . .

On Living a Modest Life

(A SAPIENTIAL WORK)

A substantial Wisdom composition, probably dating to the second century BCE, has survived in six fragmentary manuscripts. Here are two examples of guidance on living a modest life.

I

Do not strike him who is without your strength
lest you stumble and your shame increase greatly.
Do not increase your appetite for wealth;
it is better for you to be a slave in spirit.
Serve your master freely
and do not sell your glory for a price.
Do not give money in pledge for your inheritance
lest it impoverish your body.
Do not satiate yourself with bread
while there is no clothing.
Do not drink wine
while there is no food.
Do not seek luxury
when you lack bread.

Do not glorify yourself in your need if you are poor
lest you degrade your life.

II

You are a poor man. Do not say:
Since I am poor, I will not seek knowledge.
Shoulder every discipline and with every . . . refine
    your heart,
and your thoughts with a multitude of understanding.
Search the approaching mystery
and consider all the ways of truth,
and behold the roots of injustice.
Then you will know what is bitter for a man

and what is sweet for a human being.
Honour your father in your poverty
and your mother in your steps.
For his father is like God to a man
and his mother like a ruler to a human being.
For they are the crucible from which you were born
and as He placed them over you as rulers
and a frame for the spirit, so serve them,
and as He has revealed to you the approaching mystery,
honour them for your honour's sake . . .

Bless, My Soul

Bless, my soul, the Lord
for all His marvels for ever,
and may His name be blessed.
For He has delivered the soul of the poor,
and has not despised the humble,
and has not forgotten the misery of the deprived.
He has opened His eyes towards the distressed,
and has heard the cry of the fatherless,
and has turned His ears towards their crying.
He has been gracious to the humble by His great kindness,
and has opened their eyes to see His ways,
and *their* ears to hear His teaching.
He has circumcised the foreskin of their heart,
and has delivered them because of His kindness,
and has directed their feet towards the way.
He has not forsaken them amid the multitude of their misery,
neither has He handed them over to the violent,
nor has He judged them together with the wicked.
He has not *directed* His anger against them,
neither did he annihilate them in His wrath.
While all His furious wrath was not growing weary,
He has not judged them in the fire of His ardour,
but He has judged them in the greatness of His mercy.
The judgements of His eyes were to try them,
and He has brought His many mercies among the nations,
and from the hand of men He has delivered them.
He has not judged them amid the mass of nations,
and in the midst of peoples He has not judged *them*.
But He hid them in *His* . . .
He has turned darkness into light before them,
and crooked places into level ground,
He has revealed to them abundance of peace and truth.
He has made their spirit by measure,
and has established their words by weight,
and has caused them to sing like flutes.

He has given them a *perfect* heart,
and they have walked in the *way of His heart,*
He has also caused them to draw near to the *way of his heart.*
For they have pledged their spirit.
And He has surrounded them with a hedge
and has commanded that no blow should smite them.
He has placed His angels around them to protect them *from
    Belial*
lest he destroy them by the hand of their enemies.

Songs of the Sage

Scraps of two manuscripts from Cave 4 represent a mixture of sapiential psalms and poems of exorcism. Their editor, M. Baillet, assigns the script to the end of the first century B C E, or the turning of the era. The first fragment preserves an interesting list of names of demons.

I

Benedictions for the King of glory. Words of thanksgiving in psalms of . . . to the God of knowledge, the Splendour of power, the God of gods, Lord of all the holy. *His* dominion is over all the powerful mighty ones and by the power of His might all shall be terrified and shall scatter and be put to flight by the splendour of the dwelling of His kingly glory. And I, the Master, proclaim the majesty of His beauty to frighten and *terrify* all the spirits of the destroying angels and the spirits of the bastards, the demons, Lilith, the howlers and *the yelpers* . . . they who strike suddenly to lead astray the spirit of understanding and to appal their heart . . . in the age of the domination of wickedness and the appointed times for the humiliation of the sons of light, in the guilt of the ages of those smitten by iniquity, not for eternal destruction but for the humiliation of sin. Exalt, O just, the God of marvels. My psalms are for the upright . . . May all whose way is perfect exalt Him.

II

Let them rejoice before the God of justice with shouts of salvation, for there shall be no destroyer in their territories, and no spirit of wickedness shall walk in there. For the glory of the God of knowledge has shone forth in His words, and none of the sons of iniquity shall endure.

III

I have hated all the works of impurity. For God has caused the knowledge of understanding to shine in my heart. Just chastisers deal with my perversity, and faithful judges with all my sinful guilt. For God is my judge . . .

IV

Does one measure by the hollow of a human hand the waters of the great ocean? Are *the heavens estimated by the span of fingers? In one third of a measure* can any contain the dust of the earth, and weigh the mountains in a balance, or the hills in scales? Man did not make these. How can he measure the spirit of *God*?

V

God shall sanctify some of the holy as an everlasting sanctuary for himself, and purity shall endure among the cleansed. They shall be priests, His righteous people, His host, servants, the angels of his glory. They shall praise Him with marvellous prodigies.

VI

As for me, my tongue shall extol Thy righteousness, for Thou hast released it. Thou hast placed on my lips a fount of praise and in my heart the secret of the commencement of all human actions and the completion of the deeds of the perfect of way and the judgements regarding all the service done by them, justifying the just by Thy truth and condemning the wicked for their guilt. To announce peace to all the men of the Covenant and to utter a dreadful cry of woe for all those who breach it . . .

May they bless all Thy works always and blessed be Thy name for ever and ever. Amen, amen.

Beatitudes

The title given to this piece of Wisdom poetry derives from the repeated use of 'Blessed' (*'ashre*), modelled on Psalm i, 1, and recalling the Beatitudes of the New Testament (Matth. v, 3–11). The main structural difference between Matthew and this poem lies in that the former each time lists the reward of the virtue for which people are blessed, whereas this Cave 4 text provides ordinary, mostly antithetic, parallelisms instead.

> *Blessed is* . . . with a pure heart
> and does not slander with his tongue.
> Blessed are those who hold to Wisdom's precepts
> and do not hold to the ways of iniquity.
> Blessed are those who rejoice in her,
> and do not burst forth in ways of folly.
> Blessed are those who seek her with pure hands,
> and do not pursue her with a treacherous heart.
> Blessed is the man who has attained Wisdom,
> and walks in the Law of the Most High.
> He directs his heart towards her ways,
> and restrains himself by her corrections,
> and always takes delight in her chastisements.
> He does not forsake her when he sees distress,
> nor abandon her in time of strain.
> He will not forget her *on the day of* fear,
> and will not despise *her* when his soul is afflicted.
> For always he will meditate on her,
> and in his distress he will consider *her* . . .

> *He will place her* before his eyes,
> so as not to walk in the ways of *folly*.

BIBLE
INTERPRETATION

● ●

Introductory Note

Five types of biblical commentary have been recovered from the Qumran caves.

The first and least developed form of exegesis is contained in the so-called 'Reworked Pentateuch' texts, consisting of a quasi-traditional text of the Bible, occasionally rearranged and supplemented. The Temple Scroll may be assigned to this group, as well as the fairly, though not strictly, literal Aramaic translations or Targums of the Hebrew Scriptures.

The second type, represented by the Genesis Apocryphon, sets out to render the Bible story more intelligible and attractive by giving it more substance, by reconciling conflicting statements, and by reinterpreting in the light of contemporary standards and beliefs any passages which might seem to give offence. In a somewhat similar manner, a Commentary on Genesis from Cave 4 attempts to adjust the chronology of the Flood to the specific sectarian calendar of the Qumran Community.

The third type of commentary departs from the biblical text and, relying on one or several passages, creates a new story. Among others, the Admonition associated with the Flood and the Words of Moses come into this category.

The fourth and most characteristic form of exegesis applies prophetic texts to the past, present and future of the sect. Normally the commentator expounds a biblical book verse by verse, e.g. Nahum, Habakkuk and the Psalms, but some works – A Midrash on the Last Days, The Heavenly Prince Melchizedek, etc. – follow the traditional Jewish example and assemble passages from different parts of Scripture in order to develop a common theme.

Finally, a substantial amount of free compositions modelled on the Bible, e.g. the Jubilees, or circulating together with the Bible, e.g. the works attributed to Noah, constitute a fifth category of exegesis. In one way, the Aramaic and Hebrew manuscripts of one of the Apocrypha, the Book of Tobit, pertain to this class.

The Targum of Job

Two books of the Hebrew Bible have survived in Aramaic translation in the Qumran caves. A small scroll, found in Cave 11 and measuring 109 cm, has preserved in Aramaic a large portion of the last seven chapters of the Book of Job. Twenty-seven smaller fragments cover parts of Job xvii, 14 to xxxvi, 33. This text, together with small remains from Cave 4 of Leviticus and of another manuscript of Job, represent the oldest extant Aramaic renderings of the Hebrew Bible. The translation of Job frequently differs from the customary text of the Hebrew Bible, but it is unclear whether the divergences are due merely to the difficulty of translating poetry, or to a Hebrew original not identical with the traditional Scripture.

Hebrew Job xl, 12
Look on every one that is proud
and bring him low;
and tread down the wicked
where they stand.

11 QarJob
And every proud spirit
you will smash;
and extinguish the wicked
below them.

It is clear, on the other hand, that the prose narrative of xlii, 9–11 displays notable departures from the text known to us, as may be seen from the following parallel translations:

Hebrew Job xlii
(9) So Eliphaz the Temanite and
Bildad the Shuhite and Zophar the
Naamathite went and did what the
Lord had told them; and the Lord
accepted Job's prayer.
(10) And the Lord restored the
fortunes of Job, when he had prayed
for his friends; and the Lord gave
Job twice as much as he had before.
(11) Then came to him all his
brothers and sisters and all who had
known him before, and ate bread with

11 QarJob
(9) . . .
. . . . . .
God. God heard the voice of
Job and forgave his
friends' sins because of him.
(10) And the Lord returned
to Job with mercy and
doubled all that he had
owned.
(11) All his friends,
brothers and acquaintances
came to Job and they ate

him in his house; and they showed
him sympathy and comforted him for
all the evil that the Lord had brought
upon him; and each of them gave him
a piece of money (or a sheep) and a
ring of gold.

bread with him in his
house; and they comforted
him for all the evil that
God had brought upon him;
and each of them gave him a
lamb and a ring of gold.

The English version provided below (Job xxxvii, 11 to xlii, 11) should therefore be read side by side with the translation of the canonical Job. It will be noticed that Job xxxix, 24 is missing from the Aramaic and xlii, 3 is replaced by xl, 5. Furthermore, in Job xxxviii, 7 the phrase 'angels' is substituted for 'sons of God', a doctrinally suspect expression since Jews rejected the idea of God having children.

Job xxxvii

11 With water He wipes the clouds,
   and brings fire out of the cloud.
12 He speaks and they listen to Him
   and proceed with their works.
   He appoints them over all
   that He has created on earth:
13 either for striking or for benefiting the earth;
   either for famine or shortage;
   or for something good to be on it.
14 Listen to this, Job, and arise!
   Observe the might of God.
15 *Do you* know what God has put on them
   and how He has made light to shine from the cloud?
16 *Do you* know how to robe the cloud with *might*?
17 Because your robe . . .
   For He possesses knowledge . . .
18 *Do you know how to* beat the cloud
   to compress *it into a* mirror?

Job xxxviii

3 Please gird *your loins* like a man,
   and I will question you and you will answer me.
4 Where were you when I made the earth?
   Explain it to me if you possess wisdom.
5 Do you know who fixed its measures?
   Who stretched a line over it?
6 Or to what were its foundations joined
   or who set its cut stone
7 when the morning stars were shining together
   and all the angels of God exclaimed together?
8 Can you shut in the sea with gates
   when it bursts forward from the womb of the abyss,
9 when the clouds were made into its robe
   and the haze its swaddling-clothes.
10 Can you set boundaries to it . . . ? . . .

25 Who fixed a time for the rain
   and a path for the quick clouds
26 to bring the rain down to a land of wilderness
   with no man on it,
27 to satiate the low-lying and isolated places
   to produce sprouting grass.
28 Has the rain a father
   and who begets the mist of dew?
29 And from whose womb did ice come out? . . .

Job xxxix

1 the mountain goats, and the birth *pangs* . . .
2 . . . their months are completed,
   and do you know when they give birth,
3 delivering their young and ejecting them,
   and do you send away their birth pangs?
4 They raise their young and make them go;
   they depart and do not come back to them.
5 Who has set the wild ass free

and who has loosed the onager's rope,

6 to whom I gave the desert for his home
and made the salty land his dwelling.

7 He laughs at the great commotion of the city
and his master's urging he does not hear.

8 He chooses for himself mountains for *pasture*
and he goes after everything green.

9 Does the wild ox wish to serve you
or will he lodge in your stable?

10 Will you tie *the wild ox* with a yoke
and will he plough in the valley *after* you?
And will you . . .
Will you depend on him *because* great is *his strength*? . . .

21 He searches out the valley, he trembles and rejoices,
and mightily advances towards the sword.

22 He laughs at fear and does not shudder,
and does not turn back from the sword.

23 Upon him hangs a lance,
a javelin and a sharp sword . . .

25 and at the sound of the trumpet, he says, Aha,
and from afar he smells the battle,
and he enjoys the rattle of the weapons and the war cries.

26 Does the hawk get excited because of your wisdom
and spread his wings towards the winds?

27 Or does *the eagle* rise at your order
and the bird of prey build *its* nest on high?

28 It dwells on the rock and nests . . .

Job xl

6 . . . and from the cloud
God answered Job and said to him:

7 Like a man, please gird your loins;
I will question you, and you will answer me.

8 Would you indeed tear up the judgement
and declare me guilty so that you may be innocent?

9 Or do you have an arm like God
or thunder with a voice like His?

10 Throw away, please, pride and haughtiness
   and you will put on splendour, glory and honour.
11 Throw away, please, the heat of your wrath
   and observe every proud man and humble him.
12 And every proud spirit you will smash
   and you will extinguish the wicked *in* their places.
13 And hide them all in the dust
   and cover *with* ashes . . .

25 Will you pull a crocodile with a hook
   or tie up its tongue with a rope?
26 Will you put a muzzle on his nose
   and will you pierce his cheek with your chisel?
27 Will he speak gently with you
   or will he speak with you pleadingly?
28 Will he make a covenant with you
   or will you handle him as a slave for ever?
29 Will you play with him like a *bird*,
   and will you bind him with a string for your daughters? . . .

Job xli

8 They cling to one another
   and no breath passes between them.
9 One holds to another,
   and they do not separate.
10 His sneezing lights fire between his eyes
   like the shine of dawn.
11 Torches come forth out of his mouth;
   they leap like tongues of fire.
12 From his nostrils smoke goes forth
   like burning thorn and incense.
13 His breath spews out coals
   and sparks come out of his mouth.
14 His strength dwells in his neck
   and vigour springs before him.
15 The folds of his flesh are clinging,
   moulded *over him* like iron . . .
26 . . . And he is king over all the reptiles.

Job xlii

1   Job answered and said before God:

2   I know that Thou canst do all things
    and dost not lack in strength and wisdom.
    (xl, 5) I have spoken once and will not revoke it,
    a second time, and I will not add to it.
    (xlii, 4) Listen, please, and I will speak;
    I will question you and you must answer me.

5   I had heard of you by the hearing of the ear
    and now my eyes see you.

6   Therefore I am melting and dissolve
    and become dust and ashes . . .

9   . . . God heard the voice of Job and forgave them their sins
    because of him.

10   And God returned to Job with mercy and doubled all that
    he had owned.

11   All his friends, brothers and acquaintances came to Job
    and they ate bread with him in his house, and they com-
    forted him for all the misery that God had brought on him
    and each gave him a ewe-lamb and a ring of gold.

A Paraphrase of Exodus

Nine fragments of a manuscript written in Hasmonaean characters contain a paraphrase of Genesis and Exodus, judging from disconnected expressions relating to the creation of the world by God's word, to various living creatures, the establishment of man as ruler over the rest of beings, the prohibition against eating from the tree of knowledge and the rebellion against God which led to the Flood. This fragment refers to the commissioning of Moses, his vision of the burning bush, Moses' and Aaron's encounter with Pharaoh and the plagues which afflicted Egypt.

. . . *And* He sent to them Moses . . . in the vision . . . in the signs and marvels . . . And He sent them to Pharaoh . . . plagues . . . marvels for Egypt . . . and they carried His word to Pharaoh to send away *their people*. But He hardened Pharaoh's heart *to* sin so that the *Men of Israel* might know for eternal *generations*. And He changed their *waters* to blood. Frogs were in all their land and lice in all their territories, gnats in their houses and they struck all their . . . And He smote with pestilence *all* their flock and their beasts He delivered to death. He put darkness into their land and obscurity into their houses so that they could not see one another. *And He smote* their land with hail and *their* soil *with* frost to cause *all* the fruit of nourishment *to perish*. And He brought locust to cover the face of the *earth*, heavy locust in all their territory to eat everything green in *their* land . . . And God hardened *Pharaoh's* heart so that he should not dismiss *them* . . . and in order to increase wonders. *And He smote their first-born*, the beginning of all *their strength*.

The Genesis Apocryphon

Found in Cave 1, the Genesis Apocryphon is an incomplete manuscript with twenty-two surviving columns of Aramaic text. The beginning of the manuscript is missing. But it would seem that the surviving section was preceded by sixteen sheets of which only the end of the last one has been preserved. If so, the story of Noah which begins the existing portion of the scroll must have been preceded by an extensive account of the creation, Adam and Eve, and the Genesis story up to Enoch and Noah. Columns II–V narrate the miraculous birth of Noah, whose father, Lamech, suspects that his wife has conceived by one of the fallen angels. Her denials fail to convince him and he asks his father, Methuselah, to travel to Paradise and obtain reassurance from his own father, Enoch. Columns VI–XV contain Noah's first-person account of the Flood and of his journeys. Column X describes Noah's sacrifice after the Flood. Column XI deals with the covenant between God and Noah with a mention of a ban on eating blood. Column XII recounts the planting of a vineyard by Noah and his tasting of wine. The badly damaged columns XIII–XV contain a vision concerning trees and its interpretation. Two further columns XVI–XVII deal with the division of the earth among the sons of Noah. Col. XVIII is completely lost. Columns XIX–XXII, corresponding to Genesis XII–XV, deal with Abraham's journey to Egypt, his return to Canaan, the war against the invading Mesopotamian kings, and the renewal to him of a divine promise of a son. This lively and delightful narrative, largely devoid of sectarian bias, throws valuable light on inter-Testamental Bible interpretation. It is a mixture of Targum, Midrash, rewritten Bible and autobiography. Most scholars assign the manuscript to the late first century BCE or the first half of the first century CE. The composition itself is generally thought to originate from the second century BCE.

II Behold, I thought then within my heart that conception was due to the Watchers and the Holy Ones . . . and to the Giants . . . and my heart was troubled within me because of this child. Then I, Lamech, approached Bathenosh *my* wife in haste and said to her, '. . . by the Most High, the Great Lord, the King of all the worlds and Ruler of the Sons of Heaven, until you tell me all

'For in the splendour of praises is the glory of His kingship'
(Song of the holocaust of the seventh Sabbath, page 238).
Fragment of the Songs for the Holocaust of the Sabbath,
from Cave 4, Qumran, mid-1st century BCE

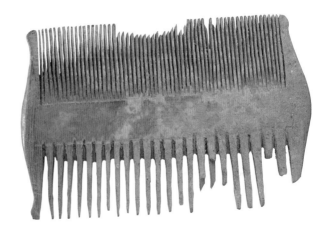

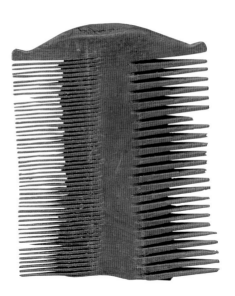

'. . . and beautiful is her face! How . . . fine are the hairs of her head!'
(The Genesis Apocryphon, page 276). Boxwood combs for combing
and delousing, from Qumran, 1st century BCE–1st century CE

things truthfully, if . . . Tell me *this truthfully* and not falsely . . . by the King of all the worlds until you tell me truthfully and not falsely.'

Then Bathenosh my wife spoke to me with much heat *and* . . . said, 'O my brother, O my lord, remember my pleasure . . . the lying together and my soul within its body. *And I tell you* all things truthfully.'

My heart was then greatly troubled within me, and when Bathenosh my wife saw that my countenance had changed . . . Then she mastered her anger and spoke to me saying, 'O my lord, O my *brother, remember* my pleasure! I swear to you by the Holy Great One, the King of *the heavens* . . . that this seed is yours and that *this* conception is from you. This fruit was planted by you . . . and by no stranger or Watcher or Son of Heaven . . . *Why* is your countenance thus changed and dismayed, and why is your spirit thus distressed . . . I speak to you truthfully.'

Then I, Lamech, ran to Methuselah my father, and *I told* him all these things. *And I asked him to go to Enoch* his father for he would surely learn all things from him. For he was beloved, and he shared the lot *of the angels*, who taught him all things. And when Methuselah heard *my words . . . he went to* Enoch his father to learn all things truthfully from him . . . his will.

He went at once to Parwain and he found him there . . . *and* he said to Enoch his father, 'O my father, O my lord, to whom I . . . And I say to you, lest you be angry with me because I come here . . .'

VI *I abstained* from injustice and in the womb of her who conceived me I searched for truth. And when I emerged from my mother's womb, I was planted for truth and I lived all my days in truth and walked in the paths of eternal truth. And the Holy One was with me . . . on my pathways truth sped to warn me off the . . . of lie which led to darkness . . . and I girded my loins with the vision of truth and wisdom . . . paths of violence . . . Then I, Noah, became a man and clung to truth and seized . . . and I took Amzara, his daughter as my wife. She conceived and bore me three sons *and daughters*. Then I took wives for my sons from among my brother's daughters, and I gave my daughters to my brother's sons according to the law of the eternal precept which the Most High *ordained* to the sons of man . . . And in my days, when according to my reckoning . . . ten jubilees had been completed, the moment came for my sons to take wives for themselves . . . heaven, I saw in a vision and was explained and made known the action of the sons of heaven and . . . the heavens. Then I hid this mystery in my heart and explained it to no man . . .

VII . . . *Until* the ark rested on one of the mountains of Ararat (HWRRT). And eternal fire . . . And I atoned for the whole earth, all of it . . .

XI . . . *Then* I, Noah, went out and walked on the earth, through its length and breadth . . . delight on her in their leaves and in their fruit. And all the land was filled with grass and herbs and grain. Then I blessed the Lord of heaven who made splendid things. He is for ever and praise is His. And I repeated the blessing on account of His grace for the earth and on account of His removing and causing to perish from it all those who do violence and wickedness and lies and on account of His rescuing the righteous man . . . *God* was revealed to me and *the Lord* of heaven spoke to me and said to me: 'Do not fear, Noah. I shall be with you and with your sons who will be like you for ever . . . of the earth and rule over them . . . and over its deserts and its mountains and all that are on them. And behold, I give all of it to you and to your sons to eat the green things and the grass of the earth. But you shall not eat any blood . . .'

XII . . . And afterwards I descended* . . . I and my sons and the sons *of my sons* . . . for the destruction was great on the earth . . . after the Flood. To my first son *Shem* was born, to begin with, a son, Arpachshad, two years after the Flood. *And* all the sons of Shem, all of them, *were Elam,* and Ashur, Arpachshad, Lud and Aram, and five daughters. *And the sons of Ham: Kush and Misrain* and Put and Canaan, and seven daughters. And the sons of Japheth: Gomer and Magog and Madai and Yavan *and* Tubal and Mashok and Tiras, and four daughters. *And* I began, I and all my sons, to fill the land and I planted a big vineyard on Mount Lubar and in the fourth year it produced wine for me . . . *And* when the first festival *came,* on the first day of the first festival in the . . . month . . . I opened this jar and I began to drink on the first day of the fifth year . . . On this day I summoned my sons, my grandsons and all our wives and their daughters, and we assembled together and we went . . . and I blessed the Lord of heaven,

* from the mountains of Ararat.

the Most High God, the Great Holy One who saved us from perdition . . .

XVII . . . And Shem, my son, divided his inheritance among his sons. And the first lot fell to Elam in the north, by the waters of the river Tigris as far as the Red Sea, whose source is in the north, and it turns to the west to Assyria as far as the Tigris . . . And after it to Aram, the land between the two rivers, as far as the top of the mountain of Ashur . . . Japheth, divided his inheritance between his sons. He gave the first lot to Gomer in the north as far as the river Tina, and afterwards to Magog, and afterwards to Media, and afterwards to Yavan, all the islands that are by Lydia. And the lot which is between the bay of Lydia and the second bay, he gave to Tubal . . . And to Meshek the sea . . .

XIX . . . And I, Abram, departed . . . and I travelled towards the south . . . until I came to Hebron *at the time when Hebron* was being built; and I dwelt there *two years.*

Now there was famine in all this land, and hearing that there was prosperity in Egypt I went . . . to the land of Egypt . . . I *came to* the river Karmon, one of the branches of the River Nile . . . and I crossed the seven branches of the River . . . We passed through our land and entered the land of the sons of Ham, the land of Egypt.

And on the night of our entry into Egypt, I, Abram, dreamt a dream; *and behold,* I saw in my dream a cedar tree and a palm tree . . . men came and they sought to cut down the cedar tree and to pull up its roots, leaving the palm tree standing alone. But the palm tree cried out saying, 'Do not cut down this cedar tree, for cursed be he who shall fell *it.*' And the cedar tree was spared because of the palm tree and *was* not felled.

And during the night I woke from my dream, and I said to Sarai my wife, 'I have dreamt a dream . . . *and I am* fearful *because of* this dream.' She said to me, 'Tell me your dream that I may know it.' So I began to tell her this dream . . . *the interpretation* of the dream . . . '. . . that they will seek to kill me, but will spare you . . . *Say to them* of me, "He is my brother", and because of you I shall live, and because of you my life shall be saved . . .'

And Sarai wept that night on account of my words . . .

Then we journeyed towards Zoan, I and Sarai . . . by her life that none should see her . . .

And when those five years had passed, three men from among the princes of Egypt *came at the command* of Pharaoh of Zoan to inquire after *my* business and after my wife . . .

During the party, the Egyptians must have seen Sarai, and on their return they praised her to the king.

XX '. . . and beautiful is her face! How . . . fine are the hairs of her head! How lovely are her eyes! How desirable her nose and all the radiance of her countenance . . . How fair are her breasts and how beautiful all her whiteness! How pleasing are her arms and how perfect her hands, and how *desirable* all the appearance of her hands! How fair are her palms and how long and slender are her fingers! How comely are her feet, how perfect her thighs! No virgin or bride led into the marriage chamber is more beautiful than she; she is fairer than all other women. Truly, her beauty is greater than theirs. Yet together with all this grace she possesses abundant wisdom, so that whatever she does is perfect.' When the king heard the words of Harkenosh and his two companions, for all three spoke as with one voice, he desired her greatly and sent out at once to take her. And seeing her, he was amazed by all her beauty and took her to be his wife, but me he sought to kill. Sarai said to the king, 'He is my brother,' that I might benefit from her, and I, Abram, was spared because of her and I was not slain.

And I, Abram, wept aloud that night, I and my nephew Lot, because Sarai had been taken from me by force. I prayed that night and I begged and implored, and I said in my sorrow while my tears ran down: 'Blessed art Thou, O Most High God, Lord of all the worlds, Thou who art Lord and king of all things and who rulest over all the kings of the earth and judgest them all! I cry now before Thee, my Lord, against Pharaoh of Zoan the king of Egypt, because of my wife who has been taken from me by force. Judge him for me that I may see Thy mighty hand raised against him and against all his household, and that he may not be able to defile my wife this night separating her from me, and that they may know Thee, my Lord, that Thou art Lord of all the kings of the earth.' And I wept and was sorrowful.

And during that night the Most High God sent a spirit to scourge him, an evil spirit to all his household; and it scourged him and all his household. And he was unable to approach her, and although he was with her for two years, he knew her not.

At the end of those two years the scourges and afflictions grew greater and more grievous upon him and all his household, so he sent for all *the sages* of Egypt, for all the magicians, together with all the healers of Egypt, that they might heal him and all his household of this scourge. But not one healer or magician or sage could stay to cure him, for the spirit scourged them all and they fled.

Then Harkenosh came to me, beseeching me to go to the king and to pray for him and to lay my hands upon him that he might live, for the king had dreamt a dream . . . But Lot said to him, 'Abram my uncle cannot pray for the king while Sarai his wife is with him. Go, therefore, and tell the king to restore his wife to her husband; then he will pray for him and he shall live.'

When Harkenosh had heard the words of Lot, he went to the king and said, 'All these scourges and afflictions with which my lord the king is scourged and afflicted are because of Sarai the wife of Abram. Let Sarai be restored to Abram her husband, and this scourge and the spirit of festering shall vanish from you.'

And he called me and said, 'What have you done to me with regard to *Sarai*? You said to me, She is my sister, whereas she is your wife; and I took her to be my wife. Behold your wife who is with me; depart and go hence from all the land of Egypt! And now pray for me and my house that this evil spirit may be expelled from it.'

So I prayed *for him* . . . and I laid my hands on his *head*, and the scourge departed from him and the evil *spirit* was expelled *from him*, and he lived. And the king rose to tell me . . . and the king swore an oath to me that . . . and the king gave her much *silver and gold* and much raiment of fine linen and purple . . . And Hagar also . . . and he appointed men to lead *me* out *of all the land of Egypt*. And I, Abram, departed with very great flocks and with silver and gold, and I went up from *Egypt* together with my nephew *Lot*. Lot had great flocks also, and he took a wife for himself from among *the daughters of Egypt*.

I pitched my camp   **XXI** *in* every place in which I had formerly camped until I came to Bethel, the place where I had built an altar. And I built a second altar and laid on it a sacrifice, and an

offering to the Most High God. And there I called on the name of
the Lord of worlds and praised the Name of God and blessed God,
and I gave thanks before God for all the riches and favours which
He had bestowed on me. For He had dealt kindly towards me
and had led me back in peace into this land. After that day, Lot
departed from me on account of the deeds of our shepherds. He
went away and settled in the valley of the Jordan, together with all
his flocks; and I myself added more to them. He kept his sheep
and journeyed as far as Sodom, and he bought a house for himself
in Sodom and dwelt in it. But I dwelt on the mountain of Bethel
and it grieved me that my nephew Lot had departed from me.
And God appeared to me in a vision at night and said to me, 'Go to
Ramath Hazor which is north of Bethel, the place where you
dwell, and lift up your eyes and look to the east and to the west
and to the south and to the north; and behold all this land which I
give to you and your seed for ever.'

The next morning, I went up to Ramath Hazor and from that
high place I beheld the land from the River of Egypt to Lebanon
and Senir, and from the Great Sea to Hauran, and all the land of
Gebal as far as Kadesh, and all the Great Desert to the east of
Hauran and Senir as far as the Euphrates. And He said to me, 'I
will give all this land to your seed and they shall possess it for ever.
And I will multiply your seed like the dust of the earth which no
man can number; neither shall any man number your seed. Rise
and go! Behold the length and breadth of the land, for it is yours;
and after you, I will give it to your seed for ever.'

And I, Abram, departed to travel about and see the land. I
began my journey at the river Gihon and travelled along the coast
of the Sea until I came to the Mountain of the Bull (Taurus). Then
I travelled from the coast of the Great Salt Sea and journeyed
towards the east by the Mountain of the Bull, across the breadth
of the land, until I came to the river Euphrates. I journeyed along
the Euphrates until I came to the Red Sea in the east, and I travelled along the coast of the Red Sea until I came to the tongue of
the Sea of Reeds* which flows out from the Red Sea. Then I pursued my way in the south until I came to the river Gihon, and
returning, I came to my house in peace and found all things pros-
perous there. I went to dwell at the Oaks of Mamre, which is at

* The modern Red Sea.

Hebron, north-east of Hebron; and I built an altar there, and laid on it a sacrifice and an oblation to the Most High God. I ate and drank there, I and all the men of my household, and I sent for Mamre, Ornam and Eshkol, the three Amorite brothers, my friends, and they ate and drank with me.

Before these days, Kedorlaomer king of Elam had set out with Amrafel king of Babylon, Ariok king of Kaptok, and Tidal king of the nations which lie between the rivers; and they had waged war against Bera king of Sodom, Birsha king of Gomorrah, Shinab king of Admah, Shemiabad king of Zeboim, and against the king of Bela. All these had made ready for battle in the valley of Siddim, and the king of Elam and the other kings with him had prevailed over the king of Sodom and his companions and had imposed a tribute upon them.

For twelve years they had paid their tribute to the king of Elam, but in the thirteenth year they rebelled against him. And in the fourteenth year, the king of Elam placed himself at the head of all his allies and went up by the Way of the Wilderness; and they smote and pillaged from the river Euphrates onward. They smote the Refaim who were at Ashteroth Karnaim, the Zumzamim who were at Ammon, the Emim *who were at* Shaveh ha-Keriyyoth, and the Horites who were in the mountains of Gebal, until they came to El Paran which is in the Wilderness. And they returned . . . at Hazazon Tamar.

The king of Sodom went out to meet them, together with the king *of Gomorrah*, the king of Admah, the king of Zeboim, and the king of Bela, *and they fought* a battle in the valley *of Siddim* against Kedorlaomer *king of Elam and the kings* who were with him. But the king of Sodom was vanquished and fled, and the king of Gomorrah fell into the pits . . . *And* the king of Elam *carried off* all the riches of Sodom and *Gomorrah* . . . and they took Lot the nephew   **XXII** of Abram who dwelt with them in Sodom, together with all his possessions.

Now one of the shepherds of the flocks which Abram had given to Lot escaped from captivity and came to Abram; at that time Abram dwelt in Hebron. He told him that Lot his nephew had been taken, together with all his possessions, but that he had not been slain and that the kings had gone by the Way of the Great Valley of the Jordan in the direction of their land, taking captives and plundering and smiting and slaying, and that they were journeying towards the land of Damascus.

Abram wept because of Lot his nephew. Then he braced himself; he rose up and chose from among his servants three hundred and eighteen fighting men trained for war, and Ornam and Eshkol and Mamre went with him also. He pursued them until he came to Dan, and came on them while they were camped in the valley of Dan. He fell on them at night from four sides and during the night he slew them; he crushed them and put them to flight, and all of them fled before him until they came to Helbon which is north of Damascus. He rescued from them all their captives, and all their booty and possessions. He also delivered Lot his nephew, together with all his possessions, and he brought back all the captives which they had taken.

When the king of Sodom learned that Abram had brought back all the captives and all the booty, he came out to meet him; and he went to Salem, which is Jerusalem.

Abram camped in the valley of Shaveh, which is the valley of the king, the valley of Beth-ha-Kerem; and Melchizedek king of Salem brought out food and drink to Abram and to all the men who were with him. He was the Priest of the Most High God. And he blessed Abram and said, 'Blessed be Abram by the Most High God, Lord of heaven and earth! And blessed be the Most High God who has delivered your enemies into your hand!' And Abram gave him the tithe of all the possessions of the king of Elam and his companions.

Then the king of Sodom approached and said to Abram, 'My lord Abram, give me the souls which are mine, which you have delivered from the king of Elam and taken captive, and you may have all the possessions.'

Then said Abram to the king of Sodom, 'I raise my hand this day to the Most High God, Lord of heaven and earth! I will take nothing of yours, not even a shoe-lace or shoe-strap, lest you say, Abram's riches come from my possessions! I will take nothing but that which the young men with me have eaten already, and the portion of the three men who have come with me. They shall decide whether they will give you their portion.' And Abram returned all the possessions and all the captives and gave them to the king of Sodom; he freed all the captives from this land who were with him, and sent them all back.

After these things, God appeared to Abram in a vision and said to him, 'Behold, ten years have passed since you departed from Haran. For two years you dwelt here and you spent seven years in Egypt, and one year has passed since you returned from Egypt. And now examine and count all you have, and see how it has grown to be double that which came out with you from Haran. And now do not fear, I am with you; I am your help and your strength. I am a shield above you and a mighty safeguard round about you. Your wealth and possessions shall multiply greatly.' But Abram said, 'My Lord God, I have great wealth and possessions but what good shall they do to me? I shall die naked; childless shall I go hence. A child from my household shall inherit from me. Eliezer son . . . shall inherit from me.' And He said to him, 'He shall not be your heir, but one who shall spring *from your body shall inherit from you.*'

A Genesis Commentary

This scroll fragment, a paraphrase of Genesis, attempts to adapt the chronology of the biblical Flood story to the solar calendar of the Qumran Community. Along more general lines, it seeks also to explain certain peculiarities of the scriptural text, e.g., why, despite Ham's disrespect to his father, it was not he, but his son Canaan, who was cursed by Noah.

I *In the* four hundred and eightieth year of the life of Noah came their end, that of antediluvian mankind. And God said, *My spirit shall not abide in man for ever and their days shall be determined to be one hundred and twenty years* (Gen. vi, 3) – until the end of the Flood. *And the waters of the Flood arrived on the earth in the six hundredth year of the life of Noah, in the second month* – on the first day of the week – *on the seventeenth* of the month. *On that day all the fountains of the great deep burst forth and the windows of the heavens were opened. And rain fell on the earth forty days and forty nights* (vii, 11–12) until the twenty-sixth day of the third month, the fifth day of the week. *And the waters prevailed upon the earth a hundred and fifty days* (vii, 24) – until the fourteenth day *of the seventh month*, the third day of the week. *And* at the end of *a hundred and fifty days, the waters had abated* – two days, the fourth and the fifth day, and on the sixth day – *the ark came to rest on the mountains of* Hurarat,* *on the seventeenth day of the seventh month* (viii, 3–4). *And the waters continued to abate until the tenth month, the first day* of the month – the fourth day of the week – *and the tops of the mountains appeared* (viii, 5). *At the end of forty days* – after the tops of the mountains had been seen – *Noah opened the window of the ark* (viii, 6) – on the tenth day of the eleventh month. *And he sent forth the dove to see if the waters had subsided* (viii, 8), *but she did not find a resting-place and returned to him to the ark* (viii, 9). *He waited another seven days and again sent her forth* (viii, 10). *She came back to him with a plucked olive leaf in her beak* (viii, 10–11) – this is the twenty-fourth day of the eleventh month, the first day of the week. *And Noah knew that the waters had subsided from the earth* (viii, 11).

* or: Turarat.

At the end of *another seven days, he sent forth the dove and it did not return again* (viii, 12) – this is the *first* day *of the twelfth* month, *the first day* of the week. At the end of three *weeks after Noah had sent forth the dove* which *did not return to him any more, the waters dried up from the earth and Noah removed the covering of the ark and looked, and behold, the face of the ground was dry* (viii, 13). This was the *first day of the first month. And it happened*   **II** *in the six hundred and first year of the life of Noah,* on the seventeenth day of *the second month that the earth was dry* (viii, 14) – on the first day of the week. On that day *Noah went forth* from the ark (viii, 18) at the end of a full year of three hundred and sixty-four days, on the first day of the week, on the *seventeenth of the second month . . . And Noah awoke from his wine and knew what his youngest son had done to him. And he said, Cursed be Canaan; a slave of slaves shall he be to his brothers* (ix, 24 – 5). But he did not curse Ham but only his son, for *God had blessed the sons of Noah. And let him dwell in the tents of Shem* (ix, 27). He gave the land to Abram, his beloved. *Terah* was one hundred and forty-five years old when he *went forth from Ur of the Chaldees and came to Haran* (xi, 31). Now *Abram was* seventy years old and for five years Abram dwelt in Haran. And afterwards Abram went forth to the land of Canaan.

Commentaries on Isaiah

Translatable fragments of four commentaries on Isaiah were discovered in Cave 4. These two deal with the Jewish opponents of the sect.

I

And there shall come forth a rod from the stem of Jesse and a Branch shall grow out of its roots. And the spirit of the Lord shall rest upon him, the spirit of wisdom and understanding, the spirit of counsel and might, the spirit of knowledge and of the fear of the Lord. And his delight shall be in the fear of the Lord. He shall not judge by what his eyes see, or pass sentence by what his ears hear; he shall judge the poor righteously and shall pass sentence justly on the humble of the earth (xi, 1–3).

Interpreted, this concerns the Branch of David who shall arise at the end of days ... God will uphold him with the spirit of might, and will give him a throne of glory and a crown of holiness and many-coloured garments ... He will put a sceptre in his hand and he shall rule over all the nations ... And his sword shall judge all the peoples.

And as for that which he said, *He shall not judge by what his eyes see or pass sentence by what his ears hear*: interpreted, this means that ... as the Priests teach him, so will he judge; and as they order, so will he pass sentence.

II

For ten acres of vineyard shall produce only one bath, and an omer of seed shall yield but one ephah (v, 10).

Interpreted, this saying concerns the last days, the devastation of the land by sword and famine. At the time of the Visitation of the land there shall be *Woe to those who rise early in the morning to run after strong drink, to those who linger in the evening until wine inflames them. They have zither and harp and timbrel and flute and wine at their feasts, but they do not regard the work of the Lord or see the deeds of His hand. Therefore my people go into exile for want of knowledge, and their noblemen die of hunger and their multitude is parched with thirst. Therefore Hell has widened its gullet and opened its mouth beyond measure, and the nobility of Jerusalem and her multitude go down, her tumult and he who rejoices in her* (v, 11–14).

These are the Scoffers in Jerusalem who have *despised the Law of the Lord and scorned the word of the Holy One of Israel. Therefore the wrath of the Lord was kindled against His people. He stretched out His hand against them and smote them; the mountains trembled and their corpses were like sweepings in the middle of the streets. And His wrath has not relented for all these things and His hand is stretched out still* (v, 24–5).

This is the congregation of Scoffers in Jerusalem . . .

Commentary on Hosea

In this fragment, the unfaithful wife is the Jewish people led astray by her lovers, the Gentiles.

She knew not that it was I who gave her the new wine and oil, who lavished upon her silver and gold which they used for Baal (ii, 8).

Interpreted, this means that *they ate and* were filled, but they forgot God ... They cast His commandments behind them which He had sent *by the hand of* His servants the Prophets, and they listened to those who led them astray. They revered them, and in their blindness they feared them as though they were gods.

Therefore I will take back my corn in its time and my wine in its season. I will take away my wool and my flax lest they cover her nakedness. I will uncover her shame before the eyes of her lovers and no man shall deliver her from out of my hand (ii, 9-10).

Interpreted, this means that He smote them with hunger and nakedness that they might be shamed and disgraced in the sight of the nations on which they relied. They will not deliver them from their miseries.

I will put an end to her rejoicing, her feasts, her new moons, her Sabbaths, and all her festivals (ii, 11).

Interpreted, this means that *they have rejected the ruling of the Law, and have* followed the festivals of the nations. But *their rejoicing shall come to an end and* shall be changed into mourning. *I will ravage her vines and her fig trees, of which she said, 'They are my wage which my lovers have given me'. I will make of them a thicket and the wild beasts shall eat them* ... (ii, 12).

Commentary on Nahum

Substantial remains of a Nahum Commentary were retrieved from Cave 4. They cover parts of chapters i and ii of the biblical book, and the first fourteen verses of chapter iii. Their historical significance has been discussed in the introduction (pp. 57–61). It is worthy of note that the commentator employs not only cryptograms (Kittim, furious young lion, etc.), but the actual names of two Greek kings (Demetrius and Antiochus). Reference to 'the furious young lion' as one who 'hangs men alive' shows that 'hanging', probably a synonym for crucifixion, was practised as a form of execution. It is also legislated for in the Temple Scroll, where it is the capital punishment reserved for traitors. In biblical law, by contrast, only the dead body of an executed criminal is to be hanged, that is, displayed in public as an example (Deut. xxi, 21).

On palaeographical grounds the manuscript is dated to the second half of the first century B C E.

He rebukes the sea and dries it up (i, 4a).

Its interpretation: the sea is all the *Kittim who are* . . . to execute judgement against them and destroy them from the face *of the earth*, together with *all* their commanders whose dominion shall be finished.

Whither the lion goes, there is the lion's cub, with none to disturb it (ii, 11b).

Interpreted, this concerns Demetrius king of Greece who sought, on the counsel of those who seek smooth things, to enter Jerusalem. *But God did not permit the city to be delivered* into the hands of the kings of Greece, from the time of Antiochus until the coming of the rulers of the Kittim. But then she shall be trampled under their feet . . .

The lion tears enough for its cubs and it chokes prey for its lionesses (ii, 12a).

Interpreted, this concerns the furious young lion who strikes by means of his great men, and by means of the men of his council.

And chokes prey for its lionesses; and it fills its caves with prey and its dens with victims (ii, 12a–b).

Interpreted, this concerns the furious young lion *who executes revenge* on those who seek smooth things and hangs men alive, . . . formerly in Israel. Because of a man hanged alive on *the* tree, He proclaims, '*Behold I am against you, says the Lord of Hosts*'.

Woe to the city of blood; it is full of lies and rapine (iii, 1a–b).

Interpreted, this is the city of Ephraim, those who seek smooth things during the last days, who walk in lies and falsehood.

The prowler is not wanting, noise of whip and noise of rattling wheel, prancing horse and jolting chariot, charging horsemen, flame and glittering spear, a multitude of the slain and a heap of carcasses. There is no end to the corpses; they stumble upon their corpses (iii, 1c–3).

Interpreted, this concerns the dominion of those who seek smooth things, from the midst of whose assembly the sword of the nations shall never be wanting. Captivity, looting, and burning shall be among them, and exile out of dread for the enemy. A multitude of guilty corpses shall fall in their days; there shall be no end to the sum of their slain. They shall also stumble upon their body of flesh because of their guilty counsel.

Because of the many harlotries of the well-favoured harlot, the mistress of seduction, she who sells nations through her harlotries and families through her seductions (iii, 4).

Interpreted, this concerns those who lead Ephraim astray, who lead many astray through their false teaching, their lying tongue, and deceitful lips – kings, princes, priests, and people, together with the stranger who joins them. Cities and families shall perish through their counsel; honourable men and rulers shall fall through their tongue's *decision*.

I will cast filth upon you and treat you with contempt and render you despicable, so that all who look upon you shall flee from you (iii, 6–7a).

Interpreted, this concerns those who seek smooth things, whose evil deeds shall be uncovered to all Israel at the end of time.

'My sons, be careful with the heritage that is handed over to you,
which your fathers have given you' (The Testament of Qahat, page 312).
Leather phylactery cases, to be worn on the head (nos 1–4) and
the arm (no. 5), from Qumran, 1st century BCE–1st century CE

'Between the two tamarisk trees in the Vale of Akhon, in their midst dig three cubits. There there are two pots full of silver' (The Copper Scroll, page 323). Twenty-four silver *shekalim* and half-*shekalim*, minted at Tyre, from a hoard of 561 coins found at Qumran, 103/2–10/9 BCE

Many shall understand their iniquity and treat them with contempt because of their guilty presumption. When the glory of
Judah shall arise, the simple of Ephraim shall flee from their
assembly; they shall abandon those who lead them astray and
shall join Israel.

They shall say, Niniveh is laid waste; who shall grieve over her?
Whence shall I seek comforters for you? (iii, 7b).

Interpreted, this concerns those who seek smooth things,
whose council shall perish and whose congregation shall be dispersed. They shall lead the assembly astray no more, and the
simple shall support their council no more.

Which was surrounded by waters, whose rampart was the sea and
whose walls were waters? (iii, 8b).

Interpreted, these are her valiant men, her almighty warriors.

Yet she was exiled; she went into captivity. Her children were
crushed at the top of all the streets. They cast lots for her honourable
men, and all her great men were bound with chains (iii, 10).

Interpreted, this concerns Manasseh in the final age, whose
kingdom shall be brought low by *Israel* . . . his wives, his children,
and his little ones shall go into captivity. His mighty men and honourable men *shall perish* by the sword.

Commentary on Habakkuk

This well-preserved and detailed exposition of the first two chapters of the Book of Habakkuk comes from Cave 1 and was published in 1950.

The palaeographical dating of the manuscript (30–1 BCE) has been confirmed by radiocarbon tests. The Habakkuk Commentary is one of the main sources for the study of Qumran origins, as well as Essene Bible exegesis and the sect's theology regarding prophecy.

Oracle of Habakkuk the prophet. How long, O Lord, shall I cry for help and Thou wilt not hear? (i, 1–2).

Interpreted, this concerns the beginning of the *final* generation . . .

Behold the nations and see, marvel and be astonished; for I accomplish a deed in your days, but you will not believe it when told (i, 5).

Interpreted, this concerns those who were unfaithful together with the Liar, in that they *did* not *listen to the word received by* the Teacher of Righteousness from the mouth of God. And it concerns the unfaithful of the New *Covenant* in that they have not believed in the Covenant of God *and have profaned* His holy Name. And likewise, this saying is to be interpreted *as concerning those who* will be unfaithful at the end of days. They, the men of violence and the breakers of the Covenant, will not believe when they hear all that *is to happen to* the final generation from the Priest *in whose heart* God set *understanding* that he might interpret all the words of His servants the Prophets, through whom He foretold all that would happen to His people and *His land.*

For behold, I rouse the Chaldeans, that bitter and hasty nation (i, 6a).

Interpreted, this concerns the Kittim *who are* quick and valiant in war, causing many to perish. *All the world shall fall* under the dominion of the Kittim, and the *wicked* . . . they shall not believe in the laws of *God* . . .

Who march through the breadth of the earth to take possession of dwellings which are not their own (i, 6b).

... they shall march across the plain, smiting and plundering the cities of the earth. For it is as He said, *To take possession of dwellings which are not their own.*

They are fearsome and terrible; their justice and grandeur proceed from themselves (i, 7).

Interpreted, this concerns the Kittim who inspire all the nations with fear *and dread.* All their evil plotting is done with intention and they deal with all the nations in cunning and guile.

Their horses are swifter than leopards and fleeter than evening wolves. Their horses step forward proudly and spread their wings; they fly from afar like an eagle avid to devour. All of them come for violence; the look on their faces is like the east wind (i, 8–9a).

Interpreted, this concerns the Kittim who trample the earth with their horses and beasts. They come *from afar,* from the islands of the sea, to devour all the peoples *like an eagle* which cannot be satisfied, and they address *all the peoples* with anger and *wrath and fury* and indignation. For it is as He said, *The look on their faces is like the east wind.*

They scoff at kings, and princes are their laughing-stock (i, 10a).

Interpreted, this means that they mock the great and despise the venerable; they ridicule kings and princes and scoff at the mighty host.

They laugh at every fortress; they pile up earth and take it (i, 10b).

Interpreted, this concerns the commanders of the Kittim who despise the fortresses of the peoples and laugh at them in derision. To capture them, they encircle them with a mighty host, and out of fear and terror they deliver themselves into their hands. They destroy them because of the sins of their inhabitants.

The wind then sweeps on and passes; and they make of their strength their god (i, 11).

Interpreted, *this concerns* the commanders of the Kittim who, on the counsel of *the* House of Guilt, pass one in front of the other; one after another *their* commanders come to lay waste the earth. *And they make of their strength their god . . .*

Art Thou not from everlasting, O Lord, my God, my Holy One? We shall not die. Thou hast ordained them, O Lord, **V** *for judgement; Thou hast established them, O Rock, for chastisement. Their eyes are too pure to behold evil; and Thou canst not look on distress* (i, 12–13a).

Interpreted, this saying means that God will not destroy His people by the hand of the nations; God will execute the judgement of the nations by the hand of His elect. And through their chastisement all the wicked of His people shall expiate their guilt who keep His commandments in their distress. For it is as he said, *Too pure of eyes to behold evil*: interpreted, this means that they have not lusted after their eyes during the age of wickedness.

O traitors, why do you stare and stay silent when the wicked swallows up one more righteous than he? (i, 13b).

Interpreted, this concerns the House of Absalom and the members of its council who were silent at the time of the chastisement of the Teacher of Righteousness and gave him no help against the Liar who flouted the Law in the midst of their whole congregation.

Thou dealest with men like the fish of the sea, like creeping things, to rule over them. They draw them all up with a fish-hook, and drag them out with their net, and gather them in their seine. Therefore they sacrifice to their net. Therefore they rejoice and exult and burn incense to their seine; for by them their portion is fat and their sustenance rich (i, 14–16).

. . . And they shall gather in their riches, together with all their booty, *like the fish of the sea*. And as for that which He said, *Therefore they sacrifice to their net and burn incense to their seine*: interpreted, this means that they sacrifice to their standards and worship their weapons of war. *For through them their portion is fat and their sustenance rich*: interpreted, this means that they divide their yoke and their tribute – *their sustenance* – over all the peoples year by year, ravaging many lands.

Therefore their sword is ever drawn to massacre nations merci-lessly (i, 17).

Interpreted, this concerns the Kittim who cause many to perish by the sword – youths, grown men, the aged, women and children – and who even take no pity on the fruit of the womb.

I will take my stand to watch and will station myself upon my fortress. I will watch to see what He will say to me and how He will answer my complaint. And the Lord answered and said to me, 'Write down the vision and make it plain upon the tablets, that he who reads may read it speedily' (ii, 1–2).

. . . and God told Habakkuk to write down that which would happen to the final generation, but He did not make known to him when time would come to an end. And as for that which He said, *That he who reads may read it speedily*: interpreted this concerns the Teacher of Righteousness, to whom God made known all the mysteries of the words of His servants the Prophets.

For there shall be yet another vision concerning the appointed time. It shall tell of the end and shall not lie (ii, 3a).

Interpreted, this means that the final age shall be prolonged, and shall exceed all that the Prophets have said; for the mysteries of God are astounding.

If it tarries, wait for it, for it shall surely come and shall not be late (ii, 3b).

Interpreted, this concerns the men of truth who keep the Law, whose hands shall not slacken in the service of truth when the final age is prolonged. For all the ages of God reach their appointed end as He determines for them in the mysteries of His wisdom.

Behold, his soul is puffed up and is not upright (ii, 4a).

Interpreted, this means that *the wicked* shall double their guilt upon themselves *and it shall not be forgiven* when they are judged . . .

But the righteous shall live by his faith (ii, 4b).

Interpreted, this concerns all those who observe the Law in the House of Judah, whom God will deliver from the House of Judgement because of their suffering and because of their faith in the Teacher of Righteousness.

Moreover, the arrogant man seizes wealth without halting. He widens his gullet like Hell and like Death he has never enough. All the nations are gathered to him and all the peoples are assembled to him. Will they not all of them taunt him and jeer at him saying, 'Woe to him who amasses that which is not his! How long will he load himself up with pledges?' (ii, 5–6).

Interpreted, this concerns the Wicked Priest who was called by the name of truth when he first arose. But when he ruled over Israel his heart became proud, and he forsook God and betrayed the precepts for the sake of riches. He robbed and amassed the riches of the men of violence who rebelled against God, and he took the wealth of the peoples, heaping sinful iniquity upon himself. And he lived in the ways of abominations amidst every unclean defilement.

Shall not your oppressors suddenly arise and your torturers awaken; and shall you not become their prey? Because you have plundered many nations, all the remnant of the peoples shall plunder you (ii, 7–8a).

Interpreted, this concerns the Priest who rebelled *and violated* the precepts *of God . . . to command* his chastisement by means of the judgements of wickedness. And they inflicted horrors of evil diseases and took vengeance upon his body of flesh. And as for that which He said, *Because you have plundered many nations, all the remnant of the peoples shall plunder you*: interpreted this concerns the last Priests of Jerusalem, who shall amass money and wealth by plundering the peoples. But in the last days, their riches and booty shall be delivered into the hands of the army of the Kittim, for it is they who shall be the *remnant of the peoples*.

Because of the blood of men and the violence done to the land, to the city, and to all its inhabitants (ii, 8b).

Interpreted, this concerns the Wicked Priest whom God delivered into the hands of his enemies because of the iniquity

committed against the Teacher of Righteousness and the men of
his Council, that he might be humbled by means of a destroying
scourge, in bitterness of soul, because he had done wickedly to His
elect.

*Woe to him who gets evil profit for his house; who perches his nest
high to be safe from the hand of evil! You have devised shame to
your house: by cutting off many peoples you have forfeited your
own soul. For the stone cries out from the wall and the beam from
the woodwork replies* (ii, 9–11).

Interpreted, this concerns the *Priest* who . . . that its stones
might be laid in oppression and the beam of its woodwork in robbery. And as for that which He said, *By cutting off many peoples
you have forfeited your own soul*: interpreted this concerns the
condemned House whose judgement God will pronounce in the
midst of many peoples. He will bring him thence for judgement
and will declare him guilty in the midst of them, and will chastise
him with fire of brimstone.

*Woe to him who builds a city with blood and founds a town upon
falsehood! Behold, is it not from the Lord of Hosts that the peoples
shall labour for fire and the nations shall strive for naught?* (ii,
12–13).

Interpreted, this concerns the Spouter of Lies who led many
astray that he might build his city of vanity with blood and raise a
congregation on deceit, causing many thereby to perform a service of vanity for the sake of its glory, and to be pregnant with
works of deceit, that their labour might be for nothing and that
they might be punished with fire who vilified and outraged the
elect of God.

*For as the waters cover the sea, so shall the earth be filled with the
knowledge of the glory of the Lord* (ii, 14).

Interpreted, *this means* . . . And afterwards, knowledge shall
be revealed to them abundantly, like the waters of the sea.

*Woe to him who causes his neighbours to drink; who pours out his
venom to make them drunk that he may gaze on their feasts*
(ii, 15).

Interpreted, this concerns the Wicked Priest who pursued the Teacher of Righteousness to the house of his exile that he might confuse him with his venomous fury. And at the time appointed for rest, for the Day of Atonement, he appeared before them to confuse them, and to cause them to stumble on the Day of Fasting, their Sabbath of repose.

You have filled yourself with ignominy more than with glory. Drink also, and stagger! The cup of the Lord's right hand shall come round to you and shame shall come on your glory (ii, 16).

Interpreted, this concerns the Priest whose ignominy was greater than his glory. For he did not circumcise the foreskin of his heart, and he walked in the ways of drunkenness that he might quench his thirst. But the cup of the wrath of God shall confuse him . . .

For the violence done to Lebanon shall overwhelm you, and the destruction of the beasts shall terrify you, because of the blood of men and the violence done to the land, the city, and all its inhabitants (ii, 17).

Interpreted, this saying concerns the Wicked Priest, inasmuch as he shall be paid the reward which he himself tendered to the Poor. For *Lebanon* is the Council of the Community; and the *beasts* are the simple of Judah who keep the Law. As he himself plotted the destruction of the Poor, so will God condemn him to destruction. And as for that which He said, *Because of the blood of the city and the violence done to the land:* interpreted, *the city* is Jerusalem where the Wicked Priest committed abominable deeds and defiled the Temple of God. *The violence done to the land:* these are the cities of Judah where he robbed the Poor of their possessions.

Of what use is an idol that its maker should shape it, a molten image, a fatling of lies? For the craftsman puts his trust in his own creation when he makes dumb idols (ii, 18).

Interpreted, this saying concerns all the idols of the nations which they make so that they may serve and worship them. But they shall not deliver them on the Day of Judgement.

*Woe to him who says to wood, 'Awake', and to dumb stone, 'Arise'!
Can such a thing give guidance? Behold, it is covered with gold
and silver but there is no spirit within it. But the Lord is in His
holy Temple: let all the earth be silent before Him!* (ii, 19–20).

Interpreted, this concerns all the nations which serve stone
and wood. But on the Day of Judgement, God will destroy from
the earth all idolatrous and wicked men.

Commentary on Psalms

Cave 1 has preserved a few scraps of a commentary on Psalms lvii and lxviii, but most of these are too small for a coherent translation. More important are two manuscripts in Herodian script which were found in Cave 4. The bulk of the text is devoted to Psalm xxxvii, in which the destiny of the just and the wicked is expounded in connection with the story of the sect and its opponents, and in particular, the struggle between the Teacher of Righteousness and the Wicked Priest.

Psalm xxxvii

. . . Be silent before the Lord and long for Him, and be not heated against the successful, the man who achieves his plans (7a).

Its interpretation concerns the Liar who has led astray many by his lying words so that they chose frivolous things and heeded not the interpreter of knowledge . . . they shall perish by the sword and famine and plague.

Relent from anger and abandon wrath. Do not be angry; it tends only to evil, for the wicked shall be cut off (8–9a).

Interpreted, this concerns all those who return to the Law, to those who do not refuse to turn away from their evil. For all those who are stubborn in turning away from their iniquity shall be cut off.

But those who wait for the Lord shall possess the land (9b).

Interpreted, this is the congregation of His elect who do His will.

A little while and the wicked shall be no more; I will look towards his place but he shall not be there (10).

Interpreted, this concerns all the wicked. At the end of the forty years they shall be blotted out and no *evil* man shall be found on the earth.

But the humble shall possess the land and delight in abundant peace (11).

Interpreted, this concerns *the congregation of the* Poor who shall accept the season of penance and shall be delivered from all the snares of Belial. Afterwards, all who possess the earth shall delight and prosper on exquisite food.

The wicked plots against the righteous and gnashes his teeth at him. The Lord laughs at him, for He sees that his day is coming (12–13).

Interpreted, this concerns the violent of the Covenant who are in the House of Judah, who have plotted to destroy those who practise the law, who are in the Council of the Community. And God will not forsake them to their hands.

The wicked draw the sword and bend their bow to bring down the poor and needy and to slay the upright of way. Their sword shall enter their own heart and their bows shall be broken (14–15).

Interpreted, this concerns the wicked of Ephraim and Manasseh, who shall seek to lay hands on the Priest and the men of his Council at the time of trial which shall come upon them. But God will redeem them from out of their hand. And afterwards, they shall be delivered into the hand of the violent among the nations for judgement . . .

And in the days of famine they shall be satisfied, but the wicked shall perish (19b–20a).

Interpreted, this *means that* He will keep them alive during the famine and the time of humiliation, whereas many shall perish from famine and plague, all those who have not departed *from there* to be with the Congregation of His elect.

And those who love the Lord shall be like the pride of pastures (20b).

Interpreted, *this concerns* the congregation of His elect, who shall be leaders and princes . . . of the flock among their herds.

Like smoke they shall all of them vanish away (20c).

Interpreted, *this* concerns the princes *of wickedness* who have oppressed His holy people, and who shall perish like smoke *blown away by the wind.*

The wicked borrows and does not repay, but the righteous is gener-ous and gives. Truly, those whom He blesses shall possess the land, but those whom He curses shall be cut off (21–2).

Interpreted, this concerns the congregation of the Poor, who *shall possess* the whole world as an inheritance. They shall pos-sess the High Mountain of Israel *for ever,* and shall enjoy *ever-lasting* delights in His Sanctuary. *But those who* shall be *cut off,* they are the violent *of the nations and* the wicked of Israel; they shall be cut off and blotted out for ever.

The wicked watches out for the righteous and seeks to slay him. The Lord will not abandon him into his hand or let him be con-demned when he is tried (32–3).

Interpreted, this concerns the Wicked *Priest* who *watched the Teacher of Righteousness* that he might put him to death *because of the ordinance* and the law which he sent to him. But God will not *abandon him and will not let him be condemned when he is tried.* And *God* will pay him his reward by delivering him into the hand of the violent of the nations, that they may execute upon him *judgement.*

Florilegium or Midrash on the Last Days

This collection of texts assembled from 2 Samuel and the Psalter, and combined with other scriptural passages, serves to present the sectarian doctrine identifying the Community with the Temple, and to announce the coming of the two Messiahs, the 'Branch of David' and the 'Interpreter of the Law'. Originating from Cave 4 and known also as 'Florilegium', the composition probably belongs to the late first century B C E.

. . . I will appoint a place for my people Israel and will plant them that they may dwell there and be troubled no more by their enemies. No son of iniquity shall afflict them again as formerly, from the day that I set judges over my people Israel (2 Sam. vii, 10).

This is the House which *He will build for them in the* last days, as it is written in the book of Moses, *In the sanctuary which Thy hands have established, O Lord, the Lord shall reign for ever and ever* (Exod. xv, 17–18). This is the House into which *the unclean shall* never *enter, nor the uncircumcised,* nor the Ammonite, nor the Moabite, nor the half-breed, nor the foreigner, nor the stranger, ever; for there shall My Holy Ones be. *Its glory shall endure* for ever; it shall appear above it perpetually. And strangers shall lay it waste no more, as they formerly laid waste the Sanctuary of Israel because of its sin. He had commanded that a Sanctuary of men be built for Himself, that there they may send up, like the smoke of incense, the works of the Law.

And concerning His words to David, *And I will give you rest from all your enemies* (2 Sam. vii, 11), this means that He will give them rest from all the children of Belial who cause them to stumble so that they may be destroyed *by their errors,* just as they came with a *devilish* plan to cause the *sons* of light to stumble and to devise against them a wicked plot, that *they might become subject* to Belial in their *wicked* straying.

The Lord declares to you that He will build you a House (2 Sam.

vii, 11c). *I will raise up your seed after you* (2 Sam. vii, 12). *I will establish the throne of his kingdom for ever* (2 Sam. vii, 13). *I will be his father and he shall be my son* (2 Sam. vii, 14). He is the Branch of David who shall arise with the Interpreter of the Law *to rule* in Zion *at the end* of time. As it is written, *I will raise up the tent of David that is fallen* (Amos ix, 11). That is to say, the fallen *tent of David* is he who shall arise to save Israel.

Explanation of *How blessed is the man who does not walk in the counsel of the wicked* (Ps. i, 1). Interpreted, this saying *concerns* those who turn aside from the way *of the people* as it is written in the book of Isaiah the Prophet concerning the last days, *It came to pass that the Lord turned me aside, as with a mighty hand, from walking in the way of this people* (Isa. viii, 11). They are those of whom it is written in the book of Ezekiel the Prophet, *The Levites strayed far from me, following their idols* (Ezek. xliv, 10). They are the sons of Zadok who *seek their own* counsel and follow *their own inclination* apart from the Council of the Community.

Why do the nations rage and the peoples meditate vanity? Why do the kings of the earth rise up, and the princes take counsel together against the Lord and against His Messiah? (Ps. ii, 1). Interpreted, this saying concerns *the kings of the nations* who shall *rage against* the elect of Israel in the last days . . . This is the time of which it is written in the book of Daniel the Prophet: *But the wicked shall do wickedly and shall not understand, but the righteous shall purify themselves and make themselves white* (Dan. xii, 10). The people who know God shall be strong.

The Heavenly Prince Melchizedek

A striking first-century BCE document, composed of thirteen fragments from Cave 11 and centred on the mysterious figure of Melchizedek, was first published by A. S. van der Woude in 1965. It takes the form of an eschatological midrash in which the proclamation of liberty to the captives at the end of days (Isa. lxi, 1) is understood as being part of the general restoration of property during the year of Jubilee (Lev. xxv, 13), seen in the Bible (Deut. xv, 2) as a remission of debts.

The heavenly deliverer is Melchizedek. Identical with the archangel Michael, he is the head of the 'sons of Heaven' or 'gods of Justice' and is referred to as *elohim* and *el*. The same terminology occurs in the Songs for the Holocaust of the Sabbath. These Hebrew words normally mean 'God', but in certain specific contexts Jewish tradition also explains *elohim* as primarily designating a 'judge'. Here Melchizedek is portrayed as presiding over the final Judgement and condemnation of his demonic counterpart, Belial/Satan, the Prince of Darkness. The great act of deliverance is expected to occur on the Day of Atonement at the end of the tenth Jubilee cycle.

This manuscript sheds valuable light not only on the Melchizedek figure in the Epistle to the Hebrews vii, but also on the development of the messianic concept in the New Testament and early Christianity.

. . . And concerning that which He said, *In this year of Jubilee each of you shall return to his property* (Lev. xxv, 13); and likewise, *And this is the manner of release: every creditor shall release that which he has lent to his neighbour. He shall not exact it of his neighbour and his brother, for God's release has been proclaimed* (Deut. xv, 2). *And it will be proclaimed* at the end of days concerning the captives as *He said, To proclaim liberty to the captives* (Isa. lxi, 1). *Its interpretation is that He* will assign them to the Sons of Heaven and to the inheritance of Melchizedek; *for He will cast* their *lot* amid the *portions of Melchizedek*, who will return them there and will proclaim to them liberty, forgiving them *the wrong-doings* of all their iniquities.

And this thing will *occur* in the first week of the Jubilee that follows the nine Jubilees. And the Day of Atonement is the *end of the* tenth Jubilee, when all the Sons of *Light* and the men of the lot of Melchizedek will be atoned for. *And* a statute concerns them *to provide* them with their rewards. For this is the moment of the Year of Grace for Melchizedek. *And* he will, by his strength, judge the holy ones of God, executing judgement as it is written concerning him in the Songs of David, who said, E L O H I M *has taken his place in the divine council; in the midst of the gods he holds judgement* (Ps. lxxxii, 1). And it was concerning him that he said, Let the assembly of the peoples *return to the height above them; God will judge the peoples* (Ps. vii, 7–8). As for that which he *said, How long will you judge unjustly and show partiality to the wicked? Selah* (Ps. lxxxii, 2), its interpretation concerns Belial and the spirits of his lot *who* rebelled by turning away from the precepts of God . . . And Melchizedek will avenge the vengeance of the judgements of God . . . and he will drag *them from the hand of* Belial and from the hand of all the *spirits of* his *lot.* And all the 'gods *of Justice*' will come to his aid *to* attend to the *destruction* of Belial . . . This is the day of *Peace/Salvation* concerning which *God* spoke *through* Isaiah the prophet, who said, *How beautiful upon the mountains are the feet of the messenger who proclaims peace, who brings good news, who proclaims salvation, who says to Zion: Your* E L O H I M *reigns* (Isa. lii, 7) . . . And *your* E L O H I M is *Melchizedek, who will save them from* the hand of Belial.

BIBLICALLY BASED
APOCRYPHAL WORKS

● ●

Jubilees

The pseudepigraphon, known prior to Qumran from a complete Ethiopic and partial Greek, Latin and Syriac translations, has surfaced for the first time in a large number of mostly small fragments in its Hebrew original in five Qumran caves. The work itself is a midrashic retelling of the story of Genesis (and the beginning of Exodus) in the form of a revelation conveyed by angels to Moses. Though most of the texts are too mutilated to provide the basis for an English translation, their chief significance lies in their attestation of a Hebrew original generally close to the account preserved in the ancient versions.

In this fragment, the author recounts the sacrifice of Isaac with details which differ from the Genesis story and display close parallels to the post-biblical representation of the Akedah or, Binding of Isaac, anticipating features known from the Palestinian Targums. The presence of angels at the sacrifice is repeatedly attested in the Targums. This scroll, therefore, provides the earliest (pre-Christian) evidence for the rabbinic story of Isaac's voluntary self-sacrifice which is thought to have supplied a model for the formulation by New Testament writers of the teaching on the sacrificial death of Jesus.

I ... *And the* Lord *said* to Abraham, 'Lift up your eyes and gaze at the stars and see and count the sand that is on the sea shore and the dust of the earth as to whether *they can be counted.*' And Abraham *believed in* God and this was reckoned for him as righteousness. And a son was born afterwards *to Abraham* and he called his name Isaac. And the prince Mastemah came *to* God and accused Abraham on account of Isaac. And God said *to Abraham,* 'Take your son, Isaac, *your* only son *whom* you *love* and offer him to me as a burnt-offering on one of the . . . mountains *which I will tell* you.' And he rose *and he went* from the wells to *Mount Moriah* . . . And *Abraham* lifted up   **II** his eyes *and behold there was* a fire. And he placed *the wood on Isaac, his son, and they went together.* And Isaac said to Abraham, *his father, 'Behold there is the fire and the wood, but where is the lamb* for the burnt-offering?' And Abraham said to *Isaac, his son, 'God will provide a lamb* for himself.' Isaac said to his father, '*Tie me well*' . . . And the angels of *Mastemah* . . . were rejoicing and saying, 'Now he, Isaac, will be destroyed . . . *we shall see* whether he will be found weak and whether *Abraham* will be found unfaithful *to God.' And God called,* 'Abraham, Abraham.' And he said, 'Here am I.' And he said, '*Now I know that it was a lie that* he, Abraham, will no longer be loving.' And the Lord God blessed *Isaac all the days of his life and he begot* Jacob, and Jacob begot Levi in the third generation.

The Book of Enoch
and the Book of Giants

Various Qumran caves have yielded for the first time the original Aramaic text of one of the major Pseudepigrapha, the Book of Enoch, which was previously known from a complete Ethiopic translation and from a Greek rendering of chapters I–XXXII and XCVII–CI, CVI–CVII, as well as from a number of Greek quotations from chapters VI to XV transmitted by the Byzantine writer George Syncellus. Qumran Cave 4 has yielded seven copies of the writing attested by, but not strictly identical to, the Ethiopic, and four further copies of the related Book of Giants. Palaeographically, all of them are dated to between 200 BCE and the end of the pre-Christian era.

The bulk of the fragments is too small for translation, and the passages included in this volume are only those which make sense in themselves. The first excerpt supplies the Aramaic names of the twenty chiefs of the fallen angels. The second relates the miraculous birth of Noah, which should be compared to the parallel accounts in the Genesis Apocryphon and in the fragments of the Book of Noah. The third and fourth extracts testify to a recension noticeably different from the corresponding Ethiopic version, while the fifth, the Astronomical Book, is considerably longer than the Ethiopic. As for the Book of Giants, it is missing from the Ethiopic, though it circulated in Manichaean, Talmudic and medieval Jewish literature.

The Book of Enoch

I

. . . And these are *the names of their chiefs.* Shemihazah who *was their head, Arataqoph,* his second; Ramtael, *third* to him; Kokabel, *fourth to him; . . . el fifth* to him; Ramael, *sixth to him;* Daniel, seventh *to him; Ziqiel, eighth* to him; Baraqel, ninth *to him;* Asael, tenth *to him; Hermoni, eleventh* to him; Matarel, twelfth *to him;* Anael, thirteenth *to him;* Stawel, fourteenth to him; Shamshiel, fifteenth to him; Shahriel, sixteenth to him; Tummiel, *seventeenth to him;* Turiel, eighteenth to him; Yomiel, nineteenth to him; *Yehaddiel, twentieth to him.* These are the chiefs of the chiefs of tens. These *and* their chiefs *took for themselves* wives from all those whom they chose and *they began to go in to them and defile themselves with them and to teach them sorcery and magic* . . . And they became pregnant by them and bore *giants* . . .

II

. . . *And* after *these shall* come a greater wickedness *than that which will have been accomplished* in *their days. For* I know the mysteries *of the Lord which* the holy ones have explained and showed me and which I read *in* the heavenly *tablets.* And I saw written in them that one generation after another will do evil in this way, and evil will last *until* generations of righteousness *arise* and evil and wickedness shall end and violence shall cease from the earth and *until good shall come on the earth* on them . . . And now, please go to your *son,* Lamech, *and explain to him* that this child is his son in truth and without lie . . .

III

. . . And behold, these are the pits for their prison. They were made thus until the day of their judgement, until the final day of the great judgement which will be imposed on them . . . There I saw the spirit of a dead man complaining and his moaning rising to heaven and crying and complaining . . .

IV

. . . *And beyond* those *mountains* roughly northwards, on their eastern side, I was shown other mountains, *full of* excellent nard, and pepperwort, and cinnamon, *and* pepper . . . And from there I was led to the east of all those mountains, far from them, to the east of the earth and I was taken over the Red *Sea* and greatly distanced myself from it and crossed over the darkness far from it. And I passed to the Paradise of righteousness . . .

V

THE ASTRONOMICAL BOOK OF ENOCH

. . . *And the moon shines in the remainder of this night with three seventh parts; and it grows during the day to four sevenths and a half; and then it sets and enters its gate and is covered for the remainder* of this day to *two* sevenths *and a half. And in the night of the twenty-fourth it is covered four sevenths and a half and four sevenths and a half* are cut off from its light. *And* then it comes out from its gate and shines in the remainder of this night two sevenths and a half. And it grows *in* this day five sevenths and then it sets and enters its gate and is covered for the remainder of this day *two sevenths* . . . And in the night, on the twenty-fifth, it is covered five sevenths, and five sevenths are cut off from its light. And then it comes out and shines for the remainder of this night two sevenths. And it grows in this day to five sevenths and a half. And then it sets *and* enters the second gate and is covered for the remainder of this day one seventh and a half . . . And in the night of the twenty-sixth it is covered five sevenths and a half and five sevenths and a half are cut off from its light.

And then it comes out of the second gate and shines for the remainder of this night one seventh and a half. And it grows in this day six sevenths. And then it sets and enters and is covered for the remainder of this day one seventh . . . And in the night of the twenty-seventh it is covered six sevenths and *six sevenths* are cut off from its light. *And then it comes out and shines for the remainder* of this night one seventh. And it grows in this day *six sevenths and a half. And then it sets and enters* . . .

And shines in the night of the eighth four *sevenths.* And then it sets and enters. In this night the sun completes the passage through all the sections of the first gate and recommences to go in and come out through its sections. *And then the moon* sets and enters. And it darkens during the remainder of this night three sevenths. And it grows in this day four sevenths and a half. And then it comes out and dominates in the remainder of this day two sevenths and a half . . . And it shines in the night of the ninth four *sevenths* and a half. And then it sets and enters. In this night the sun recommences to go through *its* sections *and to set* in them. And then *the moon* sets and enters the fifth gate and darkens in the remainder of this night *two* sevenths and a half. And it grows in this day five *sevenths* and in it the light equals five sevenths . . . equals in full. *And then it comes out* of the *fifth* gate . . .

The Book of Giants

. . . the giants searched for one to explain to them *the dream* . . . *to Enoch*, the interpreter scribe that he might interpret to us the dream . . .

Then Ohiyah, his brother, confessed and said before the giants, I, too, saw a wonder in my dream this night. Behold the Ruler of heaven descended to earth . . .

. . . Here is the end of the dream. *Then all the giants* . . . were terrified *and* called Mahawai and he came to them. And the giants *asked him* and sent him to Enoch, *the interpreter scribe* and said to him, Go . . . listen to his voice and say to him that he should explain *to you and* interpret the dreams . . .

An Admonition Associated with the Flood

This is a rewritten account of the Noah story based on Genesis vi–ix; two fragmentary columns have survived, only the first of which is suitable for translation. Palaeographically, it is said to be late Hasmonaean, i.e. from the first half of the first century BCE, but the composition itself is pre-Qumran. Both the Tetragram and the divine name '*el* are used.

And He crowned the mountains with *produce* and poured food on them, and he satisfied every soul with good fruit. 'Whoever does my will, let him eat and be satisfied', says *the* Lord. 'And let them bless *my holy* name. But, behold, they have done what is wicked in my eyes,' said the Lord. They rebelled against God through their actions, and the Lord judged them according to all their ways, and according to the thoughts of the inclination of their *evil* hearts. And He thundered at them in *His* power, and all the foundations of the earth trembled, *and the* waters burst forth from the abysses. All the windows of heaven opened, and all the abysses overflowed *with* mighty waters. And the windows of heaven *emptied out* rain and He destroyed them by the Flood . . . Therefore everything *perished* on the dry land; and men, beasts, birds and winged creatures *died*. And the *giants* did not escape . . . And God made *a sign . . . and* set His bow *in the cloud* that He might remember the covenant . . . *that there might no more be on earth* waters of flood . . . and that the mass of waters *might not be let loose* . . .

The Testament of Qahat

The Testament of Qahat is an Aramaic work of which two columns, one complete and one damaged, have survived. It is a typical example of moralising death-bed literature, similar to the Testaments of the Twelve Patriarchs, but characterised, like the Testaments of Levi and Amram, by its priestly perspective. The script has been palaeographically dated to the end of the second century B C E, but the carbon 14 test, performed in 1990, places it considerably earlier, possibly to 388–353 B C E, or more probably to 303–235 B C E. It is not a sectarian composition. This translation is taken from the first column.

Now, my sons, be careful with the heritage that is handed over to you, which your fathers have given you. Do not give your heritage to strangers, and your inheritance to knaves so that you become humiliated and foolish in their eyes and they despise you, for, although sojourners among you, they will be your chiefs. So hold to the word of Jacob, your father, and seize the laws of Abraham and the righteousness of Levi and mine. And be holy and pure of all fornication in the community. And hold the truth and walk straight, and not with a double heart, but with a pure heart and a true and good spirit. And you will give me a good name among you, and a rejoicing to Levi, and joy to Jacob, delight to Isaac, and glory to Abraham, because you will keep and walk in the heritage which your fathers will have left you: truth and righteousness and uprightness and perfection and purity *and* holiness and the priesthood according to all that you have been commanded . . .

The Words of Moses

Fragments of four very mutilated columns of a manuscript from Cave 1 have been skilfully reconstructed by J. T. Milik. They form a farewell discourse of Moses which takes its inspiration from various passages of Deuteronomy and is chiefly remarkable for the emphasis laid on the appointment of special teachers, or interpreters, of the Law (Levites and Priests). This translation comes from the first two columns.

God spoke to Moses in the *fortieth* year after *the children of* Israel had come *out of the land of* Egypt, in the eleventh month, on the first day of the month, saying:

'*Gather together* all the congregation and go up to *Mount Nebo* and stand *there*, you and Eleazar son of Aaron. Interpret *to the heads* of family of the Levites and to all the *Priests*, and proclaim to the children of Israel the words of the law which I proclaimed *to you* on Mount Sinai. Proclaim *carefully* into their ears all that I *require* of them. And *call* heaven and *earth to witness against* them; for they will not love what I have commanded *them to do*, neither *they* nor their children, *during all* the days they shall *live upon the earth*.

For I say that they will abandon *Me, and will choose the abominations of the nations*, their horrors *and their idols. They will serve* false gods which shall be for them a snare and a pitfall. *They will sin against the* holy *days*, and against the Sabbath and the Covenant, *and against the commandments* which I command you to keep this day.

Therefore I will smite them with a mighty *blow* in the midst of the land *which they* cross the Jordan *to possess*. And when all the curses come upon them and catch up with them to destroy them and *blot* them out, then shall they know that the truth has been *fulfilled* with regard to them.'

Then Moses called Eleazar son of *Aaron* and Joshua *son of Nun and said to them*, 'Speak *all these words to the people* . . . :

Be still, O Israel, and hear! This *day shall you become the people* of God, your *God. You shall keep My laws* and My testimonies *and My commandments which I* command you to *keep* this day. *And when you* cross the *Jordan so that I may give* you great *and good cities,* and houses filled with all *pleasant things, and vines and olives* which *you have not planted, and* wells which you have not dug, *beware,* when you have eaten and are full, that your hearts be not lifted up, and that *you do not forget what I have commanded you to do this day. For* it is this that will bring you life and length of *days.'*

And Moses *spoke to the children* of Israel *and said to them*:

'*Behold,* forty *years have passed since* the day we came out of the land *of Egypt, and today has God,* our God, *uttered these words* from out of His mouth: *all* His *precepts and all His* precepts.

'*But how shall I carry* your loads *and burdens and disputes alone*? When I have *established* the Covenant and commanded *the way* in which you shall walk, *appoint wise men whose* work it shall be to expound *to you and your children* all these words of the Law. *Watch carefully* for your own sakes *that you keep them, lest* the wrath *of your God* kindle and burn against you, and He stop the heavens above from shedding rain *upon you,* and *the water beneath the earth from* giving you *harvest.'*

And Moses *spoke further* to the children of Israel. 'Behold the commandments *which God has* commanded you to keep . . .'

Pseudo-Moses

In this apocryphal narrative, purporting to be a divine speech, no doubt addressed to Moses (hence the suggested title), the future of Israel is foretold in a framework of jubilees. Consequently, the kinship with the Book of Jubilees is undeniable. The account is also reminiscent of the opening paragraph of the Damascus Document. Two largish fragments form the basis of the translation. The script is considered Herodian, but on the basis of historical allusions contained in other fragments pertaining to the same composition, Devorah Dimant tentatively suggests a second century BCE date, not later than the rule of John Hyrcanus I (134–104 BCE).

The sons of Aaron will rule over them and they will not walk *in* My ways which I command you, Moses, that you may testify against them. They will also do what is evil in My eyes just as Israel did in the earlier times of her kingdom, apart from those who will first come up from the land of their captivity to build the Sanctuary. I will speak in their midst, and will send them a commandment, and they will understand all that they and their fathers have forsaken. And from the completion of that generation in the seventh jubilee of the devastation of the land they will forget the precept, and the appointed time, and the sabbath, and the Covenant. They will break all of them and will do what is evil in My eyes. I will hide My face from them and will give them into the hands of their enemies, and will deliver *them* to the sword. But I will cause a remnant to remain so that they will not be destroyed *by My fury* and by My hiding My face from them. The angels of Persecution will rule over them . . . *and they* will come *back* and will do *what is* evil in *My* eyes. They will walk in the *stubbornness of their heart* . . .

. . . And the dominion of Belial will be on them to hand them over to the sword for a week of years . . . *And in* that jubilee, they will break all My precepts and all My commandments which I will have commanded them . . . *by the hand of* My servants the prophets, *and they will* . . . to contend one with another for seventy years from the day of breaking the *Law and the* Covenant which they will break. I will give them *into the hand of the* angels of Persecution, and they will rule over them, and they will not know and understand that I am furious with them because of their transgressions *by which they will have* forsaken Me and will have done that which is evil in My eyes, and will have chosen that which I do not desire, striving for wealth and gain *and . . . , one* stealing that which is his fellow's, and one oppressing another. They will pollute My Sanctuary and profane My sabbaths . . .

Tobit

Prior to the Qumran finds, the Book of Tobit existed among the Apocrypha in two, a long and a short, Greek recensions and in various secondary ancient versions. Cave 4 has revealed remains of four Aramaic and one Hebrew manuscripts, of which two scrolls in particular have yielded copious extracts. They all basically represent the Semitic original from which the longer Greek recension, attested by the fourth-century CE Codex Sinaiticus, and the Old Latin version were made.

The following illustrate some of the differences between the Aramaic (A), and the Greek (G) Tobit:

ii, 1 (A) On the day of the Festival of Weeks
      (G) At the feast of Pentecost which is the sacred festival of the seven weeks
vi, 6 (A) Also he salted the rest for the journey. Both of them were going together
      (G) and left part of it salted. And they journeyed both of them together
vi, 12 (A) and her father loves her
      (G) and her father is an honourable man
xiv, 2 (A) He was fifty-eight years old when he lost his sight and afterward he lived fifty-four years
      (G) He was sixty-two years old when he was maimed in his eyes (Sinaiticus). He was fifty-eight years old when he lost his sight and after eight years he regained it (Vaticanus)

The following passages come from the more complete sections of the Scrolls.

Tobit ii, 1–2

1 And in the days of king Esarhaddon, when I returned to my home and Hannah my wife and Tobiah my son were restored to me, on the day of the Festival of Weeks, *I* had an excellent meal and I reclined to *eat.*
2 And they put a table in front of me and I saw the many

delicacies placed on it, *and I* said *to* Tobiah my son, My son, go and bring all those among our brothers *whom you* can find . . . my son, go and bring them. Let him be brought here and eat *together* with me . . .

Tobit vi, 2–11

2 . . . *and the angel* was with him and . . . *and they went* together. And *night* came *and they reached* the Tigris.

3 And the young man went down . . . *and* a big *fish jumped* out of *the water to swallow* the foot of the young man . . .

4 . . . Catch the *fish! And* the young man seized *the fish and brought* it to the dry land. And *the angel said to him,*

5 *Cut* it open and remove *its gall and* its *heart and its liver. Keep* them, but *throw away its* entrails. *Its gall,* its *heart* and its liver are *medicament.*

6 And *he cut out its gall and* its heart and *its liver* . . . the fish and he ate it. Also he *salted the* rest for the journey. Both of them were going together *until they* reached Media . . .

7 The young man asked the angel *and* said to him, Azariah my brother, what kind of medicament is in the heart of the fish and in its liver *and in its gall*?

8 *If you* smoke it in front of a man or a woman smitten by a demon or an *evil* spirit . . . they will never come by again.

9 The gall is for applying to the eyes *of a man* . . . white film and he will recover.

10 And when they entered Media and he was already *nearing Ecbatana,*

11 *Raphael said to the young* man, Tobiah my brother. And he said to him, Here am I. And he said to him, In the house *of Raguel we shall stay. And the* man is from the house of our father. And he has a beautiful daughter . . .

Tobit vi, 12–18

12 . . . *wise, strong* and very beautiful, and her father loves *her* . . . her father. And a just decision has been made concerning you

13 to *marry her* . . . You will speak about this young girl tonight.

You will retain her and take her to be your wife . . . *And when we return from Rages we shall make for her* a wedding-feast. And I know that Raguel cannot refuse her to you for he knows . . . and to marry his daughter than any other man. *For he* knows that if he were to give her to *another* man *this would be against the law in the Book* of Moses. And now *let us speak about* this *young* girl tonight and let us retain her *for you* . . .

14 *Then Tobiah replied and said to Raphael*, Azariah my brother, I have heard . . . that she had seven husbands who all died when they went in to her . . .

15 And now I am afraid of this demon who loves her . . . the demon kills them . . .

16 *And now* listen to me, my brother. Do not be afraid of this demon and marry her tonight . . .

17 take from the heart *of the fish* . . .

18 . . . the demon *will smell* it and will *flee* . . . When you go in *to be* with her, rise *up* . . . *And do* not be afraid *for* she has been allotted to you and for you . . . you will save *her*.

Tobit vii, 1–6

1 And when they entered Ecbatana, Tobiah *said* to him, *Azariah my brother, lead* me straight away to the house of Raguel our brother. He led him there and *they* went *to the house* of Raguel and *they* found Raguel sitting in front of the gate of his home. And first they greeted him and he said to them, In peace you have come. Enter in peace, my brothers. And he brought them into his house.

2 Then he said to Edna his wife, How much this young man resembles Tobit, the son of my uncle.

3 And Edna asked them and said to them, Where are you from, my brothers?

4 And they said to her, From among the children of Naphtali *who* are captives in Niniveh. And she said to them, Do you know Tobit our brother? And they said to her, We know him. Is he well?

5 And they said, He is well. *And* Tobiah said, He is my father.

6 And Raguel jumped to his feet and kissed him and cried.

Tobit x, 7–8

7 *And when* the fourteen days of the *wedding* were completed for them which Raguel had sworn to make for Sarah his daughter, Tobiah came *to him* and said to him, Send me away for I already know that *my father does not believe* nor does my mother believe that she will see me again. And now I request you, my father, that you send me away that I may go to my father. Already I have recounted to you how I left them.

8 And Raguel said to Tobiah, My son, remain with me and I will send messengers to Tobit your father . . .

Tobit xiii, 1–4

1 Then Tobit spoke and wrote a psalm of praise, and *said, Blessed be* the living *God* whose kingdom is for all eternity:

2 He who *strikes and who* is merciful;
He who causes to descend to the nethermost hell,
and He who brings up from the great abyss.
And who is there who can escape from His hand?

3 Give Him thanks, children of Israel, *in front of the nations,* you who are exiled among them.

4 Recite there *His greatness and extol Him before all* the living. For He is your Lord, and He is *your* God . . .

Tobit xiv, 1–2

1 And *Tobit's words of praise were* completed, *and he* died in peace aged *one hundred and twelve years.*

2 He was fifty-eight years old when he lost his sight *and* afterward *he lived fifty*-four *years.*

THE COPPER SCROLL

· ·

The Copper Scroll

BURIED TREASURE

The Copper Scroll, which has stimulated much curiosity and speculation, was found by archaeologists in Cave 3 during the excavations of
1952, but the metal had become so badly oxidised during the course of
the centuries that the scroll could not be unfolded. It was therefore sent
to Professor H. Wright Baker of the Manchester College of Science and
Technology who, in 1956, carefully divided it into longitudinal strips
and, in the same year, returned it to Jordan.

The inscription lists sixty-four hiding-places, in Jerusalem and in various districts of Palestine, where gold, silver, Temple offerings, scrolls,
etc., are said to have been deposited. J. M. Allegro reckons that the treasure must have amounted to over three thousand talents of silver, nearly
one thousand three hundred talents of gold, sixty-five bars of gold, six
hundred and eight pitchers containing silver, and six hundred and nineteen gold and silver vessels. In other words, using the post-biblical value
of the talent as a yard-stick, the total weight of precious metal must have
added up to sixty-five tons of silver and twenty-six tons of gold.

Who could have possessed such a fortune? Was there ever any truth
in it?

J. T. Milik thinks not. He believes that the exaggerated sums indicate
that the scroll is a work of fiction and that its chief interest to scholars
lies in the fields of linguistics and topography. He dates it from about
100 CE, thus ruling out any connection with the rest of the Qumran
writings since the latter were placed in the caves not later than 68 CE.

The treasure was a real one according to other scholars, representing
the fortune of the Essenes (A. Dupont-Sommer, S. Goranson) or the
Temple treasure (J. M. Allegro, N. Golb). According to Allegro, the
Zealots were responsible for the concealment of the gold and silver and

for the writing of the scroll. It has also been suggested that we are dealing here with funds collected for the rebuilding of the Temple after
70 CE, or with the hidden treasure of Bar Kokhba, leader of the second
Jewish revolution against Rome in 132–5 CE.

Milik's argument would certainly seem to account for the vast quantities of treasure mentioned. It does not, however, explain two of the
document's most striking characteristics, namely, the dry realism of its
style, very different from that of ancient legends, and the fact that it is
recorded on copper instead of on the less expensive leather or papyrus.
For if it is, in fact, a sort of fairy-story, the present text can only represent
the outline of such a tale, and who in their senses would have engraved
their literary notes on valuable metal?

The contention that the treasure was a real one is supported by the
very arguments which undermine Milik's. From the business-like approach, and the enduring material on which the catalogue is inscribed, it
might sensibly be supposed that the writer was not indulging some frivolous dream. Again, in view of the fact that the Copper Scroll was found
among writings known to come from Qumran, Dupont-Sommer and
Goranson would appear justified in allocating the fortune to the Essenes. It requires, by comparison, a strong feat of the imagination to
accept that all this wealth belonged originally to the treasure chambers
of the Temple, and that it was placed in hiding, in a hostile environment,
in 68 CE, before, that is to say, there was any immediate danger to the
capital city of Jerusalem. Allegro bypassed this objection by presuming
that, as Qumran was by then in the hands of the Zealots, it was no longer
unfriendly to the Jerusalem authorities. But it has not yet been explained why the sack of the Temple and city should have been foreseen,
and provided for, so early. In favour of the Temple treasure hypothesis,
it is nevertheless possible to envisage that the Jerusalem sanctuary
possessed such riches as these, whereas, despite Dupont-Sommer's undoubtedly true remarks concerning the apparent compatibility of religious poverty and fat revenues, it is still hard to accept that the Essenes,
a relatively small community, should have amassed such disproportion-
ate wealth.

Here are some samples chosen from the twelve columns:

I

1 A Horebbah which is in the Vale of Achor under the stairs

which go eastwards forty cubits: a box filled with silver weighing in all seventeen talents.

3 In the great cistern which is in the courtyard of the little colonnade, at its very bottom, closed with sediment towards the upper opening: nine hundred talents.

4 At the hill of Kohlit, containers, sandalwood and priestly garments. The total of the offering and of the treasure: seven talents and second tithe rendered unclean. At the exit of the canal on the northern side, six cubits towards the cavity of immersion.

5 In the hole of the waterproofed refuge, in going down towards the left, three cubits above the bottom: forty talents of silver.

II

6 In the cistern of the esplanade which is under the stairs: forty-two talents.

7 In the cave of the old Washer's House, on the third platform: sixty-five gold bars.

8 In the underground cavity which is in the courtyard of the House of Logs, where there is a cistern: vessels and silver, seventy talents.

9 In the cistern which is against the eastern gate, which is fifteen cubits away, there are vessels in it.

10 And in the canal which ends in it: ten talents.

11 In the cistern which is under the wall on the eastern side, at the sharp edge of the rock: six silver bars; its entrance is under the large paving-stone.

12 In the pond which is east of Kohlit, at a northern angle, dig four cubits: twenty-two talents.

IV

17 In the great cistern which is in the . . . , in the pillar on its northern side: 14 *talents*.

19 Between the two tamarisk trees in the Vale of Akhon, in their midst dig three cubits. There there are two pots full of silver.

20 In the red underground cavity at the mouth of the 'Aslah: 200 tal. of silver.

21 In the eastern underground cavity at the north of Kohlit: 70 tal. of silver.

22 In the heap of stones of the valley of Sekhakha dig . . . cubits: 12 tal. of silver.

VI

27 *In* the eastward-looking cave of the Pillar with two entrances, dig at the northern entrance three cubits; there is a pitcher there, in it a book, under it 22 tal.

28 In the eastward-looking cave of the base of the Stone dig nine cubits at the entrance: 21 tal.

29 In the Dwelling of the Queen on the western side dig twelve cubits: 27 tal.

30 In the heap of stones which is at the Ford of the High Priest dig nine *cubits*: 22 . . . tal.

VII

31 In the water conduit of Q . . . *the greater* northern reservoir, in the four directions measure out twenty-four cubits: four hundred talents.

32 In the nearby cave in the proximity of Bet ha-Qos dig six cubits: six silver bars.

33 At Doq under the eastern corner of the guard-post dig seven cubits: 22 tal.

34 At the mouth of the water exit of Koziba dig three cubits towards the rock: 60 tal., two talents of gold.

VIII

35 *In the* water conduit on the road east of Bet Ahsor, which is east of Ahzor, vessels of offering and books and a bar of silver.

36 In the outside valley . . . at the stone dig seventeen cubits underneath: 17 tal. of gold and silver.

37 In the heap of stones at the mouth of the Pottery ravine dig three cubits: 4 tal.

38 In the westward-looking stubble-field of ha-Sho, on the south

side, at the underground chamber looking northwards dig twenty-four cubits: 66 tal.

39 In the irrigation of ha-Sho, at the stone sign in it, dig eleven cubits: 70 tal. of silver.

IX

40 At the 'dovecot' (small opening?) at the exit of ha-Notef, measure out from its exit thirteen cubits, two tusks and, on seven smooth stones, bars corresponding to four staters.

44 At the 'sound of waters' (waterfall) close to the edge of the gutter on the east side of the exit dig seven cubits: 9 tal.

46 At the 'dovecot' which is at Mesad, at the *water* conduit,

X

southward at the second stair descending from the top: 9 tal.

47 In the cistern next to the canals fed by the Great Wady, at the bottom: 12 tal.

48 At the reservoir which is in Bet Kerem going to the left of ten notches: sixty-two talents of silver.

49 At the pond of the valley of 'YK on its western side is a ma'ah coin coupled with two ma'ahs. This is the entrance: three hundred talents of gold and twenty pitched vessels.

51 At the pond of the privy of Siloa under the watering-trough: 17 tal.

XI

53 Next to them under the corner of the southern portico at the tomb of Zadok under the pillar of the covered hall: vessels of offering of resin and offering of senna.

XII

61 On Mount Gerizim under the stairs of the higher underground cavity a box and its contents and 60 tal. of silver.

62 At the mouth of the spring of Bet-Sham vessels of silver and vessels of gold of offering and silver. In all, six hundred talents.

63 In the great underground duct of the sepulchral chamber towards the house of the sepulchral chamber. The whole weighing 71 talents and twenty minas.

64 In the underground cavity which is in the smooth rock north of Kohlit whose opening is towards the north with tombs at its mouth there is a copy of this writing and its explanation and the measurements and the details of each item.

MAJOR EDITIONS OF QUMRAN MANUSCRIPTS

• •

(listed in order of the date of publication)

Microfiche Edition

E. Tov, ed., *The Dead Sea Scrolls on Microfiche*, Leiden, 1992; *A Companion Volume to the Dead Sea Scrolls Microfiche Edition*, Leiden, 1995.

CD-ROM Edition

T. H. Lim et al., The Dead Sea Scrolls Reference Library, I (3 CD-ROMs), Oxford and Leiden, 1997.

Photographic Edition

Robert H. Eisenman and James M. Robinson, eds, *A Facsimile Edition of the Dead Sea Scrolls*, I–II, Washington, 1991.

Computer Reconstructed Edition

B. Z. Wacholder and M. G. Abegg, *A Preliminary Edition of the Unpublished Dead Sea Scrolls* I–III, Washington, 1991–5.

Cave 1

M. Burrows, J. C. Trever and W. H. Brownlee, *The Dead Sea Scrolls of St Mark's Monastery*, I, New Haven, 1950 (contains the Commentary on Habakkuk); II/2, New Haven, 1951 (contains the Community Rule Scroll). There is no II/1.

E. L. Sukenik, *The Dead Sea Scrolls of the Hebrew University*, Jerusalem, 1954–5.

D. Barthélemy and J. T. Milik, *Discoveries in the Judaean Desert, I: Qumran Cave 1*, Oxford, 1955.

N. Avigad and Y. Yadin, *A Genesis Apocryphon*, Jerusalem, 1956.

E. Ulrich et al., *Discoveries in the Judaean Desert, XXXII: Qumran Cave 1, II: The Isaiah Texts* (forthcoming).

Caves 2–3 and 5–10

M. Baillet, J. T. Milik and R. de Vaux, *Discoveries in the Judaean Desert of Jordan, III: Les petites grottes de Qumrân*, Oxford, 1963 (contains fragments and the Copper Scroll).

Cave 4

J. M. Allegro and A. A. Anderson, *Discoveries in the Judaean Desert of Jordan, V: Qumran Cave 4, I (4Q158–4Q186)*, Oxford, 1968 (contains mostly exegetical fragments). For editorial improvements, see J. Strugnell, 'Notes en marge du volume V des *Discoveries in the Judaean Desert of Jordan*', *Revue de Qumrân*, 7 (1970), 163–276.

J. T. Milik, *The Books of Enoch: Aramaic Fragments of Qumran Cave 4*, Oxford, 1976.

R. de Vaux and J. T. Milik, *Discoveries in the Judaean Desert, VI: Qumrân Grotte 4, II: I. Archéologie. II. Tefillin, Mezuzot et Targum (4Q128–4Q157)*, Oxford, 1977.

M. Baillet, *Discoveries in the Judaean Desert, VII: Qumrân Grotte 4, III (4Q482–4Q520)*, Oxford, 1982 (contains fragments of the War Rule and remains of liturgical and sapiential compositions).

Carol Newsom, *Songs of the Sabbath Sacrifice: A Critical Edition*, Atlanta, 1985.

Judith E. Sanderson, *An Exodus Scroll from Qumran: 4QpaleoExod^m and the Samaritan Tradition*, Atlanta, 1986.

Eileen M. Schuller, *Non-Canonical Psalms from Qumran: A Pseudepigraphic Collection*, Atlanta, 1986.

P. W. Skehan, E. Ulrich and Judith E. Sanderson, *Discoveries in the Judaean Desert, IX: Qumran Cave 4, IV: Palaeo-Hebrew and Greek Biblical Manuscripts*, Oxford, 1992.

R. H. Eisenman and M. Wise, *The Dead Sea Scrolls Uncovered*, Shaftesbury and Rockport, Mass., 1992; London, 1993.

E. Qimron and J. Strugnell, *Discoveries in the Judaean Desert, X: Qumran Cave 4, V: Miqsat Ma'ase Ha-Torah*, Oxford, 1994.

E. Ulrich, F. M. Cross et al., *Discoveries in the Judaean Desert, XII: Qumran Cave 4, VII: Genesis to Numbers*, Oxford, 1994.

H. Attridge et al., *Discoveries in the Judaean Desert, XIII: Qumran Cave 4, VIII: Parabiblical Texts, Part I*, Oxford, 1994 (in fact 1995).

M. Broshi et al., *Discoveries in the Judaean Desert, XIX: Qumran Cave 4, XIV: Parabiblical Texts, Part II*, Oxford, 1995.

E. Ulrich and F. M. Cross, *Discoveries in the Judaean Desert, XIV: Qumran Cave 4, IX: Deuteronomy, Joshua, Judges, Kings*, Oxford, 1996.

J. M. Baumgarten, *Discoveries in the Judaean Desert, XVIII: Qumran Cave 4, XIII: The Damascus Document (4Q266–273)*, Oxford, 1996.

G. Brooke et al., *Discoveries in the Judaean Desert XXII: Qumran Cave 4, XVII: Parabiblical Texts, Part III*, Oxford, 1996.

T. Elgvin et al., *Discoveries in the Judaean Desert, XX: Qumran Cave 4, XV:, Sapiential Texts, Part I*, Oxford, 1997.

E. Ulrich et al., *Discoveries in the Judaean Desert, XV: Qumran Cave 4, X: The Prophets*, Oxford, 1997.

E. Eschel et al., *Discoveries in the Judaean Desert, XI: Qumran Cave 4, VI: Poetical and Liturgical Texts, Part I*, Oxford, 1998.

E Puech, *Discoveries in the Judaean Desert, XXV: Qumrân Grotte 4, XVIII: Textes Hébreux (4Q521–4Q528, 4Q576–4Q579)*, Oxford, 1998.

P. S. Alexander and G. Vermes, *Discoveries in the Judaean Desert, XXVI: Qumran Cave 4, XIX: Serekh Ha-Yahad and Two Related Texts*, Oxford, 1998.

E. Ulrich, *Discoveries in the Judaean Desert, XVI: Qumran Cave 4, XI: Psalms to Chronicles* (forthcoming, 1999).

E. Chazon et al., *Discoveries in the Judaean Desert, XXIX: Qumran Cave 4, XX: Poetical and Liturgical Texts, Part II* (forthcoming, 1999).

J. Strugnell et al., *Discoveries in the Judaean Desert, XXXIV: Qumran Cave 4, XXIV: Sapiential Texts, Part II* (forthcoming, 1999).

J. Baumgarten et al., *Discoveries in the Judaean Desert, XXXV: Qumran Cave 4, XXV: Halakhic Texts* (forthcoming, 1999).

M. Bernstein et al., *Discoveries in the Judaean Desert, Va: Qumran Cave 4, I (4Q158–4Q186)* (forthcoming).

F. M. Cross et al., *Discoveries in the Judaean Desert, XVII: Qumran Cave 4, XII* (forthcoming).

S. Talmon et al., *Discoveries in the Judaean Desert, XXI: Qumran Cave 4, XVI: Calendric Texts* (forthcoming).

D. Dimant et al., *Discoveries in the Judaean Desert, XXX: Qumran Cave 4, XXI: Parabiblical Texts, Part IV* (forthcoming).

E. Puech, *Discoveries in the Judaean Desert, XXXI: Qumran Cave 4, XXII: Textes en Araméen, Tome I (4Q529–4Q549)* (forthcoming).

D. Pike et al., *Discoveries in the Judaean Desert, XXXIII: Qumran Cave 4, XXIII: Unidentified Fragments* (forthcoming).

P. Alexander, G. Vermes et al., *Discoveries in the Judaean Desert, XXXVI: Qumran Cave 4, XXVI: Miscellaneous Texts* (forthcoming).

E. Puech, *Discoveries in the Judaean Desert, XXXVII: Qumran Cave 4, XXVII: Textes en Araméen, Tome II (4Q550–4Q555)* (forthcoming).

Cave 11

J. A. Sanders, *Discoveries in the Judaean Desert of Jordan, IV: The Psalm Scroll of Qumran Cave 11*, Oxford, 1965.

J. P. M. van der Ploeg, A. S. van der Woude and B. Jongeling, *Le Targum de Job de la grotte XI de Qumrân*, Leiden, 1971.

Y. Yadin, *Megillat ha-Miqdash* I–III, Jerusalem, 1977 (English edition, *The Temple Scroll* I–III, Jerusalem, 1983).

D. N. Freedman and K. A. Matthews, *The Paleo-Hebrew Leviticus Scroll (11QpaleoLev)*, Winona Lake, 1985.

E. Qimron, *The Temple Scroll: A Critical Edition with Extensive Reconstructions* (Beer-Sheva and Jerusalem, 1996).

F. García Martínez et al., *Discoveries in the Judaean Desert, XXIII: Qumran Cave 11 (11Q2–18, 11Q20–31)*, Oxford, 1998.

Murabba'at

P. Benoit, J. T. Milik and R. de Vaux, *Discoveries in the Judaean Desert, II: Les grottes de Murabba'at*, Oxford, 1961.

Nahal Hever

E. Tov, *Discoveries in the Judaean Desert, VIII: The Greek Minor Prophets from Nahal Hever*, Oxford, 1990.

H. M. Cotton et al., *Discoveries in the Judaean Desert, XXVII: Aramaic, Hebrew and Greek Documentary Texts from Nahal Hever and Other Sites with an Appendix Containing Alleged Qumran Texts (The Seiyâl Collection II)*, Oxford, 1997.

Wady ed-Daliyeh

M. J. Winn-Leith, *Discoveries in the Judaean Desert, XXIV: Wadi Daliyeh I: The Wadi Daliyeh Seal Impressions*, Oxford, 1997.

D. Gropp, *Discoveries in the Judaean Desert, XXVIII: Wadi Daliyeh II: The Samaria Papyri from Wadi Daliyeh* (forthcoming).

Unidentified Cave

Y. Yadin, *Tefillin from Qumran (XQPhyl 1–4)*, Jerusalem, 1969.

Damascus Document

M. Broshi, *The Damascus Document Reconsidered*, Jerusalem, 1992.

Miscellaneous

H. Cotton et al., *Discoveries in the Judaean Desert, XXXVIII: Miscellaneous Texts from the Judaean Desert* (forthcoming).

E. Tov, ed., *Discoveries in the Judaean Desert, XXXIX: The Texts from the Judaean Desert: Introduction and Indices* (forthcoming).

GENERAL
BIBLIOGRAPHY

* *

(arranged alphabetically under author/editor)

1. Qumran Bibliographies

J. A. Fitzmyer, *The Dead Sea Scrolls: Major Publications and Tools for Study*, Missoula, Montana, 1975; 2nd edn, 1977; Atlanta, 1990.

B. Jongeling, *A Classified Bibliography of the Finds in the Desert of Judah: 1958–1969*, Leiden, 1971.

F. García Martínez and D. W. Parry, *A Bibliography of the Finds in the Desert of Judah 1970–1975*, Leiden, 1996.

2. General Studies and Monographs

G. J. Brooke, ed., *Temple Scroll Studies*, Sheffield, 1989.

G. J. Brooke, ed., *New Qumran Texts and Studies*, Leiden, 1995.

M. Burrows, *The Dead Sea Scrolls*, New York, 1955.

M. Burrows, *More Light on the Dead Sea Scrolls*, New York, 1958.

P. R. Callaway, *The History of the Qumran Community*, Sheffield, 1988.

J. G. Campbell, *The Use of Scripture in the Damascus Document 1–8, 19–20*, Berlin, 1995.

J. G. Campbell, *Deciphering the Dead Sea Scrolls*, London, 1996.

J. G. Charlesworth et al., eds, *Qumran-Messianism*, Tübingen, 1998.

F. H. Cryer and T. L. Thompson, eds, *Qumran between the Old and New Testaments*, Sheffield, 1998.

F. M. Cross, *The Ancient Library of Qumran and Modern Biblical Studies*, New York, 1958; Grand Rapids, 2nd edn, 1980; 3rd edn, Sheffield, 1996.

P. R. Davies, *Qumran*, Guildford, 1982.

P. R. Davies, *Behind the Essenes: History and Ideology in the Dead Sea Scrolls*, Atlanta, 1987.

P. R. Davies, *Sects and Scrolls: Essay on Qumran and Related Topics*, Atlanta, 1996.

R. de Vaux, *The Archaeology of the Dead Sea Scrolls*, London, 1973.

D. Dimant, 'Qumran Sectarian Literature' in M. Stone, ed., *Jewish Writings of the Second Temple Period*, Assen and Philadelphia, 1984.

D. Dimant and U. Rappaport, eds, *The Dead Sea Scrolls: Forty Years of Research*, Leiden, 1992.

G. R. Driver, *The Judaean Scrolls*, Oxford, 1965.

A. Dupont-Sommer, *The Essene Writings from Qumran*, Oxford, 1961.

H.-J. Fabry et al., *Qumranstudien*, Göttingen, 1996.

J. A. Fitzmyer, *Responses to 101 Questions on the Dead Sea Scrolls*, London, 1992.

F. García Martínez, *Qumran and Apocalyptic: Studies on the Aramaic Texts from Qumran*, Leiden, 1992.

F. García Martínez, *The Dead Sea Scrolls Translated: The Qumran Texts in English*, Leiden, 1994.

F. García Martínez and J. Trebolle Barrera, *The People of the Dead Sea Scrolls*, Leiden, 1995.

T. H. Gaster, *The Dead Sea Scriptures in English Translation*, Garden City, New York, 1956; 3rd edn, 1976.

N. Golb, *Who Wrote the Dead Sea Scrolls?* London, 1995.

D. J. Harrington, *Wisdom Texts from Qumran*, London and New York, 1996.

J.-P. Humbert et al., *Fouilles de Khirbet Qumrân et de Aïn Feshkha I, Album de photographies – Répertoire du fonds photographique – Synthèse des notes de chantier du Père Roland de Vaux OP*, Fribourg and Göttingen, 1994.

J. Kampen and M. J. Bernstein, eds, *Reading 4 QMMT*, Atlanta, 1996.

M. A. Knibb, *The Qumran Community*, Cambridge, 1987.

J. Maier, *Die Qumran-Essener: Die Texte vom Toten Meer* I–II, Munich, 1995.

S. Metso, *The Textual Development of the Qumran Community Rule*, Helsinki, 1996.

J. T. Milik, *Ten Years of Discovery in the Wilderness of Judaea*, London, 1959.

G. W. E. Nickelsburg, *Jewish Literature Between the Bible and the Mishnah*, Philadelphia and London, 1981.

B. Nitzan, *Qumran Prayer and Religious Poetry*, Leiden, 1994.

D. W. Parry and S. D. Ricks, eds, *Current Research and Technological Developments on the Dead Sea Scrolls*, Leiden, 1996.

S. E. Porter and C. A. Evans, eds, *The Scrolls and the Scriptures*, Sheffield, 1997.

L. H. Schiffman, ed., *Archaeology and History in the Dead Sea Scrolls*, Sheffield, 1990.

L. H. Schiffman, *Reclaiming the Dead Sea Scrolls*, Philadelphia, 1994.

H. Shanks, ed., *Understanding the Dead Sea Scrolls*, Washington, 1992.

H. Stegemann, *Die Essner, Qumran, Johannes der Täufer and Jesus*, Freiburg, 1993.

A. Steudel, *Der Midrasch zur Eschatologie aus der Qumrangemeinde (4QMidrEschat[a,b])*, Leiden, 1994.

D. D. Swanson, *The Temple Scroll and the Bible: The Methodology of 11QT*, Leiden, 1995.

S. Talmon, *The World of Qumran from Within*, Jerusalem and Leiden, 1989.

J. Trebolle Barrera and L. Vegas Montaner, eds, *The Madrid Qumran Congress 1991*, Vols I–II, Leiden, 1992.

E. Ulrich and J. C. VanderKam, eds, *The Community of the Renewed Covenant*, Notre Dame, 1994.

J. C. VanderKam, *The Dead Sea Scrolls Today*, Grand Rapids and London, 1994.

G. Vermes, *Discovery in the Judean Desert*, New York, 1956.

G. Vermes, *The Dead Sea Scrolls: Qumran in Perspective*, London, 1977; Philadelphia, 1981; 2nd edn, London, 1982; 3rd edn, London, 1994.

G. Vermes, *The Complete Dead Sea Scrolls in English*, London, 1997.

B. Z. Wacholder, *The Dawn of Qumran: The Sectarian Torah and the Teacher of Righteousness*, Cincinnati, 1983.

Edmund Wilson, *The Dead Sea Scrolls 1947–1969*, London, 1969.

M. O. Wise, *A Critical Study of the Temple Scroll from Qumran Cave 11*, Chicago, 1990.

M. Wise, M. Abegg and E. Cook, *The Dead Sea Scrolls: A New Translation*, London and San Francisco, 1996.

J. Zimmerman, *Messianische Texte aus Qumran*, Tübingen, 1998.

3. *The Scrolls and the New Testament*

M. Black, *The Scrolls and Christian Origins*, London, 1961.

M. Black, ed., *The Scrolls and Christianity*, London, 1969.

J. H. Charlesworth, ed., *John and Qumran*, London, 1972; New York, 1990.

J. H. Charlesworth, ed., *Jesus and the Dead Sea Scrolls*, New York and London, 1992.

R. Eisenman, *Maccabees, Zadokites, Christians and Qumran*, Leiden, 1983.

R. Eisenman, *James the Just in the Habakkuk Pesher*, Leiden, 1986.

N. S. Fujita, *A Crack in the Jar: What Ancient Jewish Documents Tell Us about the New Testament*, New York, 1986.

J. Murphy-O'Connor, ed., *Paul and Qumran*, London, 1968; New York, 1990.

M. Newton, *The Concept of Purity at Qumran and in the Letters of Paul*, Cambridge, 1985.

K. Stendahl, ed., *The Scrolls and the New Testament*, London, 1958.

G. Vermes, *Jesus and the World of Judaism*, London, 1983; Philadelphia, 1984.